The urgent need to reform fossil fuel prices to combat global warming, reduce air pollution deaths, and strengthen fiscal balances is widely understood – how to get it done in practice is not. Drawing on extensive economic analysis and country experiences, this rich and easily digestible book provides a comprehensive toolkit for overcoming the barriers to reform. It will be especially valuable reading for those in government, international organizations, and the research community engaged in moving reform forward.

—**Ian Parry**, *Principal Environmental Fiscal Policy Expert,*
International Monetary Fund

The reform of fossil fuel subsidies is a top priority for many resource rich emerging economies, but the challenges of implementation have proven to be significant. This book provides policy makers with an in-depth analysis of the economic implications at the household, firm, and macro levels, and demonstrates how these link with common political economy challenges. The analysis of the impacts of subsidy reforms on firms are particularly novel, and could guide future studies on this under-researched topic. Overall, this book offers evidence-based, concrete, and practical guidance for designing and implementing effective reforms.

—**Bassam Fattouh**, *Director, Oxford Institute for Energy Studies;*
Professor, School of Oriental and African Studies, University of London

[…] fossil fuel subsidies cause severe economic distortions that compromise countries' prospects of achieving equitable and sustainable development. Yet, the sheer magnitude of fossil fuel subsidies being paid globally also hints at the size and complexity of the challenge. To reform subsidies entails to understand and gauge economic and political trade-offs, to mitigate adverse effects on vulnerable households, to assist firms with implementing efficiency enhancing measures, and to ensure the long-term contribution of subsidy reform to sustainable development. This book explores these issues, with the objective of informing the preparation, design, and implementation of effective fossil fuel subsidy reforms.

—**Marianne Fay**, *Chief Economist, Sustainable Development,*
The World Bank

This book is a must read for anyone wanting to understand how to address the proverbial elephant in the room – fossil fuel subsidies reform. Ignoring Dr Rentschler's insights could well render our efforts to achieve a sustainable energy future completely ineffective.

—**Nigel Jollands**, *Associate Director, Energy Efficiency and Climate Change,*
European Bank for Reconstruction and Development (EBRD)

While you will find many articles and books explaining *why* keeping energy prices artificially low is a bad idea, there are not so many that will help you understand *how* to improve the situation. However, this is the key question: Fossil fuel subsidies are not so widespread for no reason; they are difficult to reform due to their large distributional impacts, and it remains challenging to manage the negative side effects of any significant reform. This book will help policy makers better understand why reforming fossil fuel subsidies is so difficult, but also help them design "policy packages" that can address the barriers to the reform. This book will support the implementation of reforms that can cancel the negative effects of energy price distortion while contributing to reducing poverty and promoting development.

—**Stéphane Hallegatte**, *Lead Economist, Climate Change Group,*
The World Bank

Phasing out fossil fuel subsidies is easier said than done. This book provides a much-needed coherent analysis from different angles, namely political economy and economics. Jun Rentschler has managed to delve into data from two emerging economies, Nigeria and Indonesia, assessing firms, private households, and regions. The book also develops a macro-economic model to account for fuel smuggling, certainly a real life ingredient for any analysis. Perhaps most importantly, the book makes a concise attempt bringing those strands together and develops an agenda for subsidy reforms. A must-read for scholars, international organisations, and public administrations.

—**Raimund Bleischwitz**, *Chair in Sustainable Global Resources and Deputy*
Director, Institute for Sustainable Resources, University College London

With policy-makers around the world pondering how to ramp up measures against climate change in the wake of the 2016 Paris Agreement, Jun Rentschler's volume is a very timely, clear and perceptive study of a key element, the reform of fossil fuel subsidies. This book brings together economic theory, data and policy analysis in a thoughtful investigation that considers key issues such as the distributional implications of reforms and includes novel aspects such as the impact on firms and the interaction of policies with illicit activities. As such, the volume will be of interest not only to fiscal, energy and climate-change specialists but also anyone involved in applying economics to policy-making in the real world.

—**Alex Bowen**, *Special Adviser, Grantham Research Institute on*
Climate Change and the Environment, London School of
Economics and Political Science (LSE)

Fossil Fuel Subsidy Reforms

Countries around the world are spending up to $500 billion per year on subsidising fossil fuel consumption. By some estimates, the G20 countries alone are spending around $450 billion on subsidising fossil fuel production. In addition, the indirect social welfare costs of these subsidies have been shown to be substantial – for instance due to air pollution, road congestion, climate change, and economic inefficiency, to name a few. Considering these numbers, there is no doubt that fossil fuel subsidies cause severe economic distortions that compromise countries' prospects of achieving equitable and sustainable development.

This book provides a guide to the complex challenge of designing, assessing, and implementing effective fossil fuel subsidy reforms. It shows that subsidy reform requires a careful balancing of complex economic and political trade-offs, as well as measures to mitigate adverse effects on vulnerable households and to assist firms with implementing efficiency enhancing measures. Going beyond the purely fiscal perspective, this book emphasises that smart subsidy reforms can contribute to all three dimensions of sustainable development – environment, society, and economy.

Over the course of eight chapters, this book considers a wide range of agents and stakeholders, markets, and policy measures in order to distil the key principles of designing effective fossil fuel subsidy reforms. This book will be of great relevance to scholars and policy makers with an interest in energy economics and policy, climate change policy, and sustainable development more broadly.

Jun Rentschler is an Economist (YP) at The World Bank working at the intersection of climate change and sustainable resilient development. He is also a Visiting Research Fellow at the Oxford Institute for Energy Studies, the Payne Institute for Earth Resources in Colorado, and the Graduate Institute for Policy Studies in Tokyo. Prior, he worked at the German Foreign Ministry and the European Bank for Reconstruction and Development (EBRD). He is a co-author of *Investing in Resource Efficiency: The Economics and Politics of Financing the Resource Transition* (2018).

Routledge Studies in Energy Policy

For further details please visit the series page on the Routledge website: http://www.routledge.com/books/series/RSIEP/

Fossil Fuel Subsidy Reforms

A Guide to Economic and
Political Complexity

Jun Rentschler

Routledge
Taylor & Francis Group

LONDON AND NEW YORK

from Routledge

First published 2018
by Routledge

2 Park Square, Milton Park, Abingdon, Oxfordshire OX14 4RN
52 Vanderbilt Avenue, New York, NY 10017

Routledge is an imprint of the Taylor & Francis Group, an informa business

First issued in paperback 2020

British Library Cataloguing-in-Publication Data
A catalogue record for this book is available from the British Library

Library of Congress Cataloging-in-Publication Data
A catalog record for this book has been requested

ISBN: 978-0-8153-8618-6 (hbk)
ISBN: 978-0-367-45900-0 (pbk)

Typeset in Times New Roman
by Apex CoVantage, LLC

Contents

Figures

Tables

Preface

In December 2015, after years of painstaking negotiations, governments from 197 countries made a historic step for international diplomacy and sustainable development by adopting the Paris Agreement on Climate Change. As part of this treaty, the international community reaffirmed their commitment to mobilise $100 billion of 'climate finance' annually, to promote renewable energies and low-carbon development. Around the same time, the International Energy Agency (IEA) released its estimate that just in the year before countries around the world had spent close to $500 billion to subsidise fossil fuel consumption. Another $450 billion had been spent in the G20 countries alone to subsidise fossil fuel production. Ironically, the same governments that would celebrate the Paris Agreement were spending a multiple of their climate finance commitment on subsidising fossil fuels.

Amidst this, the International Monetary Fund (IMF) shocked everyone, when it estimated the annual cost of global fossil fuel subsidies at $5.3 trillion – or 6.5% of global GDP. By not only accounting for active subsidy provision like the IEA, but also for indirect external costs (such as air pollution, road congestion, and climate change), the IMF's estimate drew attention to the severe social welfare costs of subsidising fossil fuels. Considering these numbers, there is no doubt that the subsidisation of fossil fuel consumption and production directly undermines any effort to mitigate climate change. What is more, fossil fuel subsidies cause severe economic distortions that compromise countries' prospects of achieving equitable and sustainable development.

Yet, the sheer magnitude of fossil fuel subsidies being paid globally also hints at the size and complexity of the challenge. To reform subsidies entails to understand and gauge economic and political trade-offs, to mitigate adverse effects on vulnerable households, to assist firms with implementing efficiency enhancing measures, and to ensure the long-term contribution of subsidy reform to sustainable development. This book explores these issues, with the objective of informing the preparation, design, and implementation of effective fossil fuel subsidy reforms.

Marianne Fay
Chief Economist, Sustainable Development,
The World Bank

Acknowledgements

The work contained in this book was conducted as part of my PhD at University College London. Hence, first and foremost, I would like to express my gratitude to Raimund Bleischwitz, Paul Ekins, Nobuhiro Hosoe, and Lars Nesheim, for their time, expert advice, and guidance throughout the duration of my PhD. As co-authors, Morgan Bazilian, Raimund Bleischwitz, Florian Flachenecker, Nobuhiro Hosoe, and Martin Kornejew have made valuable contributions to the studies underlying this book. I would like to thank Dayang Abu Bakar, Theo Arvanitopoulos, Mook Bangalore, Morgan Bazilian, Enrico Botta, Frank Convery, Carel Cronenberg, Craig Davies, Stijn van Ewijk, Bassam Fattouh, Jan Christoph von der Goltz, Michael Grubb, Stéphane Hallegatte, Laurence Harris, Nigel Jollands, Majid Kazemi, Thomas Kenyon, Martin Kornejew, Karlygash Kuralbayeva, Sung-Ah Kyun, Nicholas Lazarou, Peter Mallaburn, George Marbuah, Will McDowall, Seyed Mehdi Mohaghegh, Gianpiero Nacci, Victor Nechifor- Vostinaru, Rahmat Poudineh, Adam Roer, Caterina Ruggeri-Laderchi, Anupama Sen, Sandy Skelton, Janna Tenzing, Neil Strachan, Adrien Vogt-Schilb, and Matthew Winning, who have all provided extremely helpful comments and/or engaged in constructive in-depth discussions on one or several of the chapters in this book. Special thanks are due to Alex Bowen, Alvaro Calzadilla, Florian Flachenecker, and Ingo Rentschler for reviewing the entire book, and providing valuable comments and feedback. Comments from many anonymous reviewers have also helped to strengthen this work. I also gratefully acknowledge helpful comments and feedback by seminar participants at the European Bank for Reconstruction and Development (EBRD), National Graduate Institute for Policy Studies (GRIPS) in Tokyo, UCL, London School of Economics, Oxford Institute for Energy Studies (OIES), Oxford Brookes University, ETH Zurich, International Institute for Environment and Development (IIED), and the World Bank. Comments by participants of the APEC Energy Working Group workshop on fossil fuel subsidy reform in Jakarta, Indonesia, of the 21st and 22nd Annual Conferences of the European Association of Environmental and Resource Economics (EAERE), of the 5th International Symposium 5 on Mineral Resources and Mine Development (AIMS) in Aachen, Germany, and of the International Conference on Minerals in the Circular Economy in Espoo, Finland, are also gratefully acknowledged. I am particularly grateful to Nobuhiro Hosoe of GRIPS, and Bassam Fattouh of OIES for hosting me as a Visiting Research Fellow in Tokyo and Oxford respectively. I am also grateful to UCL ISR for providing a doctoral stipend and research budget, which enabled me to conduct this research. I thank OIES for funding the research in Chapter 3 as part of the Saudi Aramco Research Fellowship; Chapters 4 and 5 are also based on research funded by OIES. Chapter 6 was supported by a JSPS KAKENHI Grant (No. 16K03613). Chapter 7 is partly based on a research partnership between UCL ISR and the EBRD, and the associated policy report by Flachenecker and Rentschler (2015), which was commissioned and funded by the EBRD. I thank UCL Open Access for sponsoring excessively expensive open access fees for the publication of Chapters 2, 3, 4, and 8. Last but not least, I am most grateful to my parents (back in the days) and Janna Tenzing (more recently), for always packing the best lunch boxes. And finally, just in case: The views expressed in this book are entirely my own, and should not be attributed to the institutions with which I am associated.

1 Introduction
And a guide for navigating this book

Jun Rentschler

1.1 Policy relevance

There is an increasingly strong international consensus that fossil fuel subsidies (FFS) are detrimental in terms of economic, social, and environmental sustainability. Organisations including the Intergovernmental Panel on Climate Change (IPCC) and the IEA consider FFS reform a prerequisite for achieving any ambitious carbon emission mitigation target. The reason for this is that FFS not only incentivise overconsumption of carbon intensive energy, but directly undermine any effort to impose a price on carbon (e.g. through carbon taxes). Moreover, institutions as wide ranging as the International Monetary Fund (IMF), the World Bank, the United Nations, Greenpeace, the Organization for Economic Co-operation and Development (OECD), and Oxfam are in agreement that the urgent need for FFS reform is not only for environmental reasons: While subsidy reform is crucial from a climate change perspective, the wide range of economic and social externalities associated with fuel subsidies also emphasises that reform is a vital contribution to sustainable development objectives more generally (IMF, 2013c).

Yet, despite strong drivers for FFS reforms – fiscal strains on national budgets, adverse environmental impacts, and international commitments – overall progress at the country level has been limited and the track record is mixed. Various countries have experienced firsthand the political challenges associated with FFS reform (covered in Chapter 2). Especially when reforms were poorly designed or implemented, strong public opposition has repeatedly forced governments to abandon reform attempts. This is not least due to the fact that energy pricing reforms will directly affect the disposable income of consumers.

At the same time, various cases of past FFS reforms illustrate that thorough planning, risk assessment, and policy design can enable successful reforms. Against this background, this book provides a comprehensive and systematic account of the factors that policy makers must consider, in order to design effective reforms. The book recognises that in practice environmental objectives often play a secondary role; instead the rationale for

FFS reforms is determined within a complex – and sometimes conflicting – context of fiscal, macroeconomic, political, and social factors. By considering FFS reforms from different perspectives and at different levels, this book provides a comprehensive and robust guideline for the analytical assessment of reforms, and thus practical advice to policy makers.

1.2   Content summary

This book provides a comprehensive answer to three interlinked questions:

1   What are the likely socio-economic impacts of FFS reform?
2   How can different compensation and revenue re-distribution schemes mitigate these impacts?
3   How should FFS reforms be designed to minimise adverse side-effects, while ensuring their long-term contribution to sustainable development?

In line with these questions, this book provides analytical estimates of the likely impacts of FFS reforms on poverty levels, household consumption, welfare, competitiveness, and macro-economic performance. For the example of Nigeria, it finds that consumption shocks incurred by poor households can be substantial, though cash transfers can provide effective compensation and social protection. For the example of Indonesia, it shows energy price increases have small but significant adverse effects on the performance of firms – even after firms have deployed various response and coping measures (e.g. efficiency measures). At the macro-level, it shows that in developing countries in particular the consideration of informal and illicit activities (including tax evasion and smuggling) can play a crucial role in determining the welfare costs of FFS reform. The book also argues that removing FFS alone may not yield the efficiency gains and environmental benefits that policy makers envisage: In practice, market distortions can create barriers for economic agents to adjust their technology and behaviour in response to increasing fossil fuel prices.

Throughout, this book makes the important distinction between FFS *removal* and *reform*: A complete FFS reform is not only about removing subsidies, but also requires an integrated strategy featuring a range of carefully designed and sequenced complementary policy measures. These are summarised in the final chapter, which distils the key insights and provides a policy blueprint for designing effective FFS reforms.

1.3   Focus areas and organisation of book

As FFS reform affects economies as a whole, its repercussions are likely to be felt throughout the economy both in the short- and long-run: In both formal and informal parts of the economy, across all income groups, and at all levels – from households to firms, and to macro-economic performance. In order to take these wide-ranging effects into account, FFS reforms must be carefully planned, designed, implemented, and evaluated; only this can ensure that adverse impacts are mitigated and development opportunities maximised.

Building on this rationale, this book focusses on different parts of the economy, in order to provide specific and practical guidance to the simulation, design, and evaluation of FFS reforms. With a particular focus on the reform of consumer subsidies in developing countries, this book considers the impacts on households, firms, key macro-economic parameters, as well as the political economy. In line with these focus areas, this book is organised as follows:

- *Chapter 2* provides a **comprehensive overview** of FFS and discusses definitions, estimates, past and current reform efforts, and drivers and barriers of reform, and sets out focus areas for the design of FFS reforms.
- *Chapter 3* focusses on the impacts of FFS reform on **households**. Using Nigeria as a case study, it considers various factors which drive exposure and vulnerability to subsidy removal (i.e. energy price shocks). Moreover, it explores the complex trade-offs between the need to win public support for reform, while protecting the livelihoods of vulnerable households.
- *Chapter 4* provides a conceptual outline and discussion of the potential **impacts of FFS reforms on firms**. It discusses the transmissions channels through which reform-induced energy price shocks affect firms, and presents the main response and coping measures available to firms.
- *Chapter 5* builds on the previous chapter by focussing on Indonesia and exploring the likely long-term effects of changes in energy prices (due to FFS reform) on the **performance of firms**. It estimates the role of different response measures applied by firms to mitigate energy cost shocks.
- *Chapter 6* returns to the case of Nigeria and focusses on general equilibrium effects at the **macro-economic level**. It analyses how FFS removal (and various methods of revenue redistribution) affects parameters such as income distribution, sectoral composition, output, consumption, and fiscal efficiency. In addition, it draws attention to the important **role of fuel smuggling and tax evasion** in the context of FFS reform.
- *Chapter 7* focusses on **market failures and inefficiencies**, which can mean that FFS reform may fail to resolve negative externalities (e.g. traffic congestion, climate change) without the implementation of complementary measures.
- *Chapter 8* draws on all of the above chapters as well as past case studies, and provides a **policy blueprint for designing effective FFS reforms**.

1.4 Methods

The wide range of focus areas and perspectives, as outlined in Section 1.3, requires a range of different methodological approaches from the disciplines of economics and political economy. Broadly speaking, econometric approaches based on survey data are apt for obtaining a disaggregated and granular picture of micro-level effects. General equilibrium models are best suited for conducting policy simulations and understanding the systemic relationships at the macro-level. Political economy analyses are needed to evaluate whether economically optimal policy recommendations are in fact politically and practically feasible. Thus, this book selects different methods depending on their strengths and the respective purpose. In particular:

- *Chapter 3* uses a household expenditure survey and an **econometric simulation model,** in order to capture partial equilibrium effects (i.e. known as direct price effects) due to FFS reform.
- *Chapter 5* uses a firm survey and conducts **micro-econometric cross-section analysis,** to estimate a series of regression coefficients (including elasticities of inter-fuel substitution).
- *Chapter 6* constructs – from scratch – a **computable general equilibrium (CGE) model,** which is tailored to the analysis of FFS reforms and takes into account illicit and informal activities, such as fuel smuggling and tax evasion.
- *Chapter 7* questions the assumption of smooth and efficient markets. It provides a systematic **political economy analysis** of the market inefficiencies and barriers, which may mean that "green" tax reform (i.e. FFS reform, or environmental taxation more generally) alone may fail to trigger the intended changes in behaviour or technology.

Together, these approaches offer a comprehensive picture of the implications and trade-offs of FFS reform, and aim to be both of high analytical rigor and policy relevance.

1.5 Contribution

This book provides a comprehensive and analytically rigorous account of the economics and political economy of FFS reform. In doing so it offers a comprehensive and practical guide to any policy maker, or analyst, who is considering FFS reforms. It provides guidance on the key challenges and opportunities of reform, and highlights areas that require particular attention or care. To researchers and policy analysts it provides novel approaches for conducting reform simulations, and estimating the likely effects of different reform designs on households, firms, and the overall economy. To policy makers it provides a blueprint for the design and implementation of FFS reforms, on the basis of empirical evidence and many reform case studies.

More specifically, the work presented in this book makes several novel contributions to the existing evidence base and policy discourse:

A disaggregated and nuanced account of household level effects. Most past studies have focussed on the national level impacts of FFS reform (such as GDP, national poverty rates, or representative income groups). This book offers the first econometric study to go beyond this approach, by providing a detailed disaggregation of the factors determining the vulnerability of households to FFS reforms. It demonstrates that effects can vary substantially depending on the region, type of income-generating activity, or access to and affordability of alternative energies. In doing so, this book challenges the common presumption that income levels alone are an adequate indicator of vulnerability to energy price shocks. It also shows that policies that focus on national averages can be severely inadequate in accounting for sub-national variation. The implications of these findings can inform and strengthen the design of social protection and compensation schemes, which are critical for mitigating energy price shocks associated with FFS reform (Chapter 3).

Conceptual and empirical insights into firm level effects. Most of the existing literature on FFS reform has focussed on the impacts on households, while overlooking the potential impacts on firms. This book contributes a conceptual framework for the systematic analysis of energy price shocks (due to FFS reform) on firms (Chapter 4). It characterises the transmission channels of energy price shocks, and the response measures available to firms. It then uses this conceptual framework to offer the first econometric study that systematically analyses the long-term effects of energy price variation on the performance of firms (Chapter 5). The results from this analysis can help policy makers to identify sectors and regions in which firms are particularly exposed to FFS removal – and provide adequate assistance where necessary, e.g. to promote fuel switching or efficiency improvements.

A detailed account of fiscal and macro effects and the role of illicit market activities. While household or firm survey data enable robust and granular analyses of FFS reform effects at the micro level, they have the drawback of ignoring the macro-economic and fiscal implications of reform. Few general equilibrium studies of FFS reform exist, often using simplified, abstract, or generic computable general equilibrium (CGE) models to simulate reforms. For the purpose of this book, a novel and dedicated CGE model was developed, with the aim of capturing characteristics that are common to resource-rich developing countries (Chapter 6). In particular, the model takes an innovative approach to account for informal and illicit activities, in particular tax evasion and fuel smuggling – an aspect that has not been considered in past studies. It shows that the welfare costs of

FFS reform can be reduced drastically when the role of smuggling and tax evasion is taken into account, thus strengthening the case for reform.

Market distortions and the need for complementary reform measures. This book also challenges the popular presumption among economists that *"getting the price right"* alone can address all negative externalities associated with fossil fuel consumption. It provides a systematic analysis of barriers that prevent economic agents (firms in particular) from adjusting their behaviour or technology in response to higher energy prices (following a FFS reform). This demonstrates that increasing the price of fossil fuels alone does not automatically result in efficiency gains and environmental benefits. This has important practical implications for the design of FFS reforms (and Pigouvian taxes more generally), as active policy measures are needed to ensure that FFS reforms not only provide short-term fiscal relief, but also a long-term contribution to sustainable development (Chapter 7).[1]

Technical contribution. Finally, besides the above-mentioned policy insights, the contribution of this book also lies in the three technical methodologies developed in this book: the disaggregated household survey analysis, the firm level analysis, and the dedicated CGE model. While in this book they have been applied to the cases of Nigeria and Indonesia, these analytical tools can enable more robust ex-ante analyses of FFS reforms in other countries.

Note

1 In line with the theory of the second best, additional measures can counteract existing market distortions and result in a more efficient outcome than the first best approach on its own.

2 Reforming fossil fuel subsidies

Drivers, barriers, and the state of progress

Jun Rentschler and Morgan Bazilian[1]

2.1 Introduction

"Getting prices right" is widely regarded to be at the heart of an effective market-based solution to the climate change challenge. This approach calls on governments to reflect the social and environmental costs of carbon-intensive activities in their prices – by removing subsidies on fossil fuels and putting a price on carbon. In fact, subsidies which reduce the price of fossil fuels have the polar opposite effect of carbon taxes which aim to dis-incentivise the overconsumption of carbon-intensive energy.

By one estimate, in 2010 36% of global carbon emissions were driven by fossil fuel subsidies (Stefanski, 2014). Another study suggests that reforming FFS by 2020 can reduce global carbon emissions by 6.4% until 2050 (Schwanitz, Piontek, Bertram, and Luderer, 2014). Merrill, Bassi, Bridle, and Toft Christensen (2015) estimate for 20 selected countries that these emission reductions can be up to 18% if a small share of reform revenues (30%) is invested in renewables and energy efficiency. Similarly, the IEA (2013) estimates that FFS reform could reduce carbon emission by 360 Mt by 2020; and identifies FFS reform as one of four key policy measures for limiting global warming to 2°C above pre-industrial levels.[2] In its latest Assessment Report the IPCC (2014, TS p.98) emphasises that fossil fuel subsidy reform can "achieve significant emission reductions at negative social cost". Overall, this suggests that FFS reform must be an integral part of climate change mitigation efforts.

FFS have entered international limelight at least since the 2009 G20 summit, when heads of state announced a joint but vague commitment to the reform of "inefficient" fuel subsidies. Subsequently, this commitment has been repeated on various international policy platforms, and is reflected in the UN's Sustainable Development Goals. This international commitment is matched by efforts at the national level, with at least 27 countries around the world planning or implementing the reform of environmentally, socially, and economically unsustainable FFS in 2014 (IEA, 2014c).

In practice, the key rationale for implementing subsidy reform has typically been fiscal rather than environmental. However, the necessity and urgency of reform can only be fully understood when considering the complete range of adverse environmental, social, and economic side-effects of FFS. Besides driving climate change, FFS dis-incentivise investments, innovation, and efficiency, escalate fiscal burdens, crowd out funds for health, education, and other public infrastructure, incentivise corruption, aggravate air pollution, and reinforce poverty and income inequality (IMF, 2013c; Whitley, 2013; Devarajan, Mottaghi, Iqbal, Mundaca, Laursen, Vagliasindi, Commander, and Chaal-Dabi, 2014). Yet, the mixed track record of past reform attempts – not few resulted in violent street protests – illustrates how difficult reforms are in practice. Indeed, experience shows that political economy obstacles can be immense – but strong government commitment, thorough preparation, careful reform design, effective communication, and timing can significantly improve the success rate.

While FFS reforms are often seen as an opportunity for quick fiscal relief in times of tight government budgets, this chapter emphasises that additional measures can help, aligning FFS reforms with climate policy and long-term sustainable development objectives. For this purpose, this chapter synthesises evidence from a series of case studies of past FFS reforms and distils key principles for designing effective reforms. It shows how severe economic, environmental, and social externalities act as strong drivers for reform, while political challenges mean that implementation can be difficult in practice. Moreover, it offers policy makers a comprehensive overview of the status quo with respect to the main definitions, assessment criteria, externalities, and recent reform progress.

The remainder of this chapter is structured as follows: Section 2.2 provides an overview of existing definitions and estimates of FFS. Section 2.3 summarises the adverse effects of FFS from an economic, environmental, and social perspective. Section 2.4 provides an up-to-date picture of efforts by the international community and national governments to implement subsidy reforms. Section 2.4 discusses how international energy prices can provide (dis-) incentives for reforming subsidies and outlines common political economy challenges. Section 2.6 summarises key lessons learnt from past reform attempts for designing and implementing FFS reforms. Section 2.7 outlines areas for future research, while Section 2.8 concludes.

2.2 Defining and estimating fossil fuel subsidies

The World Trade Organization (WTO, 2006) broadly defines subsidies as any government programme which confers a benefit on its recipients. More specifically, Kojima and Koplow (2015) define FFS as any policy action which targets fossil fuels, or fossil fuel based electricity or heat, and causes one or more of the following effects: (i) a reduction of net energy costs, (ii) a reduction of energy production or distribution costs, (iii) an increase in the revenues of energy suppliers.

While FFS can take various forms, they can be broadly categorised into two types: consumer and producer subsidies (Whitley, 2013; GSI, 2010a,b; IEA, 2014c). Consumer subsidies refer to fiscal measures that lower the price of fossil fuel products below their market price (e.g. the international market price, or cost-recovery threshold), thus making them more affordable to end-users. As both market prices and domestic subsidised prices can be directly observed or estimated, consumer subsidies are more easily assessed with available data than producer subsidies. Consumer subsidies generally do not account for the cost of externalities (e.g. due to carbon emissions).

Producer subsidies are more difficult to observe and quantify, as they refer to different kinds of preferential treatment of fossil exploration and extraction firms, or other energy intensive companies, industries, or products (Bast, Doukas, Pickard, Van Der Burg, and Whitley, 2015; Bast, Makhijani, Pickard, and Whitley, 2014; GSI, 2010a). Producer subsidies could be explicit, such as grants, low-interest loans, direct payments (e.g. upstream support for oil exploration), or tax exemptions; or they may be implicit (in-kind), such as credit subsidies, government guarantees to protect investment, derivatives and subsidies through government procurement (guaranteed contracts), research, and public investment (UNEP, 2003; Whitley, 2013; OECD, 2011). The GSI has estimated producer subsidies for a series of countries, but estimates vary widely due to data issues (e.g. GSI, 2012b). Overall, producer subsidies are thought to be in the range of $80 B to $285 B annually in emerging and developing countries, and $452 B in G20 countries (Bast et al., 2015; OECD, 2015a, 2013; Whitley, 2013).

Based on these definitions, there have been several estimates of the global magnitude of subsidies and their implications.[3] These estimates, by the World Bank, IMF, OECD, IEA, GSI, and others range from $250 B to more than $5 T (Kojima and Koplow, 2015). The wide range illustrates the differences in scope, definitions, and methodology. For instance, the IEA (2014c) estimates that consumer subsidies in 2013 amounted to $548 B (Figure 2.1), but this figure increases to almost $1 T when producer subsidies are included. These figures must be seen in comparison with the (strenuously negotiated) commitment by governments under the Paris Climate Agreement to raise $100 B annually in climate financing by 2020.

While international market prices are a common benchmark for estimating subsidisation rates, in oil producing countries the cost of domestic production is often used as the reference point for setting prices.[4] Countries in the Middle East and North Africa have particularly high subsidies relative to the cost of supply; in 2014 Saudi Arabia (78.9%), Iran (73.8%), Iraq (62.4%), Libya (80.2%), Algeria (56.7%), and Egypt (53.7%) had some of the highest subsidisation rates in the world (IEA, 2014a).[5] The World Bank estimates that 48% of global FFS are paid in this region (Devarajan et al., 2014).[6] Figure 2.1 shows the 25 largest providers of fossil fuel consumption subsidies.

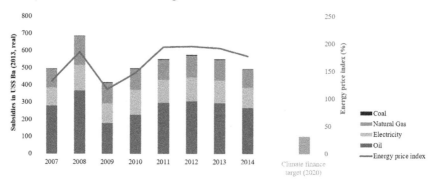

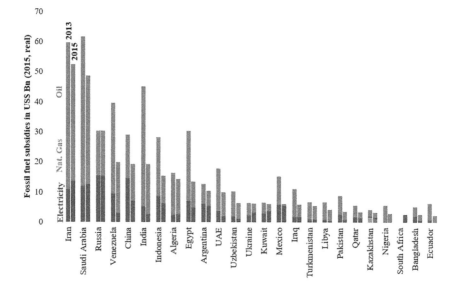

Figure 2.1 **Top:** Global consumer subsidies for fossil fuels amounted to $548 B in 2013. Subsidies generally move in line with energy prices (red line, indexed on right axis). For comparison, the climate finance commitment under the Paris Agreement amounts to $100 B per year. (IEA, 2014c) **Bottom:** The 25 largest providers of consumption subsidies to fossil fuels in 2013 and 2015 (IEA, 2016).

Comparing national diesel prices as a proxy for consumer subsidies offers a complete picture: Besides countries in the Middle East and North Africa, oil and gas exporting economies in Africa, Latin America, and Southeast Asia can be identified as heavy subsidisers of consumption (GIZ, 2014).[7] It is important to bear in mind that while consumer subsidies are mostly paid in resource-rich developing countries, numerous developed economies have large producer subsidy schemes in place; e.g. the UK

($9.0 B), Germany ($2.8 B), Australia ($5.0 B), and the USA ($20.5 B) in 2014 (Bast et al., 2015).[8]

In addition to the conventional definition of FFS, the IMF provides the measure of "post-tax subsidies" (IMF, 2013c; Coady, Parry, Sears, and Shang, 2015b, 2017). This not only accounts for consumer and producer subsidies, but also includes an estimate of the negative externalities associated with FFS (including the social cost of carbon emissions, local pollution and road congestion). By including negative externalities, the IMF interprets governments' failure to price negative externalities from fossil fuel usage as an implicit subsidy. Specifically, the "post-tax subsidy" definition also includes reduced energy tax rates, such as in the UK, where energy is taxed, albeit at a reduced rate from other consumption goods (5% VAT rather than 20%; HM Revenue and Customs, 2014).

Following this definition, the IMF estimates the cost of FFS at $5.3 T, where local and global environmental impacts constitute more than 75% of total costs (Coady et al., 2015b). This emphasises that removing conventionally defined subsidies alone is unlikely to bring fuel prices to their social optimum. The IMF definition is thus particularly relevant from an environmental perspective, as it draws attention to the substantial external costs which result from FFS (e.g. pollution, carbon emissions) – but should not be interpreted as an exact and fully robust quantification of externalities.

2.3 Fiscal, economic, environmental, and distributional costs of fossil fuel subsidies

Subsidies are typically implemented with the justification of alleviating poverty, redistributing national wealth, or promoting economic development by supporting energy-consuming industries (e.g. Strand, 2013; Commander, 2012). However, evidence suggests that FFS perform poorly at achieving these objectives, and are generally detrimental to the economic, social, and environmental dimensions of sustainable development (IMF, 2013c; UN, 2015b).

In many emerging economies, the primary objective behind fuel subsidy policies has been the promotion of industrialisation. Examples include Nigeria and Brazil, where the key objective in maintaining low energy prices was to facilitate industrialisation by conferring an advantage on domestic energy-intensive firms (De Oliveira and Laan, 2010). However, while these objectives are well-intentioned, FFS engender excessive energy use, and perpetuate inefficient technology and behaviour. In the longer term, this reduces private sector competitiveness, thus having an adverse effect on overall growth prospects (IMF, 2013c).

FFS have also been shown to distort prices, aggravate fiscal imbalances, and reduce aggregate welfare, regardless of whether the country is an oil importer or exporter (Plante, 2014). In addition, FFS have particularly

Table 2.1 Despite best intentions: fossil fuel subsidies have severe adverse effects on all three dimensions of sustainable development. This figure provides an overview of the most prominent effects.

Justification & typical rationale: • Alleviate poverty • Promote industrialisation & economic development	► Fossil Fuel Subsidies ▼ Unintended effects	
Economic:	**Social:**	**Environmental:**
• Obstruct innovation & suppress competitiveness • Discourage investment in energy infrastructure • Lock in inefficient technology & behaviour • Drain state budgets for energy importers • Encourage fuel adulteration & smuggling	• Disproportionally benefit the rich, thus aggravate inequality • Crowd out funds for public spending, incl. infrastructure, education & health services	• Encourage wasteful consumption of energy & energy-intensive resources (e.g. water) • Create barriers to clean clean energy & efficiency investments • Increase greenhouse gas emissions • Exacerbate local pollution and health risks

► **Obstruct implementation of Sustainable Development Goals**

adverse effects on the balance of payments in oil importing countries, as they exacerbate the difficulties in mitigating the effects of international energy prices (Gelb, 1988; IMF, 2008a, 2013c,a). Overall, soaring oil prices have turned fuel subsidies into an unsustainable financial burden to governments. Ukraine, Venezuela and Uzbekistan allocate approximately 10%, 20% and 30% of their annual GDP respectively to FFS (IEA, 2014c). Moreover, the IMF(2013c) and IEA (2014c) provide evidence that subsidies eliminate the incentives and financial sources for investments in the energy sector, as low consumer prices do not warrant sufficient returns, thus leading to severe inefficiency and energy shortages.

In addition, fuel subsidies have been shown to have a wide range of other unintended consequences including fuel adulteration and smuggling (Victor, 2009; IEA, 2010; Calvo-Gonzales, Cunha, and Trezzi, 2015). Evidence from Egypt and Yemen shows that fuel subsidies cause substantial external costs through traffic congestion, local pollution, and associated health impacts, but also deplete scarce water resources in the agricultural sector (Commander, 2012; Coady et al., 2017). Moreover, subsidies crowd out other productive public investments (e.g. in health, education or transport infrastructure) more generally. In Uzbekistan and Turkmenistan for instance, subsidy expenditure in 2012 exceeded public spending on health and education by a factor 10 (IMF, 2013c).

Much of the public discourse on fuel subsidies in developing countries has focused on the impact on the poor (e.g. Gangopadhyay, S., Ramaswami, B., Wadhwa, 2005; Rao, 2012; Dube, 2003; IMF, 2013c; World Bank, 2010; IEA, 2011; Ruggeri Laderchi, Olivier, and Trimble, 2013;

Adam and Lestari, 2008; Mourougane, 2010). While a common political justification for FFS is to support the poor through subsidised energy supply, the literature is clear in showing that most subsidies are regressive, i.e. in absolute terms most subsidies are received by the rich. Yet. Relative to income, adverse effects of subsidy removal are likely to be greatest for the poor (IEA, OPEC, OECD, and World Bank, 2010b; World Bank, 2010; Ruggeri Laderchi et al., 2013; Arze del Granado, Coady, and Gillingham, 2012).

For 20 developing countries Arze del Granado et al. (2012) show that poorer households consume a disproportionately small fraction of total fuel and electricity supply. In fact, households in the top income quintile spent nearly 20 times more (per capita) on most energy goods than households in the bottom quintile. Kerosene is the only exception, with broadly evenly distributed consumption across income quintiles. This implies that the bottom income quintile receives on average about 7% of the overall subsidy benefit. In contrast, the richest quintile alone receives on average almost 43% of the overall subsidy volume.

This is illustrated by household data from Nigeria (Figure 2.2): While overall expenditure on energy products is spread across different energy goods, certain energy sources are consumed to a disproportionate share by the highest income quintile. The top income quintile, for instance, accounts for 75% of overall petrol consumption, while the bottom income quintile accounts for 1%. This stark ratio can be attributed to vehicle ownership, and highlights how petrol subsidies disproportionately benefits the rich. Chapter 3 provides a more detailed study of the distribution of FFS benefits in Nigeria, and of the likely impacts of reform on different income groups.

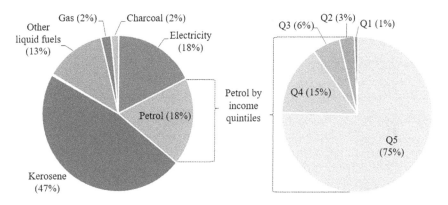

Figure 2.2 **Left:** Composition of average household energy expenditure in Nigeria; **Right:** Petrol expenditure broken down according to income quintiles, with "Q5" representing the top income quintile (National Bureau of Statistics, 2013).

Overall, the data for Nigeria confirm for petrol what various studies have documented more generally: Subsidies are highly regressive and the largest share of the financial benefit is conferred to the rich.

Apart from substantial economic and social costs, FFS are also associated with severe negative externalities on the environment – which in turn can adversely affect human and economic development in the long run. By artificially lowering the price of fossil fuel products, governments incentivise overconsumption and remove incentives for investing in energy efficiency, modern electricity infrastructure, and low-carbon energy sources (incl. renewables) (IEA, 2014c). The IEA (2014c) identifies the reform of FFS as one of the key measures for stabilising global warming at 2 degrees above pre-industrial levels; and estimates that even a partial removal of FFS could reduce global GHG emissions by 360 m tons. The IEA, OECD, and World Bank (2010a) estimate that removing global fuel subsidies would result in a 5% net reduction in the global use of energy within 10 years.

For India UNEP (2003) estimates that subsidy removal would reduce long-run energy usage by 34%. In Indonesia, Durand-Lasserve, Campagnolo, Chateau, and Dellink (2015) estimate that fossil fuel related GHG emissions could be cut by up to 12.6% by 2020 if subsidies are removed. Merrill et al. (2015) estimate potential savings from FFS reform in 20 selected countries at 2.8Gt of CO2e by 2020. At the local level, removing subsidies can help curbing traffic congestion, local pollution and associated health threats (Davis, 2013; IMF, 2013c; Commander, 2012; Coady et al., 2017). Moreover, research on the 'resource nexus' has shown that cheap energy (e.g. due to FFS) not only incentivises overconsumption of energy goods, but also encourage the inefficient use of energy-intensive materials (e.g. steel) and services in a wide range of fields, including water, transportation, and agriculture (Commander, Nikoloski, and Vagliasindi, 2015; Bleischwitz, Hoff, Spataru, van der Voet, and VanDeveer, 2017).

2.4   Reform progress: what's being done?

2.4.1   *Galvanising action: international communities and institutions*

FFS have entered international limelight at least since the G20 summit in 2009.[9] In the Pittsburgh Joint Ministerial Declaration (G20, 2009), G20 governments committed to phasing out FFS, while providing protection to the poor. Subsequently, this commitment has been reaffirmed repeatedly by numerous governments of both developing and developed countries around the world. While energy security and climate change provided the main rationale for initial commitments, in developing countries the arguments for action increasingly include goals of poverty reduction, social equity, and sustainable development more generally (Bowen and Fankhauser, 2011; Hallegatte, Fay, and Vogt-Schilb, 2013; Fay, Hallegatte, Vogt-Schilb, Rozenberg,

Narloch, and Kerr, 2015; Hallegatte, Bangalore, Bonzanigo, Fay, Narloch, Vogt-Schilb, and Rozenberg, 2014). For instance, this was highlighted most prominently through discussions and declarations of the UN Rio+20 convention in 2012, which recognise the importance of FFS reforms as a vital element of sustainable development. Subsequent multinational conventions, including the APEC Leaders' Summit in 2013, the 2014 G20 summit in Brisbane, or the 'Friends of Fossil Fuel Subsidy Reform' group of 40 governments also reflect this notion (APEC, 2013; G20, 2014; FFFSR, 2015).

Several international organisations, including the UN, World Bank, IMF, IEA, and IPCC have become strong proponents of subsidy reform in support of climate change mitigation and sustainable development. The UN's (2015b) Sustainable Development Goals for the post-2015 development agenda also includes FFS reform as a 'sub-goal':

> **Goal 12.c:** *Rationalise inefficient fossil-fuel subsidies that encourage wasteful consumption, [. . .][while] taking fully into account the specific needs and conditions of developing countries and minimizing the possible adverse impacts on their development in a manner that protects the poor and the affected communities.*

At the UN's 2015 *Financing For Development* Summit in Addis Ababa, governments have again reaffirmed their commitment to phasing out FFS and curbing wasteful consumption, while supporting the needs of the poor (UN, 2015a). While such commitments include both consumer and producer subsidies, policy attention has focused on the reform of consumer subsidies in resource-rich developing countries. Commitments by the G20 have thus far failed to galvanise action on reforming producer subsidies (Bast et al., 2015).

While the UNFCCC's 2015 Paris Agreement on climate change makes no explicit reference to fossil fuels or subsidies, it signals the strong commitment to a low-carbon energy transition, and provides a framework for accelerated action on FFS reform. In particular the Nationally Determined Contributions (NDCs), outlining country-level commitments on climate change policy actions, demonstrate that FFS reforms and other green fiscal measures can play a critical role in implementing the Agreement. Table 2.2 lists all 13 countries which explicitly integrate FFS reform into their climate policy packages. Terton, Gass, Merrill, Wagner, and Meyer (2015) further emphasise that overall 67 countries refer to green fiscal reforms (including FFS reforms) for implementing NDCs.

Following the G20 Summit in 2009 a range of international organisations and think tanks have played an important role in analysing subsidies and advocating reforms (Arze del Granado et al., 2012; IMF, 2013c; IEA, 2014c; OECD, 2011; World Bank, 2014; GSI, 2012b; CFR, 2015). These contributions have included definition and quantification of FFS, and discussions of data gaps and challenges in measurement, the socio-economic,

Table 2.2 FFS reform are explicitly integrated in the NDCs of 13 countries (Terton et al., 2015). Not all offer concrete targets and associated emission reduction estimates.

	Estimated potential GHG reduction relative to baseline (%)		
	2020	2025	2030
Burkina Faso			
China	0.8	0.7	
Egypt	14.9	12.6	
Ethiopia			
Ghana	2.8	2.5	
India	3.2	2.7	
Morocco			6.6
New Zealand			
Senegal			
Sierra Leone			
Singapore			
UAE	14.4	13.0	
Vietnam	1.7	1.9	

environmental and sectoral impacts of removing subsidies, the role of transitional policies, and case studies to highlight lessons on how to implement reforms. Whitley and van der Burg (2015) provide an overview of institutional support to FFS reform processes, including efforts by the IMF, IEA, World Bank, and OECD.

2.4.2 *Implementing subsidy reforms: country-level action*

Despite strong drivers for FFS reforms – fiscal strains on national budgets, adverse environmental impacts, and international commitments – overall reform progress at the country level has been limited and the track record mixed. In reviewing 22 case studies of recent reforms the IMF (2013a) finds that only 12 reform endeavours succeeded in permanently removing consumer subsidies without causing major economic or social disruptions. The successes and failures of past subsidy reforms illustrate the economic and political complexities, and underscore the need for country-specific reform designs. However, despite the lack of a coordinated international approach, a number of governments – primarily driven by fiscal imbalances – are making significant progress in phasing out fuel subsidies (Table 2.3).

As the momentum for FFS reform builds, governments can draw on the lessons of a rich collection of case studies of attempted subsidy reforms. While case studies of resource-rich developing countries predominate, analyses include countries of all sizes and levels of development, resource rich and poor economies, and cover all continents. In-depth reviews and analyses are offered by Vagliasindi (2012b) for 20 FFS reform case studies, and more recently by Kojima (2016) for 35 countries. The IMF (2013a) also provides a comprehensive account of recent FFS reform efforts, covering fuel, electricity, and coal sectors, and including both successful and failed reforms. Further regional reviews have analysed recent progress with FFS reforms in Sub-Saharan Africa, the Middle East and North Africa (Sdralevich, Sab, Zouhar, and Albertin, 2014; IMF, 2013b). In addition to multi-country reviews, various single-country analyses have reviewed specific reform experiences in detail, such as Salehi-Isfahani, Wilson Stucki, and Deutschmann (2015) for Iran. The GSI (e.g. 2012b) and IEA (2014c) also provide a rich collection of individual case study analyses.[10] It is striking that these studies almost exclusively cover reforms of consumer subsidies. Indeed, reforms of producer subsidies are lagging behind, and lack comprehensive analysis and documentation.

Especially for consumer subsidies, there is an up-to-date and thorough literature on reform experiences, based on which key lessons learnt and strategies for future reforms can be distilled. Several countries have successfully put other countries' lessons learnt into practice, and implemented effectively designed and publically accepted FFS reforms. The Philippines and Iran effectively managed the downside risks of FFS reforms, by using reform revenues to compensate vulnerable households with cash transfers, and support energy intensive firms with implementing energy efficiency measures. These compensation measures played a key role in catalysing public support for the reform process (Salehi-Isfahani et al., 2015; IMF, 2013c).

The IEA (2014c) reports that in 2014 there were 27 governments actively pursuing FFS reforms (also see Table 2.3). Notably, some of the most recent and comprehensive reforms were being implemented in Asia: following gradual increases, India fully liberalised diesel prices in 2014, and halved gas subsidies; Indonesia increased gasoline, diesel, and electricity prices by up to 44% in 2014; further subsidy reforms were implemented in 2013 and 2014 in Malaysia, Nepal, China, Bangladesh, Myanmar, and Thailand (IEA, 2014c; Fay et al., 2015). In an attempt to cut a fiscal deficit, the United Arab Emirates too have moved to remove all subsidies on transport fuel in 2015 (Carpenter and Khan, 2015). Overall, the last few years have shown encouraging signs that FFS reforms are being debated or implemented (even under challenging political conditions) in developing and emerging economies around the world, including those with some of the largest subsidy schemes (including Russia, Ukraine, Egypt, and Iran). However, developed economies with large producer

Table 2.3 FFS reforms between 2013 and 2015: announcements, commitments, NDCs, implementation (based on IEA, 2014c; Terton et al., 2015). For details on each case study refer to Kojima (2016).

	Status	Energy type	Price increase (subsidy reduction)
Angola	Completed	Gasoline	25%
		Diesel	25%
Argentina	Implementation ongoing	Natural gas	(20%)
Bahrain	Completed	Petrol	56%
		Diesel	(100%)
		Kerosene	(100%)
Bangladesh	Implementation ongoing	All refined oil products	(67%)
		Electricity	64%
Burkina Faso	NDC commitment		
China	Planning & piloting (NDC)	Energy pricing reform	
Ecuador	Ongoing	Electricity	
Egypt	Completed	Gasoline	41%
	Further actions	Diesel	63%
	under NDC	Natural gas Electricity	30–70%
Ethiopia	NDC commitment		
Ghana	Completed	Gasoline	(100%)
	Further actions under NDC	Diesel	(100%)
India	Completed	Diesel	(100%)
	Further actions under NDC	LNG	(50%)
Indonesia	Completed	Gasoline	44%
		Diesel	
		Electricity	
Iran	Implementation ongoing	Gasoline	75%
		Diesel	40%
		LNG	32%

(Continued)

Table 2.3 (Continued)

	Status	*Energy type*	*Price increase (subsidy reduction)*
Kuwait	Completed	Diesel	(100%)
		Kerosene	(100%)
Malaysia	Implementation ongoing	All fuels	(100%)
Mexico	Ongoing	Gasoline	
		Diesel	
Morocco	Completed	Gasoline	(100%)
	Further actions under NDC	Diesel	
Myanmar	Planning	Electricity	
Nepal	Implementation attempted & ongoing	All fuels	
New Zealand	NDC commitment		
Nigeria	Planning	All fuels	
Oman	Implementation ongoing	Petrol	(64%)
		Diesel	
Russia	Planning	Natural gas	5%
Saudi Arabia	Completed	Gasoline	66%
		Diesel	79%
		Natural gas	67%
Senegal	NDC commitment		
Sierra Leone	NDC commitment		
Singapore	NDC commitment		
Sudan	Completed	Gasoline	68%
		Diesel	75%
		LPG	66%
Thailand	Implementation ongoing	Diesel	
		CNG	
Tunisia	Completed	Gasoline	6%
Turkmenistan	Implementation ongoing	Natural gas	

(*Continued*)

Table 2.3 (Continued)

	Status	Energy type	Price increase (subsidy reduction)
Ukraine	Implementation ongoing	Natural gas	29%
United Arab Emirates	Further actions under NDC		
Uzbekistan	Implementation ongoing	Diesel	11%
Yemen	Implementation ongoing	Gasoline	60%
		Diesel	95%
Vietnam	NDC commitment		

subsidies (e.g. USA, UK) are notable absences among ongoing FFS reform efforts.

The above reform efforts refer to the removal or reduction of active subsidy schemes. In addition, the World Bank (2014) reports that about 40 national and 20 sub-national jurisdictions are introducing or operating carbon pricing schemes – in the Pigouvian sense, the next step following upon subsidy removal.

2.5 Reforms: drivers and barriers

2.5.1 The role of prices in driving reforms

Considering the economic, social and environmental costs of FFS, there is a clear rationale for reforms. However, whether policy makers are actually willing to take on the political challenges of a FFS reform is often determined by the gravity of fiscal imbalances, and urgency of the economic costs of FFS (e.g. Jordan in 2005–2008; Vagliasindi, 2012b). In practice, this implies that international energy prices can be the key drivers of action and complacency likewise: Particularly for importers, high oil prices increase the need for reform, thus galvanising action, but also aggravate the political obstacles, thus prolonging inaction. On the contrary, low oil prices reduce political obstacles, making it easier to remove subsidies – but they also remove the fiscal urgency to do so.

Since the early 2000s, increasing fossil fuel prices have turned FFS into an unaffordable commitment, especially for cash-strapped developing countries with high subsidisation rates. FFS move in line with energy prices (Figure 2.1), and accordingly 2008 has seen peaks in oil prices and subsidy bills likewise. Many governments that are committed to FFS schemes allocate substantial shares of their public budgets to subsidies, and increasing energy prices can exacerbate this burden. Especially under precarious fiscal and economic conditions rising energy prices can drive reform action, or even make it inevitable.

However, high fossil fuel prices also increase the political stakes of a FFS reform – which has typically been the main reason for inaction (Benes, Cheon, Urpelainen, and Yang, 2015). With high free market prices, subsidy removal is more likely to result in a substantial energy price shock domestically. Thus, the higher energy prices are, the stronger the opposition from low- and high-income households and political interest groups is likely to be. If economically possible, policy makers are tempted to leave such difficult and unpopular reforms to their successors.

As oil prices fell around 70% between Q3 2014 and Q1 2016 the political stakes of subsidy reform were significantly reduced (World Bank, 2015a; Baffes, Kose, Ohnsorge, and Stocker, 2015). Several countries capitalised on this opportunity: Malaysia (Dec. 2014), India (Sept. 2014), and Indonesia (Nov. 2014) have implemented partial or full fuel subsidy reforms without triggering notable public opposition (Benes et al., 2015). In fact, low international energy prices meant that diesel prices in India fell by 5.7% as a consequence of price liberalisation, thus entirely avoiding adverse price shocks on consumers – for the time being (Michael, 2014). However, particularly in energy importing countries, low energy prices also relieve governments of high FFS bills and remove the urgency of subsidy reform. As the Economist (2015) puts it, "whether low [oil] prices help to galvanise reform or simply make it easier for governments to procrastinate still remains up in the air".

In several fossil fuel exporting countries low energy prices in fact increased fiscal pressures – not due to increasing FFS, but due to dwindling export revenues. For these countries the opportunity costs of FFS (i.e. foregone export revenues) are highest under high energy prices. However, fiscal pressures due to reduced resource exports during low international energy prices can outweigh the fiscal pressures due to subsidy payments during high prices. This has pushed the UAE, Bahrain and Oman to remove subsidies in 2015/2016 (Carpenter and Khan, 2015).

Energy prices not only matter in levels, but also in terms of volatility: By running a FFS system, governments introduce the volatility on international markets into their national accounts, and obstruct forward-looking budgeting. This means that increased energy price volatility can also act as a driver of FFS reforms (Kojima, 2009, 2016; Vagliasindi, 2012b). By deregulating energy prices governments pass on price volatility to firms and households, who will then incorporate price signals into their decisions – e.g. by substituting away from volatile energy sources (see Section 8.3.5 for how governments can smoothen price shocks).

Overall, experience suggests that FFS reforms are most likely to be implemented when they are needed as a fiscal relief measure in the face of mounting fiscal burdens; and evidently fiscal burdens due to subsidies tend to be the largest when fuel prices are high. However, successful subsidy reforms in the past have been implemented under both high and low oil prices, suggesting that low oil prices are a conducive opportunity but no necessity for reform.

2.5.2 Public opposition and political economy

Experience shows that political economy challenges create some of the most serious barriers to reforming both producer and consumer subsidies (Dansie, Lanteigne, and Overland, 2010; Kojima, Bacon, and Trimble, 2014; Fattouh and El-Katiri, 2013; Cheon, Lackner, and Urpelainen, 2015; Koplow, 2014). Often this is aggravated by the fact that policy designs tend to be focussed on being technically sound and administratively feasible – rather than politically supportable (Pritchett, 2005; Strand, 2013). Especially consumption subsidies tend to be paid in countries with weak institutional capacity and poor governance, and are a common political tool for luring voters or influential interest groups, rather than being sound economic policy (Cheon, Urpelainen, and Lackner, 2013; Commander, 2012). In addition, Lockwood (2015) notes that FFS play a key role in manifesting and centralising a state's political power. This resonates with Kim and Urpelainen (2015), who argue that especially autocratic states with low-density urbanisation tend to implement FFS for securing power. Overall, the political economy obstacles of reforming fuel subsidies and raising prices to cost-recovery levels are closely linked to those of carbon taxes (Hammar, Lofgren, and Sterner, 2004; Fay et al., 2015).

The recent case of Nigeria's attempted fuel subsidy removal illustrates the immense political challenges of subsidy reforms as discussed by Victor (2009): In 2012 the government's decision to remove subsidies on fossil fuel imports caused fuel prices to more than double. The extensive strikes and public protests which followed, prompted the government to immediately reintroduce subsidies (Bazilian and Onyeji, 2012; Siddig, Aguiar, Grethe, Minor, and Walmsley, 2014). Similarly, governments of Bolivia (2010), Cameroon (2008), Venezuela (1989), and Yemen (2005 and 2014) were all forced to abandon reform attempts following heavy public protests, particularly by low-income population groups (Segal, 2011, 2012; IEA, 2014c). Chapter 3 illustrates how regions with high energy dependency (in particular urban areas) can be affected particularly strongly by FFS reform, and thus become hotspots of public opposition and protests. Overall, this highlights how subsidies create deeply-rooted interests among domestic industries and households benefitting from cheap energy (Victor, 2009; IEA, 2011; World Bank, 2010).

Reforms of subsidies and pricing mechanisms can have various adverse effects, particularly in the short-term, requiring careful attention by policy makers. Without adequate measures for mitigating these effects, and without comprehensive consultation and communication, reforms are likely to face significant resistance. Past reform attempts have shown that political economy challenges can have a range of reasons, including (World Bank, 2010):

- **Hardship on poor and vulnerable:** Subsidy reforms risk inflicting significant hardship on poor and vulnerable groups, who might be heavily dependent on the subsidies, particularly in the case of kerosene or gas (see Chapter 3).
- **Influential stakeholders:** FFS especially benefit the upper and middle classes and industry; these influential stakeholders tend to be strongly opposed to subsidy reforms, and are often better organised to exert political pressure.
- **Macro-economic impacts:** Inflationary impacts of FFS reforms can be significant as energy prices are a critical input to the cost of production for most sectors, and cost increases may be passed onto consumers.
- **Reduced competitiveness:** Energy-intensive industries could face reduced competitiveness as a result of reduced subsidies. Higher fuel and electricity prices may necessitate costly energy and material efficiency investments, affecting costs and output in manufacturing (see Chapters 4, 5, and 7).
- **Employment impacts:** FFS reduction is bound to cause structural and sectoral shifts in the economy (see Chapter 6). Such structural shifts may result from the loss of competitiveness of energy intensive industries and lead to job losses. However, in the longer term jobs may also be created, as investments increase in energy systems, renewable energy, and energy efficiency
- **Substitution with unsafe, inferior fuels:** The reduction of FFS may force poor and middle-income households to shift towards cheaper and lower grade energy sources, with significant health and environmental impacts.
- **Poor governance, accountability, and service quality:** Governments may struggle to reduce subsidies and increase prices, while service quality remains poor and key sectors continue to lack accountability and transparency.

Crucially, the above adverse effects (and associated political challenges) may vary significantly depending on the type of fuel subsidy. For instance, in many developing countries petrol is predominately consumed by the rich, while kerosene is an essential cooking and lighting fuel for the poor (Soile and Mu, 2015). Rentschler (2016) demonstrates that adverse price shocks due to subsidy removal vary significantly not only across income groups, but also across different types of fuel subsidies, across geographical regions and between urban and rural sectors (see Chapter 3). This emphasises that the nature, location, and extent of political economy challenges and political opposition can vary for the reform of different (consumer) subsidies, thus requiring tailored compensation measures, e.g. through flexible cash transfer schemes.

These challenges also highlight the crucial role played by political and administrative institutions, which must possess the authority to initiate and oversee reforms, but also the diligence to consider and mitigate potential adverse reform effects (Acemoglu and Robinson, 2010). Behind such institutions, strong political will and credibility of the government forms the foundation for successfully implementing a FFS reform and safeguarding livelihoods.

2.6   Focus areas for the design of subsidy reforms

The most common driver of past FFS reforms have been mounting fiscal pressures, which make subsidy reform an attractive rescue measure (Vagliasindi, 2012a,b). Environmental objectives have at most played a secondary role. As a result, past reform efforts (and their evaluations) have focussed strongly on managing the downside risks of FFS reform, for instance through communication and compensation strategies (IMF, 2013c,a). While these measures are indeed indispensable, they do not necessarily guarantee that the development potential and environmental benefits of a subsidy reform are maximised. Hence, "success" of a subsidy reform should not only reflect whether a subsidy was successfully removed – but whether it ensures a contribution to long-term economic development objectives, rather than mere short-term fiscal relief.

This section draws on past reform experiences and provides a brief overview of key focus areas for designing FFS reforms that contribute to long-term sustainable development objectives. The specific features of any FFS reform must be determined by a thorough analysis of country characteristics, the nature of current subsidies, and the potential impacts of a reform on households and firms. Yet, the lessons learnt from past reform attempts – both failed and successful – illustrate that several issues require particular attention:

Assessment of subsidies and pricing mechanisms: The basis of any reform effort is a thorough assessment of existing subsidies. This includes a coherent subsidy definition, and a precise understanding of the quantity of subsidies and their beneficiaries. Based on this, decision makers can prioritise the reform of certain subsidy types, determine a suitable reform timeline, and assess the likely impacts of a reform. Most importantly, this includes simulating the effect of energy price shocks on small businesses and low-income households.

Building public acceptance: Moreover, case studies show that timely and transparent communication, public engagement, and consultation processes are critical (Chapter 8; IMF, 2013c,a; Vagliasindi, 2012a). Whether a reform can win public and political support typically hinges on how effectively the benefits of reform are communicated to the population.

Social protection and compensation: In addition, communication strategies must clearly indicate how subsidy removal will be paired with effective social protection and compensation schemes which mitigate adverse effects on the population and affected firms. Several studies have shown that income shocks due to subsidy removal can be substantial, thus – if uncompensated – resulting in significant increases of poverty rates (Araar, Choueiri, and Verme, 2015; Rentschler, 2016). Hence, policy makers must strike a careful balance between raising reform revenues while ensuring affordability and protecting livelihoods (Ruggeri Laderchi et al., 2013).

Cash transfers have proven to be one of the most effective and practical instruments for compensating low-income households vulnerable to energy price hikes (IMF, 2013a,b). Such cash transfers are either issued universally to the whole (or majority) of a population, or targeted to selected recipients – typically the most affected households (Salehi-Isfahani et al., 2015). How exactly such a cash compensation scheme is designed and delivered depends greatly on country characteristics and needs (e.g. the level of vulnerability of households, their location, availability of poverty data with nation-wide coverage and attributable identification, the existence of appropriate financial infrastructure). Especially in the case of producer subsidies, targeted measures for strengthening competitiveness and energy efficiency can help firms to cope with price shocks.

Revenue redistribution and reinvestment: In order for a FFS reform to contribute to sustainable development and climate change mitigation, sustainable management, reinvestment, and redistribution of reform revenues are critical. FFS reforms create an opportunity to implement transparent institutions and prudent public finance strategies for reinvesting reform (and natural resource) revenues in line with long-term development goals, e.g. through sovereign wealth funds.

Complementary measures: Moreover, while subsidy removal will help to relieve national budgets, further actions will likely be needed to trigger investments in more efficient technology or changes in behaviour. The reason is that in practice, even if subsidies are reduced and fuel prices increased, significant barriers may exist (incl. information, capacity and financial constraints) preventing households and firms from adjusting their behaviour or investing in more efficient technology (see Chapters 4 and 7). Governments can address these barriers with complementary measures, which facilitate and stimulate low-carbon innovation and investments, and ensure that subsidy reforms contribute to low-carbon development. Such complementary measures have been argued to be crucial for ensuring the effectiveness of price-based environmental instruments – i.e. FFS reforms and carbon taxes likewise (Fay et al., 2015).

Timing and price smoothing: Overall, the insights derived from past experiences highlight that a complete FFS reform is not only about removing subsidies, but requires an integrated strategy featuring a range of carefully designed and sequenced policy measures. Indeed, issuing compensation pay-ments before subsidies are removed, and phase-wise reduction of subsidies can be critical for signalling political commitment to social protection and mitigation of price shocks. Despite differing priorities and political dynamics, these principles are applicable to both producer and consumer subsidy reforms. For instance, regardless which type of subsidy is removed, both households and firms are likely to face price shocks – albeit to different degrees (e.g. depending on firms' pass-through of price changes).

The wide range of focus areas discussed above provides the motivation for this thesis to consider a wide range of perspectives, and to use a diverse range of analytical methods (see Section 1.4). Chapter 8 (and Ren-tschler and Bazilian, 2017) offers a more detailed account of the above focus areas, and distils guiding principles for the design of effective FFS reforms by drawing on existing literature, case studies, and the insights pre-sented in this thesis.

2.7   Areas for future research

Existing literature has focused particularly on documenting the wide-ranging adverse effects of FFS. More research is required to better under-stand the determinants of successful reforms, and hence inform the design of future FFS reforms. Based on the literature presented and discussed in this chapter, at least six areas can be identified that require further research:

- **Country-level studies for all major subsidising economies:** Concrete country-level studies for all major subsidising economies are needed to inform the design of specific subsidy reforms. Such analyses need to shed light on the potential distributional and socio-economic effects of reforms, and evaluate existing social protection schemes for their suitability to mitigate price shocks. Potential price shocks need to be understood with respect to their variability across income groups, geographical locations, and occupations. Section 8.3.1 provides an overview of several such country case studies. Chapters 3, 5, and 6 offer examples of such FFS reform analyses and simulations using the cases of Nigeria and Indonesia.
- **Integrating reforms into long-term sustainable development strategies:** While experience is building on how to tackle the short-term political economy challenges of reform, a better understanding is needed on how fuel subsidy reforms can be integrated into long-term sustainable development objectives. Rather than just offering immediate fiscal bene-fits, subsidy reforms can offer a range of opportunities for complemen-tary actions, e.g. for sustainable management and reinvestment of natural resource rents, institutional reform, or effective social protection schemes. This issue is discussed in depth in Chapters 7 and 8.

- **Role of tax evasion, smuggling, and informal activities:** Studies on FFS reforms have largely overlooked activities, which may not feature in standard economic theory, but can be of substantial magnitude. FFS have long been associated with smuggling and corruption, yet these activities are not accounted for in most studies. Similarly, studies fail to consider the role of tax evasion and informality, which can significantly affect the effects of subsidy reforms. The study presented in Chapter 6 addresses these issues using a specially developed computational general equilibrium (CGE) model.
- **Impact on firms:** Empirical evidence is needed to better understand the impact of FFS reform – and thus energy price increases – on firms, and to what extent response measures can mitigate potential adverse effects. The concern that higher energy prices would harm the competitiveness of firms is a common argument of political opponents of FFS reform (IMF, 2016b). This issue is covered – both conceptually and empirically – in Chapters 4 and 5.
- **Role in emission reduction strategies (NDCs):** There is a need to evaluate the role of FFS reforms as part of comprehensive policy packages for climate change mitigation. A better understanding is needed of the potential contribution of FFS reforms in emission reduction commitments (under the NDCs), and how they may pave the way for implementing fuel or carbon taxes. The analysis in Chapter 7 shows how policy simulations can estimate the reductions in fossil fuel usage (hence GHG emissions) due to FFS reform – yet, further studies are needed to link such results to climate change mitigation targets.
- **Producer subsidies:** The evidence (and public awareness) has been disproportionately focussed on consumption subsidies, while producer subsidies – particularly in developed countries – remain insufficiently researched (and reformed). Coherent definitions and quantifications are needed, alongside analyses of political economy challenges, case studies of past reforms, and estimates of potential reform impacts. While the analytical approaches (Chapters 3, 5, and 6) and principles for effective reform design (Chapter 8) presented in this thesis are relevant to both consumer and producer subsidies, the overall focus of this thesis is on consumer subsidies.

2.8   Conclusion

Fossil fuel subsidies (FFS) have entered international limelight at least since the 2009 G20 summit in Pittsburgh when governments committed to the reform of unsustainable fuel subsidies. While subsidy reform is crucial for achieving any ambitious carbon emission reduction, the wide range of negative externalities associated with fuel subsidies emphasises that reform is a vital contribution to sustainable development objectives more generally. With the inclusion in the UN's Sustainable Development Goals, FFS reform has fully entered the mainstream sustainable development agenda.

This chapter provides a policy-oriented overview of the state-of-the-art on FFS. It shows how severe economic, environmental, and social externalities act as strong drivers for reform, while political economy challenges mean that implementation can be difficult in practice. It offers decision makers an overview of the main definitions, assessment criteria, externalities, and recent reform progress. This also provides the context and background for the subsequent analytical studies presented in this thesis. Overall, this chapter offers several key insights for policy makers implementing reform:

- **Definitions:** There is a range of approaches to defining fuel subsidies, and not all are coherent. For designing targeted reform measures, policy makers must clearly define, identify, and estimate relevant subsidies (e.g. consumer or producer subsidies, or different fuel types). This is critical for understanding the magnitude of potential reform benefits and adverse side-effects (on both firms and households), as well as designing adequate reform features.
- **Adverse effects:** The evidence is strong – FFS are detrimental to all three dimensions of sustainable development; economic, environmental, and social. For policy makers it is critical to exactly understand the adverse effects of subsidies specific to their country. This should extend beyond short-term fiscal considerations, and cover social and environmental issues, as well as longer-term competitiveness and development. This is also crucial for enabling credible and effective communication of the necessity of reform to critics.
- **Reform efforts:** With a dedicated sub-goal in the Sustainable Development Goals, and repeatedly stated commitment by the G20, there is an increasing momentum for reforming FFS. While this has been particularly true for consumer subsidies, there has been little progress in reforming producer subsidies in developed countries. As subsidies uphold inefficient and uncompetitive industries, policy makers should consider the implications of inaction, including the risk of declining international competitiveness.
- **The role of low oil prices:** Low oil prices are a conducive opportunity but no necessity for reform – successful subsidy reforms in the past have been implemented under both high and low oil prices. Rather, experience suggests that the key driver of most reforms are escalating fiscal burdens; just as with carbon taxes, implementing FFS reforms is likely to yield significant fiscal benefits. This means that policy makers should prepare a foundation for subsidy reform through careful planning, as this allows swift implementation once an opportunity presents itself (e.g. in the form of low oil prices). However, by

focussing on fiscal benefits policy makers may fail to implement complementary measures that help to maximise the potential of a FFS reform to contribute to broader sustainable development objectives (see Chapter 7).

- **Political economy challenges are substantial** and often underestimated; they require policy makers to consider a series of measures: Transparent communication and compensation are crucial for protecting low-income households, and securing public support for subsidy reform. Dedicated support to firms (e.g. through energy efficiency measures) can help manage private sector opposition. Timing and price smoothing can further mitigate price shocks.
- **Effective reform design:** Overall, reform case studies show that an effective fuel subsidy reform requires policy makers to implement a package of dedicated and carefully timed measures. They include (step-wise) subsidy removal, communication, compensation, revenue redistribution measures, and further complementary policies – all of which must be carefully timed. Smart timing and price smoothing can further mitigate price shocks. In this way policy makers can minimise the downside risks of subsidy removal (e.g. due to price shocks), while maximising the contribution to sustainable development.

Last, this chapter suggests several **areas for future research**; in particular, (i) country case studies of the distributional effects of FFS removal; (ii) the integration of FFS reforms into long-term sustainable development strategies (e.g. through institutional reforms, or sustainable management of natural resource rents); (iii) the role of tax evasion, smuggling, and informality in determining the effectiveness of reforms; (iv) the impacts of FFS reform on firms; (v) the contribution of FFS reform to national GHG emission reduction targets (e.g. as part of NDCs); and (vi) the reform of producer subsidies. While it is beyond the scope of this thesis to fill all these gaps, subsequent chapters will address the most important issues and present methodologies for conducting further studies.

Notes

1 *An abridged version of this chapter has been published as* Rentschler, J. E., Bazilian, M. (2016). Reforming fossil fuel subsidies: Drivers, barriers, and the state of progress. *Climate Policy*. Vol. 17(7), pp. 891–914.
2 For a detailed discussion of these estimates see Burniaux and Chateau (2014).
3 Stefanski (2014) takes an entirely different approach: instead of empirical measurement, the author infers global subsidies volumes theoretically by using a structural transformation model and comparing predictions with observed emission intensities.
4 Note that this notion acknowledges the break-even price but does not account for the opportunity cost of export revenues.

5 The IEA (2017) defines the cost of supply based on the import parity price (export parity price in the case of net oil exporters). This refers to the price of a good at the nearest international hub, plus transportation costs to the net importer, plus the cost of domestic distribution and any value-added tax (VAT). In the case of net exporters, the subsidies calculated in this way are implicit, as they are an opportunity cost rather than a budgetary expense.

6 See Chattopadhyay and Jha (2014) for an overview for South-east Asian countries.

7 See Whitley (2013) for an overview of different definitions and data.

8 See Johnston, Heffron, and McCauley (2014) for a detailed discussion of energy subsidies in the UK.

9 Members of the G20 include Argentina, Australia, Brazil, Canada, China, EU, France, Germany, India, Indonesia, Italy, Japan, Mexico, Russia, Saudi Arabia, South Africa, South Korea, Turkey, UK, and USA.

10 The GSI provides in-depth country studies as part of its "Fossil fuel subsidies: At what cost?" publication series (GSI, 2012b). Also see GIZ (2014), who publish a series of International Fuel Prices Observatory factsheets, focused on fuel price changes in the Middle East and Africa, East Asia and the Americas.

3 The impacts on households
The regional variation of poverty effects due to fossil fuel subsidy reform – evidence from Nigeria

Jun Rentschler[1]

3.1 Introduction

Fossil fuel subsidies have been documented to be highly regressive, as they predominantly benefit the rich, thus having substantial implications for the distribution of wealth. The reason is that high-income households consume larger quantities of subsidised products – energy in particular – thus siphoning off a disproportionately large share of overall subsidies (Arze del Granado et al., 2012). As a necessary consequence the removal of fuel subsidies is also likely to trigger significant distributional impacts and income shocks. If unmitigated, these adverse effects can be felt across all income groups, with the poorest often being the most vulnerable.

Nigeria's attempted fuel subsidy removal in 2012 illustrates how the mismanagement of such adverse effects can jeopardise entire reforms: The government's decision to remove subsidies on fossil fuel imports caused fuel prices to more than double. Strikes and violent public protests followed, prompting the government to immediately reintroduce subsidies (Bazilian and Onyeji, 2012; Siddig et al., 2014). Similarly, governments of Bolivia (2010), Cameroon (2008), Venezuela (1989), and Yemen (2005 and 2014) were all forced to abandon reform attempts following heavy public protests, particularly by low-income population groups (IEA, 2014c; Segal, 2011, 2012).

These cases confirm that it is critical to understand the incidence of existing subsidy benefits, and the potential welfare impacts of a reform. Carefully designed compensation measures are essential for mitigating energy price shocks, ensuring the affordability of fuel, and protecting livelihoods of vulnerable households (Ruggeri Laderchi et al., 2013). Indeed, several successful subsidy reforms have demonstrated that – besides timely and credible communication of reform benefits – effective compensation is crucial for securing public support for reform (IMF, 2013c; Vagliasindi, 2012a).

This chapter focuses on Nigeria and uses the statistical simulation model by Araar and Verme (2012) to estimate the regional variability of direct welfare effects of removing fuel subsidies. It finds that an uncompensated removal of fuel subsidies can increase the national poverty headcount rate by 3-4%. The chapter investigates different compensation strategies and their effect on poverty rates both at the national and state level.

Crucially, this chapter shows that uniform cash compensation that appears effective when considering national averages fails to mitigate price shocks in 16 of 37 states – thus putting livelihoods at risk, and provoking public opposition. Notably, states identified to incur the largest price shocks were hotspots of violent public protests in 2012. As an alternative this chapter presents a tailored compensation strategy which ensures for all states that price shocks are mitigated, and poverty rates are either unchanged or lower than before the reform. Overall, the analysis shows the need for thorough, disaggregated analyses of subsidy reforms, and tailored reform strategies.

The remainder of this chapter is structured as follows: Section 3.2 provides more detailed information about Nigeria's fossil fuel sector and subsidy program. Section 3.3 presents a disaggregated analysis of energy consumption patterns in Nigeria, thus highlighting underlying inequalities. Section 3.4 presents an empirical subsidy simulation. Section 3.4.1 presents the methodology, followed by an outline of the (hypothetical) reform scenarios in Section 3.4.2. Section 3.4.3 presents the results both at the national level and disaggregated to the state-level. Section 3.5 concludes.

3.2   Fossil fuel subsidies in Nigeria

As a developing country with substantial fossil resource wealth and a mixed track record of fiscal prudence and transparency, Nigeria is a frequently cited case for studying fossil fuel subsidies and natural resource management more generally. This section briefly outlines why Nigeria – which is in close competition with South Africa for the title of Africa's largest economy – signifies many of the maladies commonly associated with FFS, thus making it a relevant case study for the pupose of this analysis. By considering Nigeria, this study aims to draw conclusions which maybe transferable to other resourse-rich developing countries.

Nigeria extracts 2.5m barrels of oil a day, which account for 70% of government revenues and 95% of total exports (World Bank, 2015b; IMF, 2013c). These oil exports make Nigeria the fifth largest oil exporter in the world. Despite abundant energy resources, only 55% of Nigerians have access to electricity (34% in rural areas); annual per capita electricity consumption in 2012 was 155 kWh (compared to 4,405 kWh in South Africa). And electricity supply is not only elusive, but also unreliable: chronic underinvestment and corruption in the electricity sector mean that the average Nigerian enterprise experiences over 36 power outages a month, wiping out 4% of annual GDP. Similar problems plague the country's four national oil refineries, which operate at just 20% to 30%

capacity. While over 70% of fuel consumption is met by imports, shortages are endemic (World Bank, 2015b; IMF, 2013c).

Through the Petroleum Products Pricing Regulatory Agency, Nigeria maintains artificially low energy prices – most notably for kerosene and petrol. The gap between fuel import costs and regulated prices are financed through the Petroleum Support Fund, which administers fuel subsidies.[2] Figure 3.1 provides estimates of the overall volume of the subsidy program, as well as fuel prices per litre; the reliability of these figures remains uncertain due to conflicting information from different national authorities and large-scale subsidy theft (GSI, 2012a; also see Section 3.4.2).[3]

At nearly 5% of GDP in 2011 subsidies are a significant expense for the government, and fail to reach Nigerians in more than one sense (IMF, 2013c): As with all fossil fuel subsidy schemes, the direct financial benefits to households are concentrated on the rich, thus failing to benefit the absolute poor (who constitute 61% of the population[4]). In addition, a complex and opaque system of intermediary dealers and political influence means that, instead of lowering the market price, subsidies are often privately appropriated before the fuel reaches the market. For kerosene, Udo (2015) suggests that the subsidised rate of N50 per litre is in fact only available to privileged individuals, while regular consumers often pay prices between N120 and N250. Finally, rampant fuel smuggling means subsidy benefits are leaking out of the country. The IMF estimates that 85% of petrol consumed in Benin in 2011 was smuggled from Nigeria (Mlachila, Ruggiero, and Corvino, 2016).

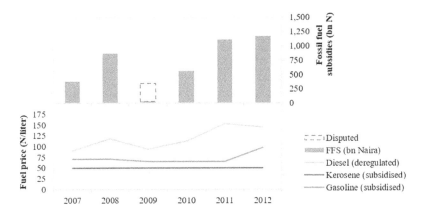

Figure 3.1 Fossil fuel subsidies in Nigeria. **Upper panel:** Estimated annual fossil fuel subsidies, primarily for oil and oil derivatives (billions of Naira). Uncertainty persists over the amount of subsidies paid in 2009 after a presidential directive to suspend kerosene subsidies. **Lower panel:** Prices for diesel, petrol, and kerosene in Naira per liter (IEA, 2014c; IMF, 2013a).

Facing mounting fiscal pressures and recognising the inefficiencies of its subsidy scheme, Nigeria attempted a radical subsidy reform in 2012. While the need for such reform was pressing, the government failed to garner sufficient public support for its reform efforts. Public opposition to the reform had two key reasons in particular: (i) A lack of credibility and transparency with respect to the handling of reform revenues, and (ii) inadequate plans for compensation and social protection, resulting from a poor understanding of the needs and vulnerability of affected energy consumers. Subsidy removal was met with extensive strikes and violent public protests, and prompted the government to swiftly reintroduce subsidies (Bazilian and Onyeji, 2012; Siddig et al., 2014).

3.3   Understanding energy demand

Understanding the patterns of energy consumption is crucial for understanding who stands to lose most from subsidy removal, and designing effective social protection schemes. This chapter uses the Harmonized Nigeria Living Standard Survey of 2009/2010, which provides consumption data for 33,775 households (or 149,261 individuals) across all 37 federal states (National Bureau of Statistics, 2013). The survey provides a detailed breakdown of household expenditure on food, education, health, energy, and other goods.

Especially in countries such as Nigeria, where existing subsidy schemes are justified as a mechanism for redistributing natural resource revenues and for supporting poor households, it is critical to understand the scale of regressivity. Various studies have highlighted how energy subsidies fail to reach poor households: Arze del Granado et al. (2012) analyse a sample of 20 developing countries from around the world and find that on average the richest 20% benefit six times more from fuel subsidies than the poorest 20% (in absolute terms). Soile and Mu (2015) confirm similar patterns for Nigeria.

The reason that the rich reap most of the subsidies is simply that they consume more energy. For instance, considering the correlation between vehicle ownership and spending on consumption goods, including energy, illustrates that richer households in Nigeria tend to own more and bigger motorised vehicles, and thus consume more petrol (Figure 3.2 top).

The level of income inequality in Nigeria is reflected in Figure 3.3. Consumption expenditure (which includes food, rent, education, energy, among others) is a common proxy for income levels, and indeed varies substantially across income deciles. In per capita terms, the data suggests that consumption expenditure by the richest 10% of the population exceeds that of the poorest 10% by a factor 10. The 2nd and 9th deciles still differ by a factor 4 – and there is little difference to this pattern between urban and rural areas.

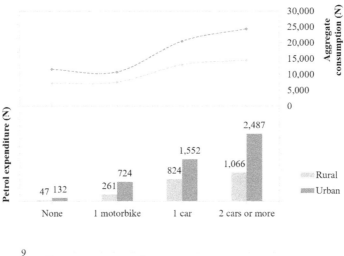

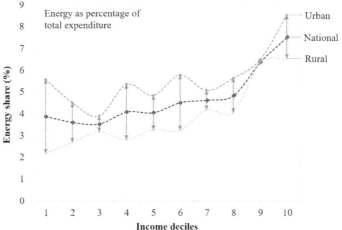

Figure 3.2 **Top:** Average household expenditure for all consumption goods (upper panel), and petrol (lower panel), according to ownership of motorised vehicles (in Naira per month). **Bottom:** Expenditure on energy goods as a share of total consumption expenditure, according to income deciles.

Considering energy consumption separately, inequality is significantly more pronounced than for aggregate consumption (Figure 3.3, right). In urban areas, the richest 10% spend 28 times more on energy consumption than the poorest 10% (factor 23 in rural areas). Notably, across the entire income distribution, average energy expenditure by urban households is consistently higher than by rural households (despite having the same level of total expenditure). This may reflect a variety of issues, including access to and availability of energy, and differing economic activities. It

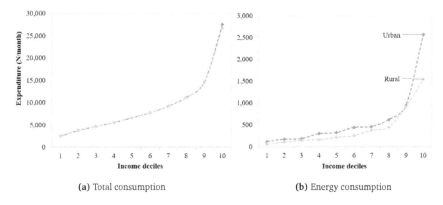

Figure 3.3 Distribution of consumption expenditure. **Left panel:** Average per capita expenditure on all consumption goods, according to income deciles. **Right panel:** Average per capita expenditure on energy goods, according to income deciles. All numbers are in Naira per month.

comes as no surprise that fuel subsidies primarily benefit the rich, and thus directly reinforce existing patterns of inequality and poverty.

Moreover, regardless of income levels, urban households spend a larger share of their income on energy than their rural counterparts (Figure 3.2 bottom). Roughly speaking, most of the urban population spends around 5% of their income on energy, while rural households spend around 3%; and in both cases the energy share is significantly larger for the highest income households.

In addition to regional differences, occupational choices can influence the extent to which households rely on energy consumption. Figure 3.4 illustrates that households that obtain their income from local trading activities (Buying & Selling) rely more on energy than households in manufacturing and agriculture. This pattern persists throughout the whole income distribution, including the poorest 40% of the population (Figure 3.4 right). For instance, even in the poorest income decile average energy expenditure differs by a factor of 2 depending on occupation.

Note, however, that these figures only reflect direct spending on energy goods (e.g. fuels and electricity), and do not take into account the energy cost of other consumption goods. In the medium to long run, changes in energy prices will indirectly affect the costs of public transport, manufacturing, distribution of goods, and other parts of the economy. Moreover, particularly for low-income households even small amounts of energy can be crucial for income-generating activities (incl. agriculture), and for ensuring access to services and markets. This means that livelihoods of the poor are likely to be more strongly affected by energy prices than the above numbers suggest. For high-income households, energy consumption is more likely to

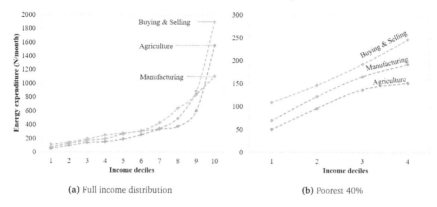

(a) Full income distribution   (b) Poorest 40%

Figure 3.4 Energy expenditure and occupations. **Left panel:** Average per capita expenditure on all consumption goods, according to income deciles and three main income generating activities. **Right panel:** Average per capita expenditure on energy goods, for the poorest 40% of households. All numbers are in Naira per month.

be "compressible", since more energy (such as transport fuels) is used for non-essential purposes.

To understand this, it is useful to disaggregate consumption patterns for different forms of energy, which typically serve very different purposes (Figure 3.6). Kerosene, for instance, is a fuel most commonly used for lighting and cooking – richer households typically substitute kerosene for cleaner energy, such as electric light. Moreover, natural constraints (e.g. on the number of meals prepared per day) mean that kerosene has a lower income elasticity than, for example, petrol which displays the characteristics of a luxury good. Indeed, petrol consumption is highly "unequal": The richest 10% consume 65.8% of all petrol used in urban areas (29.7% in rural areas), while the poorest 10% consume a mere 0.03% (1.9% in rural areas). In contrast, kerosene consumption is more evenly distributed.

Across all fuels types, consumption inequality is less pronounced in rural than in urban areas (Figure 3.6, left). In terms of average expenditure, rural households spend less than urban households, particularly on electricity and kerosene. Again the fact that total energy consumed in rural areas is considerably less than in urban areas may reflect issues around access and availability.

This difference hints at a more complex underlying pattern, which the binary *rural–urban* distinction may not fully capture. Even at the same income level, regional differences may have a substantial influence on energy consumption. Figure 3.5 illustrates the sharp regional differences: For each state, it maps the average monthly expenditure by poor people (here defined as total consumption expenditure being under N55,000 per year) for energy overall, petrol, kerosene, and electricity. Expenditure

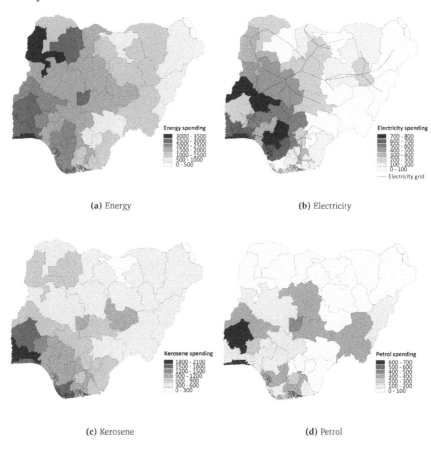

(a) Energy   (b) Electricity

(c) Kerosene   (d) Petrol

Figure 3.5 These maps display the average monthly per capita spending on energy
by all Nigerians living below the absolute poverty line (here defined as
total consumption expenditure below 55,000 Naira per year, which
roughly corresponds to $1 per day in 2010). All numbers are in Naira
per month.

levels differ significantly across states, and across different energy goods.
In general, poor people in the more developed South-West spend more
on energy than those in the North-East, suggesting stronger reliance on
energy products.

The data presented in this section allow for several observations on
energy consumption in Nigeria: (i) Absolute spending on energy goods is
more unequally distributed than overall consumption and income. The
highest income decile accounts for 37.5% to 66% of total expenditure
(depending on which energy good is considered). (ii) Energy expenditure
relative to income is increasing with income. Top income households
spend the highest income share on energy. (iii) Roughly speaking, poor

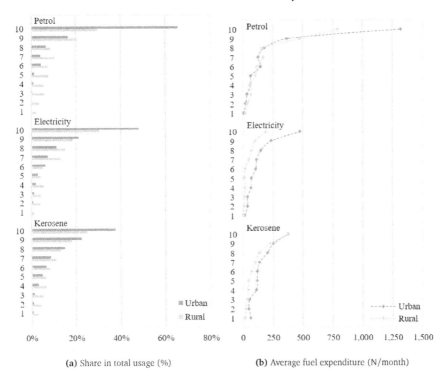

(a) Share in total usage (%) **(b)** Average fuel expenditure (N/month)

Figure 3.6 Different fuels, different usage patterns. **Left:** Share in total expenditure, according to income deciles and different fuels. **Right:** Average monthly per capita spending on different fuels, according to income deciles.

people in the more industrialised Southern states spend significantly more on energy than poor people in Northern states.

It is reasonable to infer that poor households, which are particularly reliant on energy for their livelihoods (e.g. for income-generating activities in the manufacturing sector), will be especially vulnerable to energy price shocks. Hence, identifying vulnerable households and assessing the level of their exposure and vulnerability is necessary for designing adequate compensation and social protection measures.

3.4 Simulating reform

This section provides the results from a subsidy reform simulation for the case of Nigeria, conducted based on the empirical simulation model by Araar and Verme (2012). The focus of this simulation is to get an indication of the magnitude of the short- to medium-term welfare effects of a subsidy removal, and understand how these effects may vary across regions.

This simulation only considers the direct welfare effects that occur when a removal of fuel subsidies increases households' cost of maintaining energy consumption. It does not account for further indirect welfare effects which are bound to occur as rising energy prices also increase the cost of other consumption goods, such as food and public transport; accounting for such indirect price effects requires the analysis of input-output tables – typically not available at the sub-national level – or use of general equilibrium models. A study by Arze del Granado et al. (2012) suggests that on average indirect effects make up about 60% of the total impacts of a subsidy removal.

Araar and Verme (2012) suggest that the omission of indirect price effects is reasonable if the focus is on short- to medium-term effects (e.g. up to 2 months) of a subsidy removal. They point out that analysing direct effects has the advantage of requiring only a single household expenditure survey, and few ex-ante modelling assumptions.[5] This chapter follows this approach and focuses on the variability of impacts across income groups and federal states.

To assess indirect effects the approach in this study would need to be extended into a model that uses input-output tables. Note that input-output tables are not available at the state-level, and the generalised use of a national input-output table would defeat the point of looking beyond national averages, as it dilutes subnational differences. Moreover, input-output models fail to reflect the fiscal policy dimension of FFS reform, as they do not take into account improvements in economic and fiscal efficiency, and instead just focus on the propagation of energy price shocks (Plante, 2014). Computational general equilibrium (CGE) models provide a more robust way of capturing the economy-wide effects of FFS reform (including indirect effects), as they reflect the fiscal efficiency benefits of FFS reform and enable more tailored policy simulations. Since the focus of this chapter is on sub-national and regional variation of effects, the focus will remain on direct effects. Chapter 6 then offers a full CGE model based analysis.

3.4.1 Methodology

The underlying theoretical framework for the analysis in this chapter is based on a standard consumer choice model, in which representative households choose consumption bundles of subsidised and unsubsidised goods subject to a budget constraint. As subsidies for certain energy goods are removed, their prices increase. Given the developing country setting, it is assumed that the majority of households cannot simply draw on savings to compensate for higher energy prices. This implies that – at least in the short to medium run – it is reasonable to assume that households' budgets are fixed; thus, households can only respond to higher prices by reducing the consumption of the (formerly) subsidised good, or by substituting it (e.g. for a cheaper type of fuel). Aggregated at the national level, these effects mean that overall consumption expenditure (i.e. welfare) would fall, and poverty increase.

This framework allows assessing the direct welfare effects of fossil fuel subsidy removal in line with the partial equilibrium approach proposed by Coady (2006). The author points out that this approach yields an estimate of "the upper bound on longer-term adverse impacts and a lower bound on beneficial impacts" (Coady, 2006, p.258).

This section presents the derivation and theoretical underpinnings of the main parameters considered in this analysis. In particular, this section outlines how price shocks due to subsidy removal affect (i) the consumption of the subsidised good (energy), (ii) the overall welfare of households, and (iii) government revenue. The theoretical exposition in this section is built on and breaks down the model presented by Araar and Verme (2012) to allow a disaggregated state by state analysis (in addition to national level analyses).

Impact on the consumption of the subsidised good (energy)

Formally, the change in consumption of the subsidised good g in state s can be expressed as

$$
\begin{aligned}
\Delta c_g^s &= \sum_{i=1}^{N}(c_{g,i}^1 - c_{g,i}^0) \\
&= \sum_{i=1}^{N}(q_{g,i}^1 p_g^1 - c_{g,i}^0) \\
&= \sum_{i=1}^{N}(q_{g,i}^1 p_g^0(1 + dp_g) - c_{g,i}^0)
\end{aligned}
\tag{3.1}
$$

In this notation N denotes the total number of households, c_g denotes consumption expenditure on the subsidised good g, q_g denotes the consumed quantity, p_g denotes the price of the good, and dp_g the relative price change due to subsidy removal. Superscripts 0 and 1 mark pre- and post-reform values respectively.

The relative price change dp_g is defined by

$$
dp_g = \frac{\Delta p_g}{p_g^0},
$$

where the absolute price change $\Delta p_g = p_g^1 - p_g^0$. Using an analogous definition for relative quantity change dq_g, the own-price elasticity of demand $\varepsilon_{g,i}$ can be derived. This elasticity reflects that households may adjust their consumption of the subsidised good in response to changing prices. Note that the elasticity is given by the ratio of the relative changes in consumed quantity and price:

$$\varepsilon_{g,i} = \frac{\Delta q_{g,i}/q_{g,i}^0}{\Delta p_g/p_g^0} \tag{3.2}$$

Hence, the change in consumption can be expressed as

$$\Delta q_{g,i} = \varepsilon_{g,i} q_{g,i}^0 dp_g. \tag{3.3}$$

Moreover, equation 3.1 can be simplified by replacing the post-reform quantity $q_{g,i}^1$:

$$q_{g,i}^1 = q_{g,i}^0 + \Delta q_{g,i} \tag{3.4}$$

Hence, using equations 3.3 and 3.4 the change in consumption of the subsidised good in state s becomes

$$\begin{aligned}
\Delta C_g^s &= \sum_{i=1}^{N} ((q_{g,i}^0 + \varepsilon_{g,i} q_{g,i}^0 dp_g)(p_g^0 + p_g^0 dp_g) - c_{g,i}^0) \\
&= \sum_{i=1}^{N} (q_{g,i}^0 (1 + \varepsilon_{g,i} dp_g)(p_g^0 + p_g^0 dp_g) - c_{g,i}^0).
\end{aligned} \tag{3.5}$$

Note that by standardising the pre-reform price to $p_g^0 = 1$, pre-reform consumption expenditure is equivalent to the consumed quantity (i.e. $c_{g,i}^0 = p_g^0 q_{g,i}^0 = q_{g,i}^0$). Moreover, the nominal change in consumption expenditure in equation 3.5, can be transformed into real change by removing the price adjustment $(p_g^0 + dp_g)$. Thus, the real change in the consumption expenditure on the subsidised good after the reform can be expressed as

$$\begin{aligned}
\Delta C_g^s &= \sum_{i=1}^{N} (c_{g,i}^0 (1 + \varepsilon_{g,i} dp_g) - c_{g,i}^0) \\
&= \sum_{i=1}^{N} \varepsilon_{g,i} c_{g,i}^0 dp_g.
\end{aligned} \tag{3.6}$$

The consumption change at the national level is easily obtained by summing state-level differences:

$$\Delta C_g = \sum_{s=1}^{S} \Delta C_g^s \tag{3.7}$$

Note that inelastic demand ($\varepsilon_g = 0$) would imply that subsidy removal does not cause households to adjust the consumed quantity of the subsidised good (yet, a fixed budget constraint due to absence of savings means that consumption of other goods must be reduced). In practice this could, for instance, be the case if the subsidised fuel is critical for income generating activities, and no alternative fuels are available. On the other hand, fully price elastic demand ($\varepsilon_g = -1$) would imply that households reduce consumption of the subsidised good at the same rate with which prices were increased.

Impact on households' overall welfare

Following common convention, expenditure on aggregate consumption is used as a proxy for a household's income and thus its level of welfare.[6] Thus, the overall change in welfare in state s (denoted ΔW^s) due to subsidy removal can be expressed as the change in consumption of both the subsidised (ΔC_g^s) and other goods (ΔC_o^s). Formally,

$$\Delta W^s = \Delta C^s = \Delta C_g^s + \Delta C_o^s \tag{3.8}$$

The assumption that households' budget constraints are fixed in the short term (i.e. no savings and no access to credit for smoothing consumption) implies that overall consumption expenditure must decrease by the extent to which subsidies are reduced. This means that irrespective of whether and how households substitute away from the subsidised good, the real decrease in welfare is equivalent to the relative change of the cost of pre-reform consumption of the subsidised good.[7] Thus, if a household's consumption of the subsidised good is relatively inelastic, the change in the consumption of the subsidised good must be matched by a change in the consumption of the other good – such that the fixed budget constraint assumption is met. Equation 3.8 can thus be re-written as[8]

$$\Delta W^s = \Delta C^s = \sum_{i=1}^{N} \varepsilon_{g,i} c_{g,i}^0 dp_g - \sum_{i=1}^{N} (1 + \varepsilon_{g,i}) c_{g,i}^0 dp_g$$
$$= -\sum_{i=1}^{N} c_{g,i}^0 dp_g. \tag{3.9}$$

This confirms that the overall change in welfare does not depend on the elasticity, i.e. it does not matter on which (combination of) goods the household decides to spend its reduced disposable income. Again, the welfare change at the national level is easily obtained by summing state-level differences:

$$\Delta W = \sum_{s=1}^{S} \Delta W^s = \sum_{s=1}^{S} \Delta C^s$$

Equation 3.9 highlights that the countrywide welfare effect of a subsidy reform depends on two main factors: the pre-reform level of consumption of the subsidised good, and the relative price change induced by subsidy removal. Both these factors can differ significantly across regions, thus leading to different welfare effects and necessitating different compensation measures.

Consumption of the subsidised good (c_g^0): In absolute terms, the more a household consumes of the subsidised good, the higher the absolute welfare effects of reform. Likewise, relative welfare effects depend on the share of the subsidised good in total consumption expenditure (c_g^0/c^0); i.e. the more a household spends on the subsidised good relative to income, the more it is "exposed" to the welfare effects due to the removal of subsidies. Thus, the exposure to energy price shocks is strongly influenced by external factors, such as occupational choices, access to energy, access to public transport, etc., all of which are likely to differ significantly across regions.

Relative price change due to subsidy removal (dp_g): The extent to which a subsidy reform affects household consumption and welfare depends on the extent to which prices increase. In principle, if the level of subsidy is known (e.g. in terms of $/litre of petrol), the price change due to subsidy removal is straightforward to establish. In practice, as in the Nigerian example, official government-set prices may vary substantially from actual prices in the market place, due to issues such as misappropriation of subsidy funds, corruption, and ineffective distribution. However, these are difficult to quantify and remain an uncertainty throughout the analysis.

Impact on government revenues

In addition to investigating consumption and welfare, it is possible to make a simple approximation of a government's reform revenue. In the formal setting introduced above, the additional revenue for a national government resulting from the removal of fuel subsidies can be expressed as

$$\Delta R = \sum_{s=1}^{S} \Delta R_s = \sum_{s=1}^{S} \sum_{i=1}^{N} c_{g,i}^0 dp_g \big(1 + \varepsilon_{g,i}(1 + dp_g)\big). \tag{3.10}$$

This expression implies that reform revenue is equivalent to the nominal aggregate change in households' consumption expenditure on the subsidised good; or in other words, the households' loss (in terms of reduced disposable income) is the governments gain (i.e. avoided payment of subsidies).

3.4.2   A hypothetical fuel subsidy reform: two scenarios

This section briefly sets out the main features of a hypothetical fossil fuel subsidy reform:

Elasticities: There are few robust estimates for price elasticities of different fossil fuels in Nigeria. The analysis is complicated by highly distorted and manipulated markets, significant supply shortages and access barriers (Iwayemi et al., 2010). Omisakin, Oyinlola, and Oluwatosin (2012) find that energy demand in Nigeria is relatively inelastic: long-run price elasticities are estimated to be -0.016 for petrol and -0.205 for kerosene. Iwayemi, Adenikinju, and Babatunde (2010) use co-integration regressions to estimate statistically significant long-run price elasticities of −0.115 for kerosene, and −0.106 for aggregate energy products (i.e. petrol, diesel and kerosene). In the short-run, they estimate price elasticities to be −0.415 for diesel, and −0.249 for petrol.

In a survey of 18 developing countries Dahl (1994) suggests that short-run price elasticities for oil demand tend to be clustered between −0.05 and −0.09, while long-run elasticities are as low as −0.3. These figures are in line with a more recent study: Arzaghi and Squalli (2015) estimate elasticities for petrol demand in 32 fuel-subsidising economies. They find short- and long-run price elasticities to be around −0.05 and −0.25 respectively.

For the purpose of this chapter a price elasticity of −0.3 is used for all energy products. This figure is comparable to values used in similar studies; e.g. Verme and El-Massnaoui (2015) conduct a subsidy reform analysis for Morocco and use a price elasticity of −0.2 for all energy products. Araar et al. (2015) conduct a similar study for Libya, and apply a price elasticity of −0.5 for all energy products. In this context, following points should be noted: In this study, estimates of overall welfare impacts do not depend on elasticities as illustrated by equation 3.9. The main results on regional heterogeneity are unaffected by the elasticity. However, the choice of elasticity plays an important role in estimating the post-reform level of energy consumption and government revenue. Figure 3.10 (top right) provides a sensitivity test for a range of elasticity values.

Energy goods and subsidies: Subsidies on petrol, kerosene, and electricity are considered. These three energy types represent over 80% of total energy consumption. In the case of Nigeria, obtaining reliable figures on consumer subsidies for these energy goods is remarkably difficult. Large-scale smuggling, black market activities, and complex intermediary retail structures mean that market prices can be significantly higher than those prescribed (and paid for) by the government.

It is also unclear how large overall subsidy payments have been (both in terms of subsidy per litre, and at the national level). For instance, while the government officially suspended kerosene subsidies in 2009, the Nigeria National Petroleum Corporation (NNPC) which administers kerosene subsidies, claims arrears of N310 bn. But it remains unclear whether or to what extent this sum was actually disbursed as subsidies. Moreover, frequently changing policies, contradicting information and data, and opaque institutions increase the margin of error. The GSI (2012a) and IMF (2013c) provide detailed accounts of energy subsidies in Nigeria, and provide the basis for the numbers used in this analysis:

- **Petrol:** The subsidised retail price is assumed to be N65 per litre for 2010 (corresponding to the year of the household survey). Subsidies are assumed to be N90 per litre.

- **Kerosene:** While the government prescribes a price of N50 per litre, the actual retail price is often significantly higher. Middlemen siphon off around N108 per litre. For this analysis an average retail price of N100 per litre is assumed, and subsidy removal is assumed to be uniformly passed on to end-users.
- **Electricity** usage varies distinctly across different regions. The pre-reform effective electricity tariff of N7/kWh is used as a baseline. As production costs are estimated to be around N23/kWh, this implies an electricity subsidy of N16/kWh.

Figure 3.7 illustrates the regressivity of the above defined subsidy levels for petrol, kerosene, and electricity. Benefits from electricity and kerosene subsidies can be seen to be concentrated disproportionately on the rich, following a similar distribution as overall income (see Lorenz curve for consumption as a reference). Benefits from petrol subsidies are significantly more concentrated on the rich than benefits from electricity and kerosene. Note that this pattern results directly from the starkly unequal distribution of energy consumption.

Two reform scenarios are considered. In both scenarios it is assumed that a subsidy reduction will cause a uniform energy price increase throughout the country. (i) In the first scenario subsidies are **reduced by 50%** on all three considered energy goods. This implies price increases of 69% for petrol, 108% for kerosene, and 114% for electricity. (ii) The second case represents complete subsidy removal, i.e. a **reduction by 100%**. This implies price increases of 138% (petrol), 216% (kerosene), and 228% (electricity). While a 100% reduction appears radical – especially considering

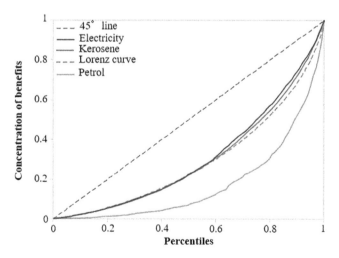

Figure 3.7 Regressivity of subsidy benefits. Subsidies predominantly benefit higher income households. Subsidies on petrol are the most regressive.

the high subsidisation rate – this is precisely what the Nigerian government attempted to implement in 2009 (kerosene) and 2012 (petrol), and again announced in 2016.

Compensation and social protection: For this analysis, a scheme is considered which mitigates adverse effects on households by directly compensating income shocks. This compensation mechanism takes the form of an universal, uniform, and untargeted cash transfer scheme. 'Uniform' cash payments imply that regardless of location or income, the same lump sum payment is made per person.

In principle, uniform and universal cash transfer schemes do not require the costly and administratively complicated targeting of beneficiaries; this makes them particularly relevant in policy environments with low administrative capacity and limited pre-existing social safety net infrastructure. By assuming that compensation payments are made universally, this study estimates an upper bound for compensation costs. Targeting compensation payments to only the most vulnerable, rather than the entire population is likely to be cheaper, especially when existing social protection infrastructure can be used to keep targeting costs low. In Nigeria, no strong social protection system exists with country-wide coverage.

Poverty line: The definition of the poverty line can make a significant difference to the estimates. In this study, total consumption expenditure of N55,000 per year or less is used for defining absolute poverty (this roughly corresponds to $1 per day in 2010).

3.4.3 Estimation results: the impacts of reform

Impacts at the national level

Arguably the most important question for a household is how the proposed subsidy reform impacts on welfare. This impact is determined by several factors, including (i) the pre-reform level of income and energy expenditure, (ii) the extent to which subsidies are reduced, and (iii) the level of cash compensation received. Figure 3.8 shows that across income groups, the reduction in welfare can be mitigated or offset by adequate cash transfers. For each income decile the figure shows the net change in consumption expenditure associated with universal and uniform cash transfers. The net change in consumption can be positive or negative, depending on the transfer level and the considered income decile. In both reform scenarios, a threshold for cash compensation is determined that ensures *net* poverty neutrality of the reform (blue dashed line); i.e. the national poverty rate does not increase due to the reform, if this lump sum compensation is transferred uniformly to each person. Note that these cash transfer levels mean that roughly the poorest 60% of the population are better off after the reform. In both scenarios the poverty neutral transfers are lower than the revenue neutral transfer level (green dashed line). However the difference between the

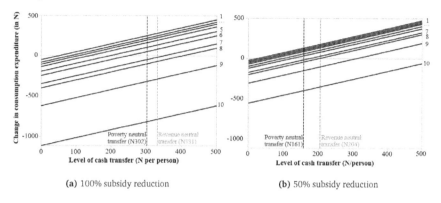

(a) 100% subsidy reduction   (b) 50% subsidy reduction

Figure 3.8 Compensation makes the difference. The solid lines reflect income deciles; the blue dashed line indicates the minimum cash transfer required to prevent an increase of the national poverty rate; the green dashed line indicates the cash transfer level that utilises all reform revenues.

two compensation levels is small. This is due to the high pre-existing poverty rate, which implies that transfers need to be paid to nearly 100 million people to maintain poverty neutrality.

At the lower end of the income distribution the welfare losses due to a subsidy reform can mean that already poor households are pushed deeper into poverty. Households that were previously just above the poverty line may be pushed into poverty, as energy prices increase and purchasing power is reduced. The extent to which subsidy removal increases poverty rates differs across energy goods (Figure 3.9 top). Increases in kerosene prices have particularly strong impacts on the overall poverty rate.

In the absence of any compensation a 100% (or 50%) reduction of subsidies is estimated to instantly increase the poverty headcount rate from pre-reform 60% to 63.3% (or 61.8%) (Figure 3.9 top); while the poverty gap increases from 25.7% to 27.8%. It comes as no surprise that any uncompensated subsidy reform tends to be met by strong public opposition. The figure illustrates further that by providing a universal (i.e. untargeted) and uniform cash transfer, the government can mitigate the increase of poverty – and above a certain level even offset and reverse it. In comparison – using the same methodology – Araar et al. (2015) estimate that full removal of energy subsidies in Libya would increase energy prices by 670% and more than double the pre-reform poverty rate of 8.5%.

In the case of a 100% removal of existing subsidies on petrol, kerosene and electricity, a total of N54 bn can be raised. With a population of approximately 163 million, this implies that a uniform and universal cash transfer of N331 per month can be provided. This redistribution of reform revenues would instantly reduce the national poverty rate by about 1%. These figures illustrate how subsidy removals can not only

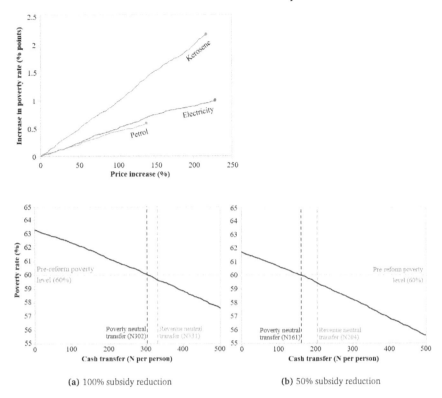

Figure 3.9 **Top:** Uncompensated price increases push up poverty levels. These lines represent the impact on poverty for each energy good separately (i.e. they are not stacked). A 100% subsidy removal corresponds to a 228% increase of electricity prices, 216% for kerosene, and 138% for petrol. However, cash transfers can mitigate a rise in poverty. **Bottom left:** In the case of a complete removal of fuel subsidies (100% reduction) a monthly cash transfer of at least N302 is necessary to avoid a post-reform increase in poverty (relative to the pre-reform poverty level of 60%). **Bottom right:** For a 50% reduction in subsidies a monthly cash transfer of about N161 is needed to prevent a poverty increase.

be poverty neutral, but directly benefit the poor. Moreover, if compensation is directly targeted to poor households (rather than provided universally), and if additional funds are used, cash transfers may deliver more significant poverty reductions than in Figure 3.9 (bottom). It is the government's responsibility to clearly communicate – and deliver – these benefits along with a subsidy reform. Note that these figures ignore potential transaction costs of cash transfers, but these tend to be lower than those of subsidies which are highly vulnerable to corruption and graft (Devarajan, Ehrhart, Le, and Raballand, 2011; Standing, 2014; Gelb and Majerowicz, 2011).

The potential revenues from subsidy removal depend on the overall demand for an energy good, and the associated pre-reform total subsidy payments. This is illustrated by Figure 3.10 (left), which reflects that the average Nigerian household spends more on kerosene than on petrol, and more on petrol than on electricity.[9] Increasing the price of kerosene will thus yield the highest reform revenues in absolute terms – but it should be noted that reducing kerosene subsidies is also associated with the highest rate of poverty increase (Figure 3.9 top), thus requiring larger cash transfers to compensate vulnerable households.

In practice, particularly in developing countries, subsidy removals without compensation are politically unviable, as price shocks have signifi-cant impacts on the welfare of a majority of the population. Thus, ulti-mately, any statement on reform revenues must account for the cost of compensation. Figure 3.10 (bottom) shows the estimated *net* government

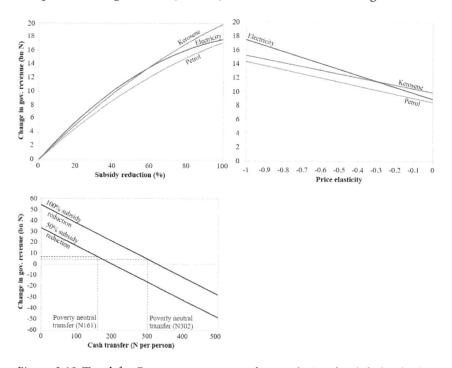

Figure 3.10 **Top left:** Government revenues from reducing fossil fuel subsidies depend on the specific energy good. Note that these lines are not stacked; they do not account for the cost of compensatory cash trans-fers. **Top right:** The sensitivity of government revenue from a 50% subsidy reduction to variation in the price elasticity of energy con-sumption. **Bottom:** Change in government revenues: Reform revenues and compensatory cash transfers: For each case, the dotted lines indi-cate the minimum universal cash transfer necessary to avoid an increase in poverty, and the associated government revenue.

revenues for both reform scenarios, with respect to the level of the per capita compensatory cash transfer. When subsidy removal is made poverty neutral through cash transfers, *net* revenues are N4.7 bn in the case of a 100% subsidy reduction, and N7 bn for a 50% reduction. In the absence of any compensation, revenues are N54 bn (100%) and N33.3 bn (50%).

These government revenue figures refer to "avoided" monthly subsidy payments which the government can realise immediately after a reform. In practice, case studies of past subsidy reforms show that compensatory cash transfers do not tend to be provided indefinitely, but are complemented with (potentially revenue generating) public investments, e.g. in infrastructure. Thus, measuring reform revenues in the long term is more complex than for the short-term, and depends greatly on redistribution and reinvestment decisions.

In countries such as Nigeria, where fossil fuel subsidies are financed through resource rents, the redistribution and reinvestment of reform revenues is closely linked to the management of natural resource revenues. A large literature exists which discusses different approaches to sustainable resource management, which in many cases calls for capital and infrastructure investments which help to diversify income streams (Gill, Izvorski, van Eeghen, and de Rosa, 2014). Notably, a series of studies have also explored and advocated the implementation of a resource dividend, in the form of a permanent uniform cash transfer (Devarajan et al., 2011; Moss and Young, 2009; Segal, 2011; Standing, 2014; Pogge, 2001). This would essentially institutionalise the short-term cash compensation suggested in this section, as a direct and long-term measure for reducing poverty and increasing welfare.

Disaggregating impacts to the state level

Like most previous studies on the impacts of subsidy removal, the analysis in Section 3.4.3 has focused on national averages. However, vulnerability to price shocks is highly context specific and a compensation policy based on national averages is likely to be inadequate for certain population groups. In fact, the household expenditure survey for Nigeria suggests that headcount rates of absolute poverty vary between 25% and 88% across different states. Thus, the consequences of subsidy removal and energy price shocks are bound to differ.

To complement studies at the national level, this section disaggregates the estimates to each of Nigeria's 37 federal states. This section considers different compensation strategies, and analyses how they may affect poverty levels across states. In particular, the purpose of this section is to show that the effects of subsidy removal differ significantly across states, and illustrate to what extent a nationally uniform compensation policies may overcompensate some, while undercompensating others.

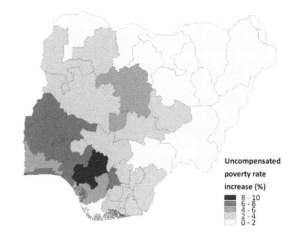

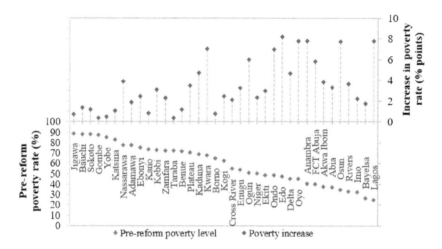

Figure 3.11 **Top:** Regional variation in poverty increase after uncompensated subsidy removal. **Bottom:** Post-reform poverty rates without compensation. A 100% reduction of subsidies increases poverty headcount rates in all states. States with lower pre-reform poverty rates tend to have larger increases in poverty.

The compensation strategies considered in this section are chosen for illustrative purposes, and are uniform at the state-level (i.e. within states, cash transfers are assumed to be of equal size, and provided to everyone). In practice, if large-scale social safety nets and poverty registers are available, these are likely to allow more efficient targeting of vulnerable households. Existing social protection channels can be used to identify and support those who are worst hit. If safety nets lack coverage or simply do not exist – as in the case of Nigeria – identifying and targeting vulnerable households may prove to be expensive and slow. For simplicity, only the scenario of 100% subsidy removal is considered in this section.

Uncompensated subsidy removal

Relative to pre-reform levels of poverty, full removal of fossil fuel subsidies is estimated to increase poverty rates most in the more developed states of Southern Nigeria; this observation holds for both the poverty headcount rate and poverty gap measures (see Figure 3.11 for headcount rate results). Low pre-reform poverty rates suggest the presence of a large group of near-poor households, who are pushed into poverty through the reform induced energy price shock. This effect is exacerbated as poor and near-poor households in these states tend to rely on energy subsidies more heavily than households of similar income levels in the North.

Poverty rates in northern states are estimated to increase less drastically. However, this must not be interpreted in the sense that subsidy removal has little impact in these states. With pre-reform poverty rates of 70% to 90%, there is less scope for the *number* of people in absolute poverty to increase. But the *severity* of poverty of those who are already poor is likely to be aggravated (Figure 3.11, top).

The attempted removal of fossil fuel subsidies in Nigeria in 2012 was accompanied by the *Subsidy Reinvestment and Empowerment Program* which was to feature a range of infrastructure investments (especially in the power, transportation, water and downstream petroleum sectors), as well as social safety nets (IMF, 2013c). However, the announcement of these vague plans for compensation and reinvestment came late, and their implementation even more so. Large parts of the population expected reform revenues to flow into wasteful government spending or feed corruption. Thus the reality, or the public's perception of it, resembled the uncompensated subsidy removal scenario outlined above. Violent protests followed the removal of subsidies, with particularly severe unrest occurring in metropolitan regions in the South (dark red in Figure 3.11, top).

Figure 3.11 highlights that the largest increases in poverty rates are estimated to occur in some of the urbanised and most populous states, including Oyo, Anambra and Lagos. While these are among the more developed states, with lower poverty rates, they are of high political importance. This illustrates the two – possibly competing – needs of a successful subsidy reform: Managing political economy challenges by ensuring adequate compensation in richer states; as well as social protection, equitable redistribution of funds, and poverty alleviation in poorer states.

Poverty neutral compensation

In the previous section, it was estimated that providing nationwide universal cash compensation of N302 could neutralise the increase in poverty that an uncompensated reform would cause. According to the estimates, this would indeed hold at the national average; however, the state level analysis suggests that the N302 cash transfer is likely to undercompensate in some states while overcompensating in others. In other words, the level of cash compensation that maintains poverty neutrality at the national level, does not actually achieve this objective in any specific state (Figure 3.12). While some states benefit from poverty reductions of up to 4%, cash transfers of N302 still leave poverty rates spiking by up to 5% in other states. Notably this includes states such Lagos and Abuja, which experienced intense public opposition to subsidy reforms in 2012.

As energy consumption patterns differ across states, so does the level of cash compensation that is needed to maintain poverty neutrality of a given subsidy removal. Figure 3.13 (top) shows the minimum cash compensation transfer that is required in each state. Note that, as shown in Figure 3.8, this estimated cash transfer threshold will prevent an increase in the state's average poverty rate; low income households are still likely to benefit overall from the reform, while high-income households are likely to lose from the reform. This emphasises that fossil fuel subsidy reform, paired with uniform cash transfers, can be a pro-poor progressive fiscal reform.

Overall, ensuring poverty neutrality is a minimum requirement for protecting the livelihoods of the poorest, and for ensuring broad public support for subsidy reforms. As Nigeria's 2012 experience illustrates, failing to communicate and deliver direct compensation can lead to the downfall of the entire reform endeavour.

However, if the government's goal is to maximise the development potential of a subsidy reform, poverty neutral cash compensation is not sufficient. Poverty neutral cash transfers that are only provided in the short term can mitigate adverse effects for poor households, but further complementary policies are critical to ensure that subsidy reforms actively benefit the poor and are invested in the foundations for future development.

One of the main concerns raised by poverty neutral cash transfers is the unequal distribution of compensation (and thus reform) benefits. States with higher energy consumption and lower pre-reform poverty rates require higher compensation payments. Consequently, states with lower pre-reform poverty rates receive a larger share of the overall compensation budget. Figure 3.14 shows how the overall compensation budget – which depends on per capita transfer levels and a state's population size – is distributed.

Revenue neutral compensation: A tailored approach

Besides poverty neutral compensation, it is also worth considering the effect of a revenue neutral compensation scheme. In this scenario, reform revenues are distributed entirely in the form of universal cash transfers. In resource rich countries fossil fuel subsidies are typically financed through resource rents; thus subsidy removal is a "gift that keeps giving" – rather than simply reducing government expenditure or yielding a one-off

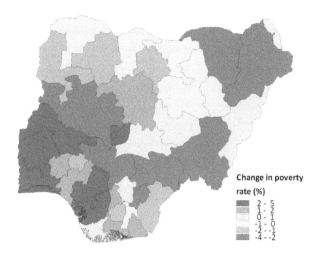

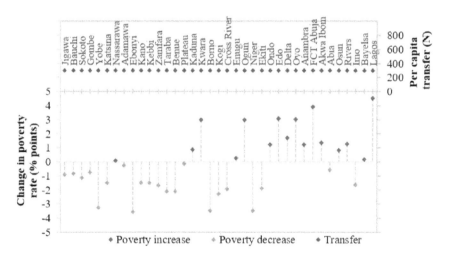

Figure 3.12 **Top:** Change in poverty rates after a universal "poverty neutral" compensation payment of N302 per person. While keeping the national poverty level constant, changes in poverty rates can be significant at the state level. **Bottom:** Paying a compensation of N302 to every Nigerian can neutralise a poverty increase at the national average. At the state level however, this cash transfer level causes poverty reductions in some states, while failing to mitigate poverty increases in others.

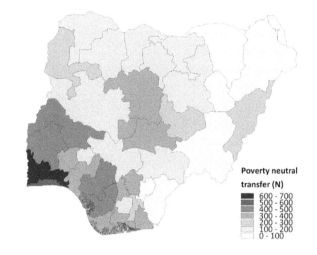

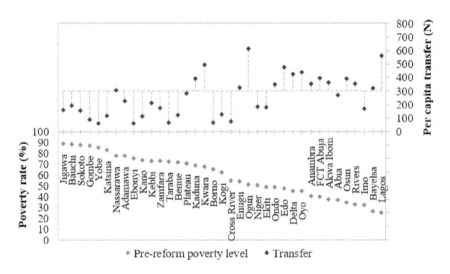

Figure 3.13 Estimated cash transfer levels that neutralise post-reform poverty increases in each state (i.e. maintain pre-reform poverty rates).

windfall, it unlocks a long-term revenue stream. By fully dedicating this revenue stream to compensation in the short-term, governments can not only mitigate adverse effects, but also deliver immediate and tangible benefits to the population and secure broad public support. In the medium- to long-term, governments can then shift their priority from compensation to reinvestment and more targeted social safety nets.

A uniform revenue neutral compensation scheme would redistribute the entire reform revenue of N54 bn at N331 per month to all Nigerians. Such

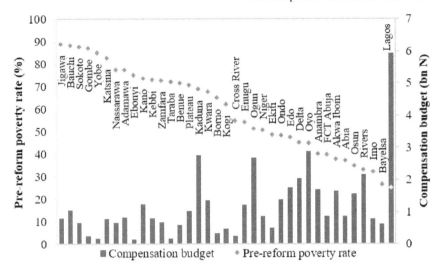

Figure 3.14 Locating the compensation budget. This figure shows the overall budget requirement in each state for implementing a state-level uniform cash transfers scheme that maintains existing poverty rates. The budget distribution favours richer states.

an approach would reduce the national poverty rate by about 1%. This average however conceals significant variation at the state-level (very similar to the poverty neutral scheme, Figure 3.12). Most notably the capital Abuja and Lagos, would still experience significant income shocks and thus increases in their respective poverty rates.

Thus, lastly, another hypothetical and revenue neutral compensation scheme is considered: Poverty neutral compensation is provided in states where revenue neutral compensation alone would not prevent increasing poverty rates (Figure 3.15). The remaining reform revenue (N31.2 bn) is redistributed at N253 per person in all other states. This compensation scheme maintains revenue neutrality and is preferable to poverty neutral compensation alone. Increases in poverty rates are avoided in all states, while a series of poorer states benefit from poverty rate reductions of up to 3%.

Figure 3.15 (top) shows that this combined compensation scheme can prevent poverty increases in richer states in the south, thus helping to secure public support for reforms in this region. At the same time, Northern states benefit from reduced poverty rates, and higher transfers of wealth than in the purely poverty neutral case.

It should be emphasised that the compensation strategies considered in this section are hypothetical and stylised. They mainly serve the purpose of highlighting the important differences at the subnational level. Taking these into account may help to design more effective and equitable subsidy reforms.

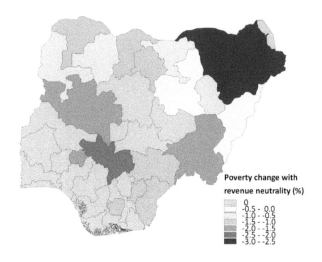

Poverty change with
revenue neutrality (%)
0
-0.5 - 0.0
-1.0 - -0.5
-1.5 - -1.0
-2.0 - -1.5
-2.5 - -2.0
-3.0 - -2.5

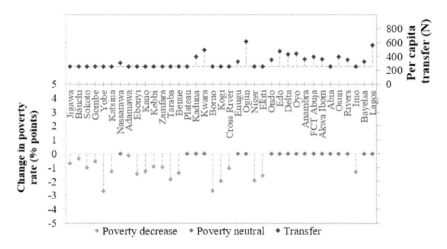

Figure 3.15 **Top:** Combined poverty and revenue neutral compensation. This map depicts impact of a combined compensation programme on state level poverty rates. **Bottom:** The poverty impacts of a tailored compensation scheme. Poverty neutral compensation is provided in states where revenue neutral compensation alone would not prevent increasing poverty rates. The remaining reform revenue is redistributed at N253 per person in other states.

3.5 Designing fossil fuel subsidy reforms: conclusions

The inclusion of fossil fuel subsidy reform in the UN's Sustainable Development Goals reflects a widespread consensus on the notion that fossil fuel subsidies are fundamentally unsustainable. Indeed, primarily driven by fiscal imbalances, in recent years several countries have made significant progress in phasing out fuel subsidies. And considering the wide range of adverse effects of fossil fuel subsidies – including market distortions, underinvestment in infrastructure and efficiency, escalating fiscal burdens, climate change, and income inequality – the need for such reforms is ever increasing. However, the possibility of major price shocks and adverse distributional effects requires policy makers to carefully design effective social protection measures.

This chapter focuses on Nigeria, and investigates the regional variability of the direct welfare effects of fuel subsidies removal. It analyses the role of different cash compensation strategies and investigates their effect on national and state-level poverty rates. Overall, the analysis in this chapter highlights several issues:

- **Inequality:** Energy consumption is highly unequal; rich households account for a disproportionately high share of total energy expenditure. The level of consumption inequality varies for different fuel types, with petrol being most and kerosene least unequal.
- **Regressivity:** Consumption inequality is the reason for the high level of regressivity of fuel subsidies; i.e. subsidies predominantly benefit the rich. Nevertheless, removing fossil fuel subsidies can have severe effects on the livelihoods of poor people. These results are in line with findings from similar studies e.g. for Morocco, Libya, and Jordan, and also reflect the insights from cross-country studies (Arze del Granado et al., 2012; Verme and El-Massnaoui, 2015).
- **Compensation is key:** The analysis shows that compensation measures play a central role in mitigating energy price shocks and thus ensuring affordability and protecting livelihoods. For instance, a countrywide universal (i.e. untargeted) cash compensation program can prevent increases in poverty rates, while still unlocking significant net reform revenues. Redistributing all reform revenues in the form of cash transfers can significantly increase welfare levels throughout the country. For targeted compensation and social protection schemes, the definition of adequate vulnerability indicators is crucial. Such indicators should go beyond income levels, and take into account factors such as geographical circumstances, food security, and the energy-dependency of income generating activities.
- **Seeing beyond national averages:** The analysis also shows that due to varying energy consumption patterns, poverty impacts and vulnerabilities can vary substantially across geographic regions. Income levels

alone may be incomplete indicators of vulnerability to energy price shocks. By considering national averages alone, policy makers may fail to recognise certain high-vulnerability groups. For instance, certain compensation measures (e.g. uniform cash compensation) that appear effective when considering national averages can still fail to adequately mitigate price shocks in certain states, risking strong public opposition and shocks to livelihoods.

- **The need for tailored strategies:** This chapter proposes a tailored compensation strategy which can help to offset the largest poverty increases in high income states, while contributing to active poverty reduction in low-income states. This highlights that there can be a trade-off between mitigating public opposition to reform, and pro-poor wealth transfers. Balancing these requirements and priorities calls for careful analysis and tailored reform design.

The practicality and effectiveness of compensation and social protection programs will depend greatly on country-specific characteristics: The availability of pre-existing social safety nets, poverty registers, and access to reliable infrastructure (incl. mobile phones and bank accounts), as well as alternative energy forms are critical factors to be considered when designing reforms. The analysis in this chapter aims to contribute to developing a more refined understanding of the impacts of subsidy reforms and show the need for a thorough, disaggregated analysis of subsidy reforms, and tailored reform strategies.

Notes

1 *An abridged version of this chapter has been published as* Rentschler, J. E. (2016). Incidence and impact: The regional variation of poverty effects due to fossil fuel subsidy reform. *Energy Policy*. Vol. 96, pp. 491–503. Rentschler, J. E. (2016). Incidence and impact: The regional variation of poverty effects due to fossil fuel subsidy reform. *Oxford Energy Working Papers*. Oxford: Oxford Institute for Energy Studies, University of Oxford.
2 The Petroleum Support Fund is managed by the Petroleum Products Pricing Regulatory Agency, and receives a set allocation in the federal budget. Contributions to the fund are made by the federal, state, and local governments. Moreover, the fund is supplemented by subsidy "surpluses", which essentially occur when international market prices exceed the government-set fuel price (GSI, 2012a).
3 For instance, there is conflicting information on the amount of subsidies provided following a 2009 government decision to remove kerosene subsidies (GSI, 2012a). The NNPC maintains that N310 bn in subsidies have been paid out, but disputes between different authorities persist.
4 This figure is based on the national absolute poverty definition, using an absolute poverty line of N54,401 (National Bureau of Statistics, 2010).
5 Araar et al. (2015) and Verme and El-Massnaoui (2015) both follow this approach to consider fuel subsidy reforms in Libya and Morocco respectively. See Siddig et al. (2014) for a CGE analysis.

6 For the purpose of household survey analyses, consumption-based welfare measures are the most common approach; see Deaton (2003).

7 Put simply, if a household's disposable income is reduced for instance by $5 due to subsidy removal, the reduction in overall consumption expenditure is also $5 (assuming limited or no savings). This is the case no matter on which (combination of) goods the household decides to spend its reduced disposable income.

8 Note that as an own price elasticity, $\varepsilon_{g,i}$ takes a negative value.

9 Note that government revenues depend on the extent of subsidy removal, and the subsequent change in demand for the subsidised good. Elasticities do not influence government revenues for full subsidy removal.

4 Subsidy reforms and the impacts on firms

Transmission channels and response measures

Jun Rentschler, Martin Kornejew, and Morgan Bazilian[1]

4.1 Introduction

In early 2016, the Kingdom of Saudi Arabia announced a significant reduction in FFS as a way to compensate shrinking government revenues – and the associated fiscal pressures – due to lower oil prices. As subsidies were removed across a range of fuel types, the subsequent price hikes hit consumers and certain industrial sectors to varying degrees. Gasoline prices increased by about 50% mainly affecting individual drivers (MEES, 2016). A 67% increase in natural gas prices principally affected electricity generators and industrial sectors. One of the highest price increases was for ethane, which rose from $0.75/MMBTU to $1.75/MMBTU or by 133%. Ethane is a key input used by the petro-chemical sector, a cornerstone of the Saudi economy.

Soon after the price increases, some of the largest petro-chemical firms published estimates for the likely impacts on their production costs or profits (MEES, 2016). Several large petro-chemical firms estimated the adverse impact on profits ranging from 6.5% to 44.1% relative to 2014. The Saudi Cement Company expected production costs to increase by $18.1 m as a direct consequence of FFS removal (Trade Arabia, 2015). While these self-reported figures may not be consistently comparable, they highlight a common political economy challenge of FFS removal: firms – and in particular large energy intensive industries – tend to oppose FFS removal and will often exert their political clout to do so. Thus, concerns about competitiveness and profitability have been an important argument of political opponents of FFS reform.[2]

However, focussing on energy cost increases alone is likely to yield an incomplete picture of the effects of FFS reform on firms. To understand how energy price changes (induced by FFS removal) affect competitiveness, both direct and indirect transmission channels for energy prices must be considered, as well as firms' ability to respond. The ability to respond depends on various mechanisms that firms may have at their disposal to mitigate (or pass on) price shocks – and thus is crucial for estimating the net consequences on firms' profitability and competitiveness.

While the adverse effects of FFS removal are increasingly well understood for households, the existing literature has largely ignored the effect of subsidy reform on firms (see Chapter 2). This appears to be a clear gap in the evidence base that should be addressed in order to enable policy makers to design and deliver FFS reforms more effectively.

As few studies exist on the effects of FFS reform on firms, this chapter provides a conceptual discussion in preparation of the empirical analysis in Chapter 5. In particular, this chapter outlines the most important transmission channels for energy price shocks, and response measures used by firms. In doing so, this chapter provides a framework for identifying adequate policy measures to mitigate potential adverse effects on firms as a consequence of FFS reform.

The remainder of this chapter is organised as follows. Section 4.2 discusses related literature on the effect of environmental taxation on competitiveness, but notes that hardly any evidence exists on the effects of FFS reforms. Section 4.3 discusses two transmission channels through which firms are affected by energy price shocks, and four response measures which firms can use to mitigate the adverse effects. Section 4.4 offers suggestions for future research – in particular on FFS reform and firms – and concludes with several policy recommendations.

4.2   Background

A comprehensive body of literature has documented the substantial economic, social and environmental costs of FFS, and argues that by removing FFS these costs could be avoided (Coady et al., 2017; Arze del Granado et al., 2012; IEA, 2014c; NCE, 2016; Rentschler and Bazilian, 2016, also see Chapter 2). The political economy challenges of subsidy reform are increasingly well understood as case studies of past reforms are studied and lessons learnt (Commander, 2012; Fattouh and El-Katiri, 2015; Kojima, 2016; Strand, 2013).

A crucial factor in determining political economy challenges and common public opposition to reforms are the potentially substantial adverse effects on livelihoods due to rising energy prices. In particular, research has been conducted on how vulnerable households can be protected from the adverse effects of FFS reforms and associated energy price shocks – and how this can increase public acceptance of subsidy reform (Arze del Granado et al., 2012; Rentschler, 2016; Ruggeri Laderchi et al., 2013, also see Chapter 3).

However, with a strong focus on households, research has given far less attention to the potential impacts of FFS reform on firms. This is true despite concerns about competitiveness and profitability, which have been an important argument of political opponents of subsidy reform (IMF, 2016b). Particularly, energy intensive manufacturing firms have been argued to experience substantial changes to their cost structures, with adverse implications for profitability (Bazilian and Onyeji, 2012). Evidently such effects can have knock-on effects on economic activity, employment, and thus on households (Kilian, 2008). The impacts of FFS reform on firms is of particular importance when considering producer subsidies – another under-researched topic (see Chapter 2; Bast et al., 2015; OECD, 2015a).

Despite these concerns, few empirical studies exist that focus on the effects on firms.[3] Using a CGE model for Vietnam, Willenbockel, and Hoa (2011) suggest that firms can cope with moderate energy price increases (5-10% per year) using common energy efficiency measures. In Egypt, a doubling of energy prices due to subsidy removal is estimated to reduce profit margins of firms in energy intensive sectors, e.g. in the cement (39% to 29% reduction), fertiliser (22%), and steel sectors (13%) (Khattab, 2007). Jamal and Ayarkwa (2014) provide evidence from Ghana suggesting that firms are strongly affected by the indirect effects of subsidy reform rather than direct energy price shocks, as the costs of transportation, raw materials capital increase, while consumers' purchasing power decreases. The same observation is made by Tambunan (2015) using a survey of Indonesian micro, small, and medium enterprises. The study also emphasises that the ultimate effect of subsidy removal depends crucially on firms' ability to mitigate price shocks – which in turn can be strengthened by dedicated policy measures.

It is useful to turn to studies on the impact of environmental taxes and regulation on firms, which can offer some relevant insights. For instance, Dechezlepretre and Sato (2014) review the evidence on the effect of environmental regulation on competitiveness, for a wide range of regulation types, industries, and countries. They conclude that environmental regulation, including carbon taxes, does not have a large adverse effect on indicators of competitiveness – neither at the firm nor the country level. Similarly, Fankhauser, Bowen, Calel, Dechezleprêtre, Grover, Rydge, and Sato (2013) show that economic growth that abides by environmental principles can strengthen the "green competitiveness" of countries.

In a comprehensive review, Arlinghaus (2015) summarises the evidence on the effects of carbon taxes on various indicators of competitiveness. The study concludes that empirical studies consistently fail to identify any significant adverse competitiveness effects from the introduction of carbon taxes. This observation holds across various indicators of competitiveness, including employment, output, profits, and exports. Several other studies also reach the conclusion that stricter environmental policies have little adverse effect on aggregate productivity or competitiveness; and – in line with the Porter Hypothesis – find that some firms may even be able to increase their productivity (Albrizio, Botta, Koźluk, and Zipperer, 2014; Ekins and Speck, 2008, 2010; Enevoldsen, Ryelund, and Andersen, 2009). In a comprehensive review of the literature, Dethier, Hirn, and Straub (2011) show that other factors such as infrastructure, finance, security, competition, and regulation play a far more significant role than energy prices in determining firms' performance.

In a recent empirical study of German electricity taxes, Flues and Lutz (2015) show that electricity taxes (EUR 14.6/MWh or EUR 44.4/t CO2) did not negatively affect common competitiveness indicators of firms, such as turnover, exports, value added, or investment and employment. In a review of earlier literature, Zhang and Baranzini (2004) also conclude that overall, the competitiveness losses due to carbon taxes are small and in many cases not significant.

Conceptually, increases in energy prices due to subsidy removal are directly comparable to increasing energy prices due to carbon or energy taxes. However, it should be noted that in the past, energy price increases due to carbon taxes have typically been significantly smaller than price increases due to subsidy removal. While depending on specific pre-existing subsidisation rates, subsidy reforms have caused energy price increases of 100% and more in the past (Fattouh, Sen, and Moerenhout, 2016; Rentschler and Bazilian, 2016). This implies that any parallels need to be drawn with caution.

4.3   Transmission channels and response measures

FFS removals typically induce energy price shocks (one-off or gradual), which affect firms and households throughout the economy. In the case of households, the literature typically distinguishes between direct and indirect price effects; i.e. the extent to which energy price changes directly affect households by increasing the cost of energy consumption, and indirectly by increasing the cost of other goods and services. In the case of firms these two channels of transmitting energy price shocks also apply. In addition to these transmission channels, several response measures (i.e. means that firms have to mitigate some of the impacts to their bottom line) play a crucial role in determining the extent to which firms are affected by subsidy removal.

This section discusses the transmission channels for energy price shocks, and presents four common response measures, as illustrated in Figure 4.1. As this section discusses, enterprise surveys can help to shed light on most of these aspects, and identify potential differences between sectors or regions. In the case of larger, publicly listed firms similar analyses can be conducted using analysis of balance sheets and accounts; this is of particular relevance when an economy or sector is dominated by a single firm which is in a strong political position to oppose reforms.

To illustrate these channels and mechanisms, this chapter provides a simple mathematical framework, which suggests entry points for quantitative estimation. This framework builds on a standard profit function of a hypothetical firm, which uses energy E and other inputs or production

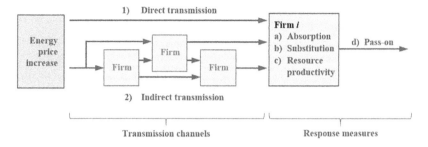

Figure 4.1 Energy price shocks due to subsidy removal: channels for shock transmission and response measures (Author's illustration).

factors F for producing output Q sold at price p^Q. Both primary (F^{pri}) and
intermediate inputs (F^{int}) are distinguished. Overall profits π are determined
by revenues R and energy, primary and intermediate factor costs (C^{ene}, C^{pri},
and C^{int} respectively):

$$
\begin{aligned}
\pi_i &= R_i - C_i^{ene} - C_i^{pri} - C_i^{int} \\
&= p^Q Q_i - p^{ene} E_i - p^{pri} F_i^{pri} - p^{int} F_i^{int}
\end{aligned}
\tag{4.1}
$$

In addition, the profit function of a firm producing intermediate inputs
F_{int}^{int} using energy is given by:

$$
\begin{aligned}
\pi_{int} &= R_{int} - C_{int}^{ene} \\
&= p^{int} F_{int}^{int} - p^{ene} E_{int}
\end{aligned}
\tag{4.2}
$$

For illustration purposes it is assumed that the intermediate firm uses
energy inputs only.[4] Note that subscript i denotes the analysed firm, subscript *int* denotes the firm producing intermediate inputs, while superscripts
denote types of input or output goods.

4.3.1   *Transmission channels of energy price increases*

1)   *Direct channel*

Removing subsidies on specific energy types (e.g. electricity), will increase
the input costs of firms. As subsidy removal affects energy prices
"instantly", directly transmitted price shocks are typically the first impact
felt by firms. This means that direct price shocks affect firms' energy
costs almost instantaneously, unless the price of energy inputs has been
hedged.[5] Such immediate cost shocks cannot typically be coped with
using longer term measures (such as technological updates to increase
energy efficiency), but require quickly deployable measures. In practice,

energy-intensive industries, such as petrochemicals, cement, steel, manufacturing, or transport, tend to be particularly exposed to subsidy reform induced price shocks.

The level of a firm's exposure to direct energy price shocks depends on the extent to which it relies on energy inputs for generating revenue. This level of exposure can be approximated quantitatively by the share of energy input costs relative to total input costs or revenues.[6] It should be noted however, that firms' energy expenditure does not necessarily increase at the same rate as energy prices. The reason for this discrepancy is that firms' reported energy expenditures may include various payments to energy suppliers that do not directly depend on energy prices (e.g. suppliers' labour costs, electricity transmission costs, or service fees; Grave, Hazrat, Boeve, von Blücher, Bourgault, Breitschopf, Friedrichsen, Arens, Aydemir, Pudlik, Duscha, Ordonez, Lutz, Großmann, and Flaute, 2015; Marcu, Genoese, Renda, Wieczorkiewicz, Roth, Infelise, Luchetta, Colantoni, Stoefs, Timini, and Simonelli, 2014). For accuracy it would thus be preferable to use physical rather than monetary measures of energy inputs, though such data may be more difficult to obtain. Moreover, it should be noted that it is important to distinguish between different types of energy inputs, as energy types are typically subsidised at different rates (and some not at all).

More formally, the direct price effect refers to the change in energy costs C_i^{ene} due to a change in the price of energy.

$$direct\ effect = \frac{\partial C_i^{ene}}{\partial p^{ene}} \Delta p^{ene}. \tag{4.3}$$

Hence, this expression depends on the (energy) price elasticity of the firm's energy costs, and measures the partial equilibrium effect of FFS reform as described by Coady(2006) and Araar and Verme (2012).

2) Indirect channel

Energy prices also affect firms indirectly, as the production costs of intermediate inputs increase. More specifically, firms producing intermediate goods will incur direct energy price shocks, which they (at least partially) pass on to other firms by increasing the price of intermediate inputs (Castagneto-Gissey, 2014; Kim, Chattopadhyay, and Park, 2010). In this way energy price shocks can progress through supply chains in the form of price increases of non-energy goods. In practice, firms relying heavily on energy intensive inputs (i.e. inputs consisting of materials with high embodied energy content, such as steel) tend to be affected most by indirect price shocks (Bassi, Yudken, and Ruth, 2009).

Indirect price effects are likely to take longer to fully materialise, as price shocks are successively passed down supply chains. Thus, how quickly any given firm will incur the full indirect price shock depends not least on the number and interactions of preceding intermediate production stages. Moreover, firms supplying intermediate goods may choose not to fully pass on energy price increases, but instead rely on other mechanisms to respond to energy price shocks.

The level of a firm's exposure to indirect energy price shocks depends above all on the energy intensity of its intermediate production inputs. This can be approximated by determining the "embodied" energy content of a firm's production inputs. Various databases exist which offer detailed estimates of the embodied energy of hundreds of the most common industrial materials (Rentschler, Flachenecker, and Kornejew, 2017). However, it should be noted that the geographical origin of materials is crucial to consider, as domestic energy price shocks due to FFS removal are irrelevant for imported materials – no matter their energy intensity.[7] The use of input-output tables, or of CGE models with detailed sectoral disaggregation can help with disentangling these aspects (Hosoe, Gasawa, and Hashimoto, 2010).

In formal notation, the indirect price effect has two elements: (i) the change in intermediate input costs C_i^{int}; note that a change in p^{ene} affects the energy costs C_{int}^{ene} of the firm producing intermediate inputs, which may choose to adjust the sales price p^{int} in response. (ii) A change in p^{ene} will change the disposable income of consumers, which in turn may affect the equilibrium output quantity Q_i; this will affect revenue R_i:

$$indirect \; effect = \frac{\partial C_i^{int}}{\partial p^{ene}} \Delta p^{ene} + \frac{\partial R_i}{\partial p^{ene}} \Delta p^{ene} \tag{4.4}$$

Besides the change in intermediate (non-energy) input costs, another potential indirect shock should be acknowledged: An increase in energy prices will (ceteris paribus) reduce the disposable income of consumers, thus potentially reducing aggregate demand (Jamal and Ayarkwa, 2014). This demand shock in turn is likely to affect firms' output and revenue levels. The magnitude of this effect will depend crucially on price elasticities of demand, and how FFS reform revenues are re-used (e.g. compensation of consumers, or government expenditure). To the firms, this effect is – strictly speaking – a demand shock, not a cost shock.

4.3.2 Four response measures

The transmission channels discussed previously determine the size of the overall cost shock faced by a firm following a subsidy reform. This section discusses four often-employed response measures that firms typically have at their disposal to respond to the overall cost shock. Three of these – *absorption, substitution, and resource efficiency* – refer to internal responses within firms; the last response measure – *price pass-on* – can help firms to forward remaining cost shocks down the value chain to other firms or households, and thus depends externally on the price elasticity of demand. Chapter 7 offers a detailed discussion of market barriers that may lead firms to be unable (or unwilling) to use these response measures.

a)   Absorption

If profit margins are large enough, firms can absorb energy price shocks by accepting smaller margins. If energy price shocks are fully absorbed into profit margins, firms can continue operations without making any adjustments to technology and production quantities, or sales prices. In this case, consumption of both the (formerly) subsidised energy type and of all other energy inputs remains constant; i.e. no behavioural response takes place. Absorbing price shocks into profits is a firm's direct analogy to a household absorbing shocks into savings (though note the difference between the stock and flow of savings).

The ability of firms to absorb energy price shocks can be approximated by comparing absolute profits with the combined direct and indirect energy price shock. Alternatively, computing the ratio of profits and energy expenditures can also provide an indication of the ability to absorb energy price shocks. In the above referenced example of Saudi Arabia, the 14 largest petro-chemical firms had jointly made total net profits of over $9bn in 2014 (MEES, 2016). It is plausible that high profits reaffirmed policy makers that energy price increases would enable these firms to absorb cost increases.

Formally, cost increases due to energy price hikes are fully absorbed when the following relationship holds:

$$\frac{\partial C_i^{ene}}{\partial p^{ene}} + \frac{\partial C_i^{pri}}{\partial p^{ene}} + \frac{\partial C_i^{int}}{\partial p^{ene}} = -\frac{\partial \pi_i}{\partial p^{ene}} \tag{4.5}$$

This expression describes that cost changes (increases) translate uniformly into a change (reduction) of profits, provided that profits are positive. In other words, firms accept a reduction in profits in order to leave sales unchanged (*ceteris paribus*). However, once excessive absorption diminishes all profits – and once all other response measures are exhausted – firms will eventually exit the market.

b)   Substitution

As subsidy reforms typically increase the price of selected energy types (e.g. electricity, petrol), firms may also respond by substituting these energy types with fuels that have become relatively cheaper. Such inter-fuel substitution can be observed in the form of changing energy shares (i.e. the energy mix) in total energy usage. However, the absolute quantity of energy consumption may remain constant, even if significant inter-fuel substitution takes place.

The ability to substitute energy types is constrained by technological characteristics of production, which can vary significantly across sectors. In fact, technological innovation and substitution has been argued to play a key role in determining how a green tax reform (e.g. FFS reform) affects competitiveness (Koskela, Sinn, and Schöb, 2001). In addition, inter-fuel substitution depends critically on the access to energy and reliability of supply, which typically can vary significantly across regions. For instance, lacking access to the electricity grid or frequent power outages in rural regions mean that rural firms may be unable to rely on electricity as a substitute for energy types that are subject to FFS reform.

Using firm surveys, the nature and magnitude of inter-fuel substitutability can be formally characterised and estimated by own and cross price elasticities, as well as Uzawa-Allen partial elasticities of substitution (Azlina, Anang, and Alipiah, 2013; Pindyck, 1979). Moreover, firm surveys frequently collect information on energy access and supply quality, which can shed light on firms' ability to substitute across regions and sectors (Arnold, Mattoo, and Narciso, 2008).

Formally, note that energy costs reflect the mix of different energy types chosen by the firm, i.e. they represent an energy aggregate $E(E_1, E_2, . . ., E_n)$. If the (exogenously determined) price of one of these energy types increases, firms can choose to adjust their energy mix by substituting this energy type for another.

c)   Resource efficiency[8]

Firms may also respond to direct energy cost increases by reducing their overall energy consumption while maintaining the pre-reform level of output, i.e. increasing energy efficiency. Moreover, increasing material efficiency can play a crucial role in responding to indirectly transmitted price shocks, which are due to embodied energy in intermediate materials (Rentschler et al., 2017; Bleischwitz, Giljum, Kuhndt, and Schmidt-Bleek, 2009; Bleischwitz, 2010, 2012). In fact, considering the fact that material costs often significantly exceed energy costs even in energy intensive manufacturing sectors, the role of material efficiency is of particular importance (Allwood, Ashby, Gutowski, and Worrell, 2011; Yilmaz, Akcaoz, and Ozkan, 2005).

Similar to the case of substitution, the ability to increase resource efficiency depends on a variety of factors, including the availability and affordability of modern technology, and support mechanisms for financing and implementing efficiency increasing measures. Moreover, various indicators exist to enable the measurement of energy or material efficiency, and hence allow a direct comparison with related sectors in other countries (Bringezu and Schütz, 2010). More complex indicators can require data which are typically not available from standard firm surveys, but by computing the quantity of output or revenue per unit of energy (or material) input can provide a basic measure for energy (or material) productivity.

Formally, energy productivity e can be defined as the marginal product of energy:

$$e = \frac{\partial Q_i}{\partial E_i} \tag{4.6}$$

And similarly, material productivity m can be described by the marginal product of intermediate inputs (which are a function of p^{ene}):

$$m = \frac{\partial Q_i}{\partial F_i^{int}} \tag{4.7}$$

These equations imply that gains in energy or material efficiency require an adjustment to the production function determining Q_i; for instance by improving production processes or technology. An efficiency increase occurs when the marginal product before the energy price change is smaller than afterwards (i.e. $e < e'$ and $m < m'$).

d) Price pass-on

While the first three response measures describe how firms respond *internally* to direct and indirect energy price shocks, the net impact on firms depends to a large extent on whether price shocks can be passed-on to *external* consumers. This response measure is specific to the analysis of firms, and does not feature in the analysis of FFS reform effects on households. In its essence, this channel refers to the extent to which firms can adjust the sales price of their output in response to changing input costs while maintaining the sales quantity. Even if energy price increases are large, if firms can pass through increasing energy prices by charging proportionally higher sales prices, the overall adverse effect on the firm may be limited.

Price pass-on can be measured as the change in the sales price p^Q in response to a change in the price of energy. Formally, based on Sijm, Neuhoff, and Chen (2006) the pass through rate can be expressed as:

$$\frac{\partial p^Q}{\partial p^{ene}} \tag{4.8}$$

Note that technically in equilibrium the sales price is equal to the consumer's demand price. Thus, a firm's ability to adjust its sales price depends on the consumer's demand choice. The ability to pass on price increases depends essentially on the price elasticity of demand; i.e. how likely are end-users (e.g. households) and other firms (consumers of intermediate goods) to substitute away from a given firm's product. This in turn can depend on a variety of factors: the degree of competition, and the availability and affordability of alternatives (Kim et al., 2010; Sijm, Neuhoff, and Chen, 2006). Reviewing the empirical evidence on the pass-through of carbon taxes, Arlinghaus (2015) concludes that across industries pass-on rates vary between 0% and over 100% of the price shock – thus highlighting the important role of sector specific conditions.

4.4 Conclusion and policy implications

4.4.1 Need for further research

By building the evidence base on FFS reforms and firms, research can strengthen the design of FFS reforms and increase the momentum for reforms. This is particularly true for the reform of subsidies to fossil fuel producers and energy intensive firms.

Country-level studies for major subsidising economies are needed to esti-mate the likely effects of FFS reform on firms. CGE models can estimate effects at the sector level, and provide insights about interaction between sectors, dynamic effects, and both direct and indirect price shocks. Firm survey analyses can also shed light on both direct and indirect price effects, if combined with input-output tables.[9] Moreover, firm survey anal-yses can be critical for benchmarking sector-level energy-intensities, and for considering how FFS reforms may affect certain types of firms (such as micro, small and medium enterprises).

When conducting *ex-ante* assessments of the potential effects of FFS reform on firms, it is important not to equate cost increases (both direct and indirect) with competitiveness losses. Empirical analyses based on firm-level survey data can be crucial for investigating the ability of firms to use the response measures outlined in this chapter. These response mea-sures determine to what extent cost increases do in fact translate into com-petitiveness losses. Thus, by computing elasticities and energy cost shares, empirical studies can provide detailed country and sector specific insights to inform the design of policy measures for strengthening coping and adjustment capacities (see Chapter 5). Research should also focus on how energy price increases may affect other firm level outcomes – employment in particular – in order to determine to what extent adverse effects of FFS reforms are passed on to households, and how they can be protected.

Micro-level approaches using household surveys have offered crucial insights into how energy shocks due to fossil fuel subsidy reforms can affect the livelihoods of households (Coady, Arze, Eyraud, Jin, Thakoor, Tuladhar, and Nemeth, 2012; Rentschler and Bazilian, 2016; Verme and El-Massnaoui, 2015). Hence, there is a clear need for empirical studies using micro-level firm data, which investigate exposure and vulnerability to high energy prices and firms' ability to respond (e.g. by reducing energy inten-sity, or substituting towards cheaper energy types); Dethier et al., 2011). Just as in the case of household studies, such studies are crucial for informing the design and implementation of energy pricing reforms in developing countries.

As policy measures are identified to mitigate the adverse effects on competitiveness, further research is also needed on how such mitigation measures can be integrated into broader efforts to strengthen the business environment in which firms operate. Enterprise surveys, such as the *Doing Business* reports by the World Bank (2016), the *Management, Organisation and Innovation* surveys by the European Bank for Reconstruction and Development (EBRD, 2010), or the *Competitiveness Reports* by the World Economic Forum (WEF, 2016) provide useful starting points for exploring the broader drivers of and barriers to competitiveness (e.g. infrastructure, finance, security, competition, institutions, administrative capacity, and labour productivity). Such research may demonstrate that FFS reforms should not only be associated with competitiveness losses due to cost shocks, but – in line with the Porter Hypothesis (Porter, 1990) – may promote efficiency, innovation, modernisation, and institutional reform, and thus increase the competitiveness of firms.

4.4.2 Implications for the design of fuel subsidy reforms

As case studies of past reforms are studied and lessons learnt, the political economy challenges of subsidy reform are increasingly well documented (Commander, 2012; Fattouh and El-Katiri, 2015; Strand, 2013). Concerns about competitiveness and profitability have been a key part of these challenges, and important argument of political opponents of subsidy reform. Particularly, energy intensive manufacturing firms have been argued to experience substantial changes to their cost structures, with adverse implications for profitability (Bazilian and Onyeji, 2012). Evidently such effects can have knock-on effects on jobs and thus on households.

Countless studies have rightly emphasised the need for social protection measures to protect vulnerable households, and thus manage political economy challenges. In addition, this chapter argues, policy makers may also need to consider actions for strengthening the ability of firms to respond to energy price shocks by applying the measures outlined in this chapter (i.e. absorption, substitution, efficiency, pass-on). In particular, measures may be needed to help firms substitute towards alternative fuel types or to increase the efficiency of energy and material usage; e.g. by providing technical assistance, information programs, and financial support for implementing efficiency investments (e.g. in modern machinery Bleischwitz et al., 2009). In addition, providing reliable and affordable access to alternative energies (e.g. through public investments in electrification) can be critical for facilitating and directing inter-fuel substitution towards modern and clean energy sources. Chapters 5 and 8 provide a more detailed account of firms' response measures and the associated policy implications.

In some cases, policy makers may decide that no major assistance measures are required, as profit margins are large enough to absorb cost shocks and finance investments in efficiency and substitution. However, especially in competitive markets profit margins cannot always be assumed to be large, thus requiring policy makers to consider measures to mitigate potential competitiveness losses. Here, it should be recalled that energy costs are only one (minor) factor among many that determine a firm's or sector's competitiveness (Dethier et al., 2011).

This implies that policy makers have a wide range of measures at their disposal to counter-balance potential competitiveness losses due to energy price increases; for instance by strengthening institutions, and administrative capacity, or by investing in infrastructure and labour productivity and ensuring a stable business environment through prudent long-term policy strategies.

Notes

1 *An abridged version of this chapter has been published as* Rentschler, J. E., Kornejew, M., Bazilian, M. (2017). Fossil fuel subsidy reforms and the impacts on firms. *Energy Policy*. Vol. 108, pp. 617–623.
  Rentschler, J. E., Kornejew, M. (2016). Fossil fuel subsidy reforms and the impacts on firms: transmission channels and response measures. *Oxford Energy Comment*. Oxford: Oxford Institute for Energy Studies, University of Oxford.
2 In this chapter the term *competitiveness* is used as a theoretical concept describing the ability of a firm to prevail and succeed in its sector. Chapter 5 offers a more detailed and concrete discussion of the concept and presents quantifiable proxies.
3 The reason for lacking analyses of impacts on firms is not least due to a lack of detailed data on firms' energy consumption. While household expenditure surveys exist for many countries, corresponding firm surveys tend to be less commonly available.
4 Including other input types would not alter the arguments made in this chapter.
5 This is typically the case for large energy intensive firms (e.g. airlines), but not relevant in the context of small and micro enterprises in developing countries.
6 For industrial enterprises in Ireland energy costs are estimated to be up to 6% of total direct costs (Fergal O'Leary, Howley, and Ó'Gallachóir, 2007).
7 Likewise, subsidisation and energy or carbon tax schemes in other countries will influence the cost of imports.
8 "Resources" comprise both energy and materials.
9 See Araar and Verme (2012) for a discussion on how input-output tables can be used in the context of household surveys.

5 Energy price variation and competitiveness
Firm level evidence from Indonesia

Jun Rentschler and Martin Kornejew[1]

5.1 Introduction

The IMF (2016b) highlights that a central concern preventing governments from implementing green fiscal reforms is that the competitiveness of domestic firms may be adversely affected. Indeed, the concern that higher energy prices may harm firms features prominently in most debates on energy pricing reforms, in particular fossil fuel subsidy (FFS) removals or energy and carbon taxes. Case studies of FFS reforms for instance show that such energy price shocks have been a key reason why policy makers have struggled to win public support for reforms (Commander, 2012; Strand, 2013). However, while the adverse effects of FFS removal are increasingly well understood for households, the existing literature has largely ignored the effects of subsidy reform – and thus of higher energy prices – on firms (see Chapter 4; Rentschler and Kornejew, 2016).

This micro-econometric study investigates whether higher energy prices do indeed reduce the long-term competitiveness of firms. It uses a large firm survey dataset for Indonesian small enterprises in manufacturing and mining sectors. By exploiting regional price differences, it investigates whether and to what extent energy prices affect the performance of firms; and how firms adapt to energy price differences using inter-fuel substitution, energy efficiency, and price pass-on.

For the purpose of this analysis, the Indonesia constitutes an ideal case study. While 90% of the population are located on five main islands, the country covers over 1.8 million square kilometres of archipelagic land mass with almost 1,000 permanently inhabited islands, distributed over 34 provinces. These geographic characteristics impose considerable obstacles to energy distribution and have resulted in heterogeneous supply patterns, which prevent an even transmission of prices (IEA, 2014b, 2015a).

In particular, regions with significant infrastructure gaps are prone to face energy shortages and high distribution costs, which raise local energy prices above the national average. Firms in such locations face higher average energy prices than their competitors elsewhere, while producing under identical regulatory conditions and supplying similar markets. As these inter-regional price differences are structural and persistent, the data allows the estimation of potential long-run effects of higher energy prices on the performance of firms. As such, this setting can yield insights as to how energy price shocks – e.g. due to FFS reform – affect firms in the long run, i.e. after having exhausted possible response measures.

The analysis in this chapter shows that most energy prices to have a small (but statistically significant) adverse effect on the long-run performance of firms. More specifically, it shows that higher energy prices are associated with reduced profit margins, though the magnitude of the effect varies for different fuel types and industries. It is also shown that firms respond to higher energy prices by increasing energy efficiency (i.e. reducing the energy intensity of output), and by passing energy costs on to consumers in the form of increased sales prices. Furthermore, it is shown that most energy types can be substituted by one another, thus allowing firms to respond to varying energy prices by adjusting their energy mix.

The remainder of this chapter is structured as follows: Section 5.2 provides an overview of the relevant literature and existing empirical evidence. Section 5.3 offers a theoretical and conceptual discussion of competitiveness. Section 5.4 presents the dataset and descriptive insights. Section 5.5 presents the analytical methodologies and results. Section 5.6 offers a discussion of the robustness of results, and Section 5.7 concludes with observations and policy recommendations.

5.2 Literature and background

The question of whether environmental policies have an adverse effect on economic activity and competitiveness has been the subject of numerous studies. As part of this literature, research has focused on energy price regulation, in particular in the form of energy or carbon taxation, and investigated how such policy measures may affect the profitability and overall performance of firms. This section provides a brief overview of the relevant literature, its insights, and its shortcomings.

Studies on the competitiveness effects of energy and carbon taxes are of particular relevance, as these policy measures typically translate into energy price shocks. Arlinghaus (2015) reviews the empirical literature on the effects of carbon taxes on various indicators of competitiveness. Based on ex-post evaluations of a wide range of carbon and energy tax case studies, the review concludes that studies consistently fail to identify any significant adverse effects on common competitiveness indicators, such as employment, output, exports, and profits. Moreover, carbon taxes are found to significantly decrease the energy intensity of firms, while pass-on rates vary across different manufacturing sectors from 0% to over 100% of the tax.

Flues and Lutz (2015) study the effects of German electricity taxes on competitiveness. Using firm-level data for 1999 to 2005 and a regression discontinuity design, they show that electricity taxes (EUR 14.6/MWh or EUR 44.4/t CO_2) did not negatively affect common competitiveness indicators of firms, such as turnover, exports, value added, investment, and employment. Similarly, reviewing evidence for OECD countries, Zhang and Baranzini (2004) also conclude that overall, the competitiveness losses due to carbon taxes are small and in many cases not significant. However, for Egypt, Khattab (2007) estimates that a doubling of energy prices due to subsidy removal would reduce profit margins of firms in energy intensive sectors, e.g. in the cement (39% to 29% reduction), fertiliser (22%), and steel sectors (13%).

Moreover, the literature on environmental policies and regulation more generally can offer further useful insights. For instance, Dechezlepretre and Sato (2014) review the evidence on the effect of environmental regulation on competitiveness, for a wide range of regulation types, industries, and countries. They conclude that environmental regulation, including carbon taxes, has no adverse effect on indicators of international competitiveness, especially trade. At the firm-level, small adverse effects on employment and productivity may occur, especially in the short term and in energy-intensive industries.

In fact, a prominent strand of literature has investigated whether stringent environmental regulation may even have a positive effect on firm performance (Albrizio et al., 2014; Ambec, Cohen, and Lanoie, 2013; Ekins and Speck, 2010, 2008; Enevoldsen et al., 2009). Porter (1990) argued that well-designed environmental regulation can in fact enhance competitiveness, as firms are incentivised to increase investments in efficiency and innovation. Ambec et al. (2013) provide a comprehensive review of the empirical evidence for this so called Porter Hypothesis, and found that its validity appears to be conflicting. In certain countries and sectors, environmental regulation and policies were found to indeed have positive effects on competitiveness – measured as productivity or profitability. However, the opposite could be found in other cases. This emphasises the importance of relying on case specific analyses for ex-ante assessments of specific policy measures.

Gonseth, Cadot, Mathys, and Thalmann (2015) show that "adaptive capacity" can play a key role in determining whether energy taxes (and environmental policies more generally) increase or reduce the competitiveness of firms. For a sample of six European countries and eleven industrial sectors they show that human capital is an important determinant of the ability to mitigate negative impacts of energy taxes. Besides human capital, the capacity for technological innovation and substitution has also been argued to play a key role in determining how a green tax reform (e.g. energy tax) affects competitiveness (Koskela et al., 2001). Using a CGE model for Vietnam, Willenbockel and Hoa (2011) suggest that common energy efficiency measures can play a key role in enabling firms to cope with moderate energy price increases (5-10% per year). In a qualitative study of Indonesian micro, small, and medium enterprises, Tambunan (2015) finds that firms are most strongly affected by the indirect effects of energy price increases, as the costs of transportation, raw materials, and capital increase. The study also emphasises that the net effect of high energy prices crucially depends on firms' ability to adapt (e.g. increasing the output price, or energy efficiency).

Overall, the evidence presented above suggests that effects of energy taxes (and thus of higher energy prices) on indicators of competitiveness tend to be small on average, and even insignificant in many cases. This confirms the view that other factors such as infrastructure, finance, security, competition, and regulation play a far more significant role than energy prices in determining firms' performance (Dethier et al., 2011). However, it is also evident that studies focus predominantly on developed economies, and use macro-econometric approaches (based on country or sector level data), rather than analysing firm level data that can yield detailed and more nuanced insights.

Dethier et al. (2011) offer a critical review of empirical studies on the determinants of enterprise performance in developing countries. The authors argue that macro-econometric data conflates important dimensions of heterogeneity, including differences across regions and firm types (e.g. firm size). Hence, by analysing national averages or the behaviour of representative firms, macro-econometric approaches often fail to capture the heterogeneous effects of external shocks, e.g. due to changes in price or the business climate (Banerjee and Duflo, 2005; Pande and Udry, 2005). Moreover, by assuming profit-maximising behaviour, some basic features of standard growth models may contradict the evidence observed in firm surveys; e.g. about marginal costs and prices of production factors (Dethier et al., 2011).

Micro-level approaches using household surveys have offered crucial insights into how energy shocks due to fossil fuel subsidy reforms can affect the livelihoods of households (see Chapter 3; Arze del Granado et al., 2012; Rentschler and Bazilian, 2016; Ruggeri Laderchi et al., 2013; Verme and El-Massnaoui, 2015). However, while the adverse effects of FFS removal are increasingly well understood for households, the existing literature has largely ignored the effect of subsidy reforms on firms (see Chapters 2 and 4; Rentschler and Kornejew, 2016). While some studies have considered economic activity and industrial sectors, their general equilibrium modelling approach lacks the granularity to offer concrete and nuanced policy recommendations for mitigating adverse effects on firms (Durand-Lasserve et al., 2015; Plante, 2014; Siddig et al., 2014; Solaymani and Kari, 2014).

Hence, there is a clear need for empirical studies using micro-level firm data, which investigate exposure and vulnerability to high energy prices and firms' ability to cope (e.g. by reducing energy intensity, or substituting towards cheaper energy types). Just as in the case of household studies, such studies are crucial for informing the design and implementation of energy pricing reforms in developing countries.

5.3 Background: competitiveness and firms' response measures

Despite being a frequently cited policy objective, competitiveness remains a concept which is neither clearly defined, nor fully understood. For the purpose of this chapter, the focus is on the impact of energy price variations on the competitiveness of firms, which is often understood as a firm's "ability to sell" or "ability to earn" (Arlinghaus, 2015). Observing and quantifying this "ability" can be difficult in practice and there is no single generally accepted approach.

Yet, for evaluating the impact of energy price variations on firms, an indicator of firm performance or competitiveness is indispensable. Recognising the difficulty of measuring the elusive concept of competitiveness per se, past empirical studies have used a variety of so called "outcome indicators", which are thought to measure outcomes or "symptoms" of competitiveness. Such indicators include revenues, profits, market share, employment, investments, exports, patents, productivity growth, and others (Arlinghaus, 2015; Dechezlepretre and Sato, 2014; Ekins and Speck, 2008; Flachenecker, 2017; Neary, 2006; Siggel, 2006; WEF, 2016; Zairi, 1994).

In practice, the choice of an adequate competitiveness indicator is driven by the considered policy issue, and limited by data availability (Arlinghaus, 2015). This chapter uses profit margins as an indicator of the performance and competitiveness of firms. Profit margins reflect both the success in cost competition, as well as potential mark-ups based on distinctive characteristics (e.g. location, product quality). Other common indicators of competitiveness, are either only weakly linked to energy price variations (such as employment or output), meaningless for micro and small enterprises (e.g. market share), or not observed in the data (e.g. exports, technology, innovation). The conceptual and theoretical underpinnings for the choice of this competitiveness indicator are outlined in this section.

5.3.1 Using profits to estimate competitiveness

In micro-economic theory, profit maximisation is the sole objective of a firm, thus providing a strong rationale to use profits as an indicator for a firm's performance or competitiveness. Hence, in practice, profits are one of the most common measures of firm level competitiveness, and most relevant to the objectives of this chapter. Profits are a key determinant of a firm's ability to operate. Prolonged periods of negative profits almost inevitably lead to the firm's exit. On the contrary, large positive profits (above sector average) indicate that a firm is outperforming its competitors producing similar products. On the contrary, prolonged periods of negative profits eventually lead to a firm's exit. Moreover, profits are directly influenced by costs, and thus are particularly suited for assessing the effect of varying energy input prices. The most basic profit-based competitiveness indicator are absolute profits.

Absolute profits refer to the size of firms' profit margins. As larger firms are bound to generate larger revenues and profits, firms' absolute profits are normalised by firm size to enable coherent comparison. Formally, absolute profits AP_i are calculated based on the revenue and aggregate cost data:

$$AP_i = \frac{\pi_i^s}{n_i} = \frac{R_i^s - C_i^s}{n_i}$$

where π_i^s denotes the total profit of firm i in sector s, and R_i^s and C_i^s denote revenues and aggregate costs respectively. Note that in this example profits are normalised by the number of employees n_i in firm i, which corresponds to the dataset's definition of firm size.

However, absolute profits do not indicate whether and to what extent a firm is outperforming competitors. For instance, it may be achieving positive profits which are significantly smaller than the industry average – in this case, the firm would be less "competitive" than its peers, but absolute profits cannot capture this.

Relative profits indicate any given firm's performance in comparison to its direct competitors, i.e. other firms in the same sector. This indicator reflects the notion that competitiveness is necessarily a relative concept, and cannot be assessed for any given firm in isolation (Zairi, 1994). In other words, the ability of a firm to compete must be benchmarked against the performance of its competitors.

Formally, this competitiveness indicator of a given firm i in sector s is computed by benchmarking a firm's absolute profit level (per employee) against the sector's average absolute profit:

$$RP_i = \frac{AP_i}{\bar{AP}_s} = \frac{\pi_i^s/n_i}{\underbrace{\sum_i (\pi_i^s/n_i)}_{I_s}}$$

where π_i^s denotes the profit of firm i in sector s, and I_s the total number of firms in sector s. Numerically, this definition will indicate whether a given firm makes negative profits ($RP_i < 0$), lower profits than the industry average ($0 < RP_i < 1$), or higher profits than the industry average ($1 < RP_i$).

It must be acknowledged that by using absolute or relative profits as a proxy for competitiveness, several simplifying assumptions are made. First, by benchmarking a given firm's profit only against the sector's average profit, the indicator assumes that no inter-sector competition takes place – even if sectors operate in related fields. Second, using profits as an indicator of competitiveness only provides a limited picture of a firm's economic performance and resilience. Other factors, including access to credit, the ability to innovate continuously, or existing assets, may play an important role in defining a firm's ability to compete (Dethier et al., 2011; Porter, 1990).

5.3.2 Normalising for firm size

Since larger firms tend to have larger revenues, profits and costs in absolute terms, it is necessary to normalise any measure of competitiveness according to firm size. The absolute and relative profits measures above address this issue by scaling profits according to the number of employees. This approach is consistent with the approach taken by the firm survey BPS Statistics Indonesia, 2015), which classifies firm size according to the number of employees. Similarly, the analysis of household expenditure surveys – which has strong parallels to the analysis of firm surveys – follows the convention of normalising using the number of household members. However, for the purpose of this chapter, using employee numbers as a measure of firm size introduces potential inaccuracies.

Note that profit per employee (π_i/n_i) is closely related to the measure of labour productivity, which is typically calculated as output divided by labour input. In other words, this measure fails to account for other factors of production, which in practice can play an important role in defining the size (i.e. output) of a firm. For instance, in the case of a tobacco farm, agricultural machinery or the size of cultivated land plays an important role in determining the quantity of output, thus revenues, thus profits.

More practically, due to a very small number of employees in the dataset (between 1 and 19), scaling by employee numbers can introduce significant variation to profit figures. For illustration, a self-employed tobacco farmer will appear as only half as profitable (i.e. competitive), if he decides to count the help by a family member as a second employee.

Note that in contrast to the absolute and relative profit expressions in the previous subsection, normalising profits by total revenues yields a more accurately scaled indicator of competitiveness. This can easily be shown, as revenues R_i can be expressed as a function of all production factors – not just labour:

$$\frac{\pi_i}{R_i} = \frac{\pi_i}{p^s Q_i} = \frac{\pi_i}{p^s f_i(K_i, L_i, N_i, O_i)} \tag{5.1}$$

Here p^s denotes the sales price, and Q_i denotes output quantity, which is given by a production function f_i of various production factors including capital (K_i), labour (L_i), natural resources (N_i), and other factor inputs (O_i). This confirms that scaling profits by overall revenues more accurately reflects the range of production factors, which determine a firm's economic size. This argument is particularly relevant in manufacturing industries, where the capacity of a firm is crucially determined by assets and machinery, or in agriculture, where the size of cultivated land significantly influences output.

5.3.3 *Profit and cost shares of revenue*

By normalising profits with respect to total revenues, the expression in equation 5.1 essentially denotes the firm's profits share, i.e. the percentage share of profits in overall revenues. By definition profit and cost shares add to unity, thus considering profit shares as a measure of competitiveness is equivalent to considering cost shares:

$$\frac{\pi_i^s}{R_i} = \frac{R_i - C_i^s}{R_i} = 1 - \frac{C_i^s}{R_i}$$

By definition, the cost share indicator for profitable firms will fall between 0 (no costs, positive revenues) and 1 (costs equal to revenues, i.e. zero profits); for firms operating at a loss the indicator will exceed 1 (costs exceed revenues). Note that the cost share is always positive, while the profit share is negative for loss-making firms. To be able to use a logarithmic regression specification, the *cost share* is used for further analysis. Moreover, it should be noted that the regression setting controls for sector fixed effects. Hence, this chapter uses the firm specific cost share as a reduced form competitiveness indicator, which does not need to be standardised by the sector average.

5.3.4 *Response measures determine impacts*

In addition to considering the effect of energy price variation on the competitiveness of firms, this chapter also investigates whether firms have deployed measures to mitigate the effect of high energy prices (as discussed in Chapter 4). Such measures can be crucial for determining whether and to what extent an energy price change translates into competitiveness losses. To summarise Chapter 4, four main response measures can be identified that firms apply to mitigate the effect of energy price changes:

1 **Absorption:** Firms may choose to accept smaller profit margins, in order to absorb increases in energy costs. The level of absorption can be analysed by considering the effect of energy price changes on profit (or cost) shares – which is also an indicator of the net effect on competitiveness as discussed above.
2 **Substitution:** In response to changes in relative prices, firms may choose to substitute towards relatively cheaper energy types or production

factors. The ability of firms to substitute depends on a series of factors (including the availability and affordability of alternative energy sources), and can be estimated using elasticities of (inter-fuel) substitution.

3 **Energy efficiency:** When facing higher energy prices, firms may increase the efficiency with which energy inputs are converted into output. Energy efficiency adjustments by firms can be estimated by analysing whether the energy intensity of revenue depends on energy price variation.

4 **Pass-on:** Firms may choose to pass on high energy costs to consumers in the form of higher unit sales prices. Firms' pass-on rate can be estimated by analysing whether unit sales prices depend on energy price variation.

In practice, firms will choose a combination of up to four of these measures. In order to understand the overall impact of energy prices changes on competitiveness, this chapter offers an empirical analysis of each of these response measures (Section 5.5).

5.4 Data and descriptive observations

This chapter is based on a large firm survey from Indonesia for 2013, entitled Survei Industri Mikro dan Kecil (BPS Statistics Indonesia, 2015). The firm survey covers 41,402 small and micro enterprises, ranging in size from 1 to 19 employees, and distributed across all Indonesian provinces.[2] The survey provides a detailed breakdown of firms' characteristics, including employment patterns, inputs, costs, sales prices, revenues, and assets. Specifically, inputs cover various types of energy, reported in both physical and monetary units, thus enabling the computation of firm-specific prices for different energy types. This preserves price variation within provinces – a key for identification under confounded province level effects. Similarly, wages from total worker remuneration and employment. Revenues comprise (without distinction) domestic and international sales. However, the latter can be assumed to play a minor role due to the small and localised nature of the considered firms. Additionally, data on provincial minimum wages is obtained (BPS, 2016).

5.4.1 Data preparation

Several data cleaning measures were taken. Specifically, 3,543 firms are omitted that the survey identifies to operate only seasonally, since the reported data may not adequately reflect average business activity (e.g. profits from active seasons may be systematically larger than the sectoral average, to compensate for inactive seasons). Additionally, 1,100 observations that do not report any costs or sales figures are dropped.

While the remaining 36,759 firms all report expenditure on materials, energy, and capital, 63% of them lack data on labour costs. To avoid massive cuts in sample size, missing wage data is constructed by multiplying a firm's employee number with the province-specific minimum wage (set and reported by local governments; BPS, 2016). For cross-validation, average wages are also computed based on reported wage bills (i.e. for the 37% of firms that report wages), and indeed their cross-province variation closely reflects the profile of province-specific minimum wages. Nevertheless, individual observations are found to frequently undercut the respective province minimum wage. This can be observed for firms with two or three employees in particular, thus suggesting informal employment. Section 5.6 shows that the overall results are not sensitive to alternative methods of constructing labour costs.

Moreover, based on reported cost and quantity data, prices for the five main types of energy are computed: electricity, petrol, diesel, kerosene, and liquefied petroleum gas (LPG), which collectively account for 78.4% of total energy costs in this sample.[3] Since prices are susceptible to potential measurement errors in either cost or quantity figures, price outliers are replaced by the 2.5[th] (or 97.5[th]) percentile value of the respective provincial price distribution.[4]

Whenever firms do not use a certain type of energy – hence preventing the computation of a firm-specific energy price – the province's average price is assigned instead. This maintains substantial and meaningful variation in energy price variables, because inter-regional differences are considerable and of statistical significance: Regressing firm-individual energy prices on the full set of province fixed effects explains up to 59% of price variation for certain energy types, and finds more than half of all province averages to deviate significantly ($p < 0.05$) from the respective national average.

5.4.2   Sectors

The surveyed firms operate in the Indonesian mining and manufacturing industries. The 24 sectors distinguished in this dataset have been aggregated to 9 individual sectors on the basis of their ISIC denomination, in order to obtain robust sample sizes for each sector. Table 5.1 provides an exact summary of the sector coverage and aggregation used in this chapter.

5.4.3   Energy prices: regional variation

Energy prices tend to display large regional variations even within countries, not least due to local supply constraints and variable distribution costs. This issue is particularly stark in Indonesia due to its geographical characteristics.

Table 5.1 ISIC sector classification and aggregation used in this chapter.

Industry classification (ISIC)	Aggregated sector	Number of firms	Contained sub-sectors (ISIC)
Mining & quarrying	1. Coal, lignite, peat	9,836	-
	2. Crude oil, gas, uranium	1,457	Extraction of crude petroleum & natural gas; service activities incidental to oil & gas extraction
			Mining of uranium & thorium ores
	3. Metal ores & others	7,224	Mining of metal ores
			Other mining and quarrying
	4. Food & beverages	1,046	-
	5. Tobacco products	6,802	-
			Textiles
	6. Light consumption goods	1,628	Wearing apparel; dressing and dyeing of fur
Manufacturing			Wood & of products of wood & cork, except furniture; manufacture of articles of straw & plaiting materials
			Paper & paper products
			Publishing, printing & reproduction of recorded media

(*Continued*)

Table 5.1 (Continued)

Industry classification (ISIC) Aggregated sector	Number of firms	Contained sub-sectors (ISIC)
7. Coke & refined petroleum products	4,686	-
		Chemicals & chemical products
		Rubber & plastics products
8. Intermediate materials	2,159	Other non-metallic mineral products
		Basic metals
		Fabricated metal products (except machinery & equipment)
		Machinery & equipment
9. Technical products	3,572	Office, accounting and computing machinery
		Medical, precision & optical instruments, watches & clocks
		Radio, television & communication devices
		Other electrical machinery

Prices for subsidised petrol, diesel, kerosene, and LPG – distributed and sold by the state-owned oil company – are set by the national government, and thus supposedly homogeneous throughout the country. Similar conditions apply to electricity supply. However, inadequate infrastructure frequently causes supply shortages, particularly in peripheral and rural regions, thus creating price pressures (IEA, 2015a; Inchauste and Victor, 2017). Existing infrastructure gaps are perpetuated by energy subsidies, which dis-incentivise investments in energy and transport infrastructure. As for electricity, missing high-voltage transmission prompt authorities to approve higher tariffs in order to unlock local small-scale supply from independent utilities (IEA, 2014b). These price pressures due to infrastructure gaps are reinforced by large distances and natural barriers (e.g. inland sea).

Using data on firm-specific energy usage and expenditure, firm-specific energy prices can be computed – and hence provincial average energy prices:

Electricity: In the case of electricity, challenges of distributing centrally generated power between islands are particularly large; local electricity prices thus depend strongly on the availability of local power generation capacity and off-grid solutions.

As shown in Figure 5.1 (top), the average province level electricity price varies significantly across all major islands. Provinces in the most developed island of Java (central Indonesia) have consistently lower electricity prices than provinces in Sumatra (western Indonesia), Borneo (North), Kalimantan (North East), or Papua (East). Some of the lowest electricity prices are found in the Javanese provinces of Yogyakarta (716 R/kWh), Banten (761 R/kWh), and Jawa Tengah (827 R/kWh), while some of the highest prices are in Maluku (1,777 R/kWh), and Kalimantan Tengah (2,376 R/kWh). This variation implies a factor 3 difference in price levels within Indonesia.

Kerosene: For further illustration, Figure 5.1 (middle) presents the provincially differentiated prices of kerosene. The pattern differs significantly from the above price patternfor electricity. Prices are significantly and consistently lower in Eastern provinces, which may suggest the presence of targeted subsidies in these less developed provinces. Note that Indonesia implemented a large-scale kerosene to LPG conversion programme from 2007 to 2012, which helped kerosene users to cope with the removal of kerosene subsidies by providing them with LPG powered appliances (especially cooking stoves GSI, 2011). This firm level dataset was collected in 2012/2013 and suggests that this conversion and subsidy removal process had not yet been concluded in Eastern provinces. Average kerosene prices range between 4,427 R/litre (Papua Barat) to 6,067 R/litre (Maluku Utara) in nine Eastern provinces. In remaining provinces, prices range from 7,293 R/litre (Kepulauan Riau) to 11,570 R/litre (Jawa Timur).

Similar to the cases of electricity and kerosene, regional price variation is also significant for other major energy types (including LPG petrol, and diesel; see Appendix A.1). This highlights that firms operating in the

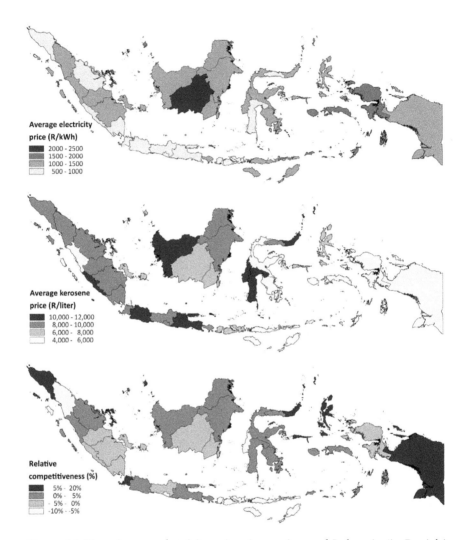

Figure 5.1 **Top:** Average electricity prices in provinces of Indonesia (in Rupiah/kWh). R 10,000 correspond to roughly US $1 in 2013. **Middle:** Average kerosene prices in provinces of Indonesia (in Rupiah/litre). **Bottom:** Average percentage deviation from national average competitiveness (defined as the relative cost share of revenue) across all Indonesian provinces. The percentage deviation is relatively small for most provinces, and competitive firms are located across the entire country.

same industrial sector, may face starkly differing energy prices depending on their location.

5.4.4 Competitiveness: regional variation

For the purpose of illustration, relative cost shares can be computed by normalising a firm's individual cost share with regard to its respective sector's average cost share (Section 5.3). Plotting these relative cost shares on a map illustrates that this indicator of competitiveness varies significantly across and within all major Indonesian islands (Figure 5.1). In a nutshell, this chapter investigates whether and to what extent this variation in competitiveness can be attributed to energy price differences (Section 5.5.1).

5.4.5 Energy intensity

In principle, energy intensive firms will be particularly exposed to variation in energy input costs. Specifically, firms' direct exposure to energy prices depends on the share of particular energy goods (e.g. electricity, petrol) in total costs (Table 5.2). As different energy types are subject to different regulation (e.g. subsidies, taxes), supply constraints, transport costs, and other factors, energy cannot be treated as a homogenous input (Figure 5.2). Overall, a firm's energy intensity will determine the magnitude of the *direct* impact of energy prices on competitiveness.

Despite covering the relatively energy intensive mining and manufacturing industries, the considered sample of firms shows that energy related costs only account for 1% to 6% of total costs in all sectors, except for coke and petroleum refineries (12%; Table 5.2). The energy share of total costs varies substantially across sectors and firm sizes (approximated by

Table 5.2 Energy intensity by sector: mean, standard deviation, and percentiles.

	Sector	*Mean*	*SD*	*1st*	*99th*
Mining & quarrying	1. Coal, lignite, peat	0.06	0.06	0	0.32
	2. Crude oil, gas, uranium	0.06	0.06	0	0.28
	3. Metal ores & others	0.01	0.02	0	0.11
Manufacturing	4. Food & beverages	0.02	0.03	0	0.12
	5. Tobacco products	0.02	0.04	0	0.24
	6. Light consumption goods	0.03	0.05	0	0.23
	7. Coke & petroleum refineries	0.12	0.12	0	0.49
	8. Intermediate materials	0.06	0.07	0	0.34
	9. Technical products	0.02	0.03	0	0.16

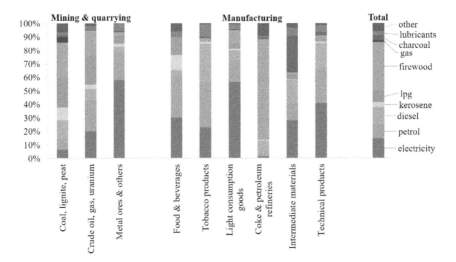

Figure 5.2 Composition of energy expenditure in manufacturing and mining sectors.

total costs), but relative to non-energy inputs, the cost of energy inputs tends to be significantly lower.

However, it must be recognised that the focus on direct energy costs necessarily neglects the embodied, i.e. indirect energy costs of other production inputs. For instance, even if a firm does not rely on energy as a direct production input, it will still rely on other goods or services (e.g. transportation, manufacturing, intermediate materials, and other parts of the local economy) – all of which rely on energy and may pass down energy price changes. This implies that especially in the longer term, firms may be affected more strongly by energy prices than these low energy intensity numbers suggest (see Section 5.5.1).

5.5 The effects of energy prices on competitiveness – and firms' response measures

Based on the discussion in Chapter 4, this section empirically assesses the link between energy price variation and competitiveness – and explores the role of response measures in determining this link. Section 5.5.1 investigates the long-term effect of high energy prices on competitiveness, using the absorption into profit shares as a proxy. Section 5.5.2 estimates firms' ability to adapt to high prices of certain fuels by substituting energy types and other inputs. Section 5.5.3 explores the role of energy efficiency as a response measure to high energy prices. Section 5.5.4 analyses to what extent firms pass on high energy costs to end-users.

5.5.1 Long-run competitiveness: energy prices and cost shares

By exploiting inter-regional energy price differentials, this section investigates whether energy prices have an enduring impact on the competitiveness of firms. The underlying argument is that high energy prices drive up production costs (directly and indirectly), thus jeopardising firms' ability to operate competitively. By basing the estimation on structural and thus persistent regional price differentials, this model measures the net effect of energy prices on firms' per-unit cost in the long run: i.e. after indirect price effects have unfolded, and after firms have implemented adaptation measures. Moreover, analysing small and micro firms – which predominantly draw on regional supply chains – ensures that the associated regional price indeed shapes indirect impacts.

Regression set-up

Specifically, the natural logarithm of the cost share of firm i is regressed on logged prices for electricity, petrol, diesel, kerosene, and LPG, indexed by e. Intuitively, higher energy prices are expected to be associated with higher cost shares, i.e. that parameter β_e is positive.[5]

$$
\ln\left(\frac{C_i}{R_i}\right) = \beta_0 + \sum_{e=1}^{5} \beta_e\left(\ln(price_{e,i})\right) + \sum_{s=1}^{21} \gamma_s sector_{s,i}
$$
$$
+ \sum_{p=1}^{32} \delta_p province_{s,i} + \varepsilon_i \qquad (5.2)
$$

Common sector impacts such as market demand shocks or the degree of competition which determines mark-ups, are controlled for by sector fixed effects.[6] Moreover, the full set of province dummies is included, as regional characteristics that drive energy prices might otherwise directly or indirectly affect cost shares.

Note that no further controls are included to isolate the *direct* energy price effect. The reason is that in order to estimate the total effect of energy prices on competitiveness, the reduced-form effect must be preserved, i.e. including both direct and indirect price effects. The indirect effect captures that energy costs are passed on along value chains, thus affecting the cost of non-energy inputs such as materials, capital, and labour. In other words, to assess the total effect of energy prices on firm performance, the energy-intensity of non-energy inputs cannot be disregarded.

The choice of the dependent also makes the regression set-up robust to issues of reverse causality or simultaneity, which are common with price regressions. Typically, prices and quantities form an endogenous link, thus biasing the analysis. Rather than focussing on absolute energy demand (which may affect energy prices, e.g. in the case of large firms), the focus is on cost and profit shares, as these are independent of firm size, and thus not systematically linked to absolute factor demand.

Results

Overall, the results – as summarised in Table 5.3 – show that higher energy prices have a small but significant adverse effect on the competitiveness of firms. Specifically, following observations can be made:

Small, but significant effect: Higher energy prices reduce competitiveness. The estimates for the total sample (first column of estimated coefficients) suggest that – on average – higher energy prices are indeed associated with higher long-run unit costs, i.e. lower levels of competitiveness. Effects are small, but significant for four out of five types of energy. Across all sectors and energy types significant coefficients are positive, thus confirming the qualitative nature of the effect.

Some energy types matter more than others. While the prices for all energy types are associated with positive coefficients, the size of the effect differs considerably across energy types. Most notably, the largest impacts come from differences in diesel and LPG prices. This pattern holds not only in the total sample but also in many sectors. On average, 1% higher diesel prices result in a 0.35% higher cost share, and 0.23% higher in the case of LPG prices. Kerosene and electricity are estimated to affect cost shares least of all, though kerosene matters greatly in certain sectors.

Different energy types matter in different sectors. Disaggregating the sample into nine sectors (as defined in Table 5.1) reveals heterogeneity masked by the overall effects. For instance, kerosene is estimated to be important for the mining of coal, lignite and peat, and the production of tobacco and technical goods – but not in other sectors. The rank order of importance of energy types varies across sectors, though the role of either LPG or diesel is estimated to be substantial in almost all sectors. The impact of electricity is relatively weak across all sub-samples.

In combination, the above observations show that effects can differ significantly depending on which sector and which energy type is considered. This is despite sectors being similar (i.e. manufacturing or mining sectors), and demonstrates that increasing prices of certain energy types is likely to have disproportionately large effects on certain sectors, due to the inherent (technological) characteristics of their production processes, which determine their ability to implement response measures.

5.5.2   *Inter-fuel substitution*

The extent to which regional energy price differences affect the long-run competitiveness of a firm, depends crucially on whether firms are able to respond by substituting away from comparably expensive energy types

Table 5.3 Estimated coefficients. Robust standard errors are reported in italics, significance levels indicated by asterisks: *** $p<0.001$; ** $p<0.01$; * $p< 0.05$. YES and NO specify the introduction of industry and province dummies. IN PARTS denote the introduction of those industry dummies that apply to the given aggregate sector; see Table 5.1 for sector classifications and aggregations.

Sample	All sectors	Mining & quarrying			Manufacturing					
		Coal, lignite, peat	Crude oil, gas, uranium	Metal ores & others	Food & beverages	Tobacco products	Light consumption goods	Coke & refined petroleum	Inter-mediate materials	Technical products
ln (electricity price)	0.052***	0.077***	0.081	0.028	0.016	0.089**	-0.087	0.015	0.016	0.023
	0.009	0.014	0.05	0.022	0.047	0.028	0.047	0.028	0.027	0.021
ln (kerosene price)	0.043	0.167**	-0.363	-0.263	-0.082	0.589*	-0.015	0.105	-0.245	0.128
	0.043	0.055	0.222	0.176	0.31	0.284	0.296	0.104	0.142	0.259
ln (LPG price)	0.232***	0.198***	0.124	0.458***	0.29	0.767**	0.091	0.568	0.095	0.059
	0.036	0.045	0.141	0.132	0.149	0.3	0.228	0.406	0.088	0.147
ln (petrol price)	0.160**	0.234*	0.207	0.400**	-0.002	-0.033	0.225	0.450**	0.229	-0.038
	0.05	0.094	0.17	0.15	0.169	0.156	0.193	0.145	0.135	0.105
ln (diesel price)	0.373***	0.568**	0.542	0.45	-0.636	0.685*	0.701	-0.117	0.564*	0.266
	0.098	0.212	0.494	0.536	0.481	0.25	0.575	0.155	0.222	0.153
industry dummies	YES	NO	IN PARTS	IN PARTS	NO	NO	IN PARTS	NO	IN PARTS	IN PARTS
province dummies	YES	YES	YES	YES	YES	YES	YES	YES	YES	YES
Observations	36,759	9,371	1,165	7,197	1,052	6,576	1,592	4,102	2,178	3,526
Adjusted R^2	0.214	0.061	0.106	0.293	0.073	0.134	0.139	0.069	0.065	0.087

(see Chapter 4; Rentschler and Kornejew, 2016). Similarly, if firms upstream the value chain are able to substitute away from expensive energy types this can dampen indirect cost propagation. In principle, substitution can refer to the replacement of energy inputs with other factors of production (e.g. labour), as well as inter-fuel substitution. In either case, the substitutability of energy will depend on firm specific technological limitations, operational requirements, and on the general availability of and access to alternative energy types.

The price coefficients obtained in the previous subsection are linked to the respective *gross input price elasticity of costs*, and can hence be interpreted as an indicator of a fuel's overall substitutability. By considering inter-fuel substitution, this subsection assesses the extent to which firms are able to substitute away from certain energy types, i.e. adapt to high energy prices by adjusting their energy mix.

The ability to substitute fuels is also of importance from an environmental perspective. It determines to what extent price based environmental policy (such as energy taxes or subsidy removal) can cause consumers to switch towards cleaner energy goods, and thus contribute to the reduction of environmental burdens such as air pollution or greenhouse gas emissions.

Partial price elasticities and elasticities of substitution

In order to quantitatively assess (inter-) fuel substitutability, this section estimates trans-log cost functions – a common approach used for example by Pindyck (1979), Andrikopoulos, Brox, and Paraskevopoulos (1989), Cho, Nam, and Pagán (2004), and Banda and Verdugo (2007). As suggested by Blackorby and Russell (1989), Chambers (1988), and Frondel (2010), partial own and cross price elasticity combinations are estimated to assess the extent to which firms are able to substitute (or complement) one energy type with another.

In line with a standard two-stage cost minimisation problem, a trans-log cost function is considered which is homothetically separable in the production factors, i.e. labour, capital, and five types of energy (Christensen, Jorgenson, and Lau, 1973; Pindyck, 1979):[7]

$$log\ C = \alpha_0 + \alpha_Q\ log\ Q + \sum_i \alpha_i\ log\ p_i + \frac{1}{2}\gamma_{QQ}(log\ Q)^2$$

$$+ \frac{1}{2}\sum_i\sum_j \gamma_{ij}\ log\ p_i\ log\ p_j + \sum_i \gamma_{Qi}\ log\ Q\ log\ p_i \quad (5.3)$$

where $Q = f(K, L, E(electricity, petrol, diesel, kerosene, lpg))$

and $i, j \in \{K, L, E\}$

For a discussion of the parameters in the translog cost function see Appendix A.4, Pindyck (1979), and Banda and Verdugo (2007). Note that the nested structure of the production function comprises capital K, labour L, and an energy aggregate E, which is a function of various energy types whose mix are optimised in the first stage. Under homotheticity, the unit cost function for aggregate energy (p_E) resulting from this first-stage-optimisation can be modelled as:

$$\log p_E = \beta_0 + \sum_m \beta_m \log p_m + \sum_m \sum_n \gamma_{mn} \log p_m \log p_n \tag{5.4}$$

where $m, n \in \{electricity, petrol, diesel, kerosene, lpg\}$

Following Shephard's Lemma, expenditure shares are obtained by differentiating respective cost functions with respect to logarithmic factor prices. Accordingly, the share s_m of fuel m in total energy expenditure can be expressed as

$$\frac{\partial \log p_E}{\partial \log p_m} = s_m$$
$$= \beta_m + \sum_n \gamma_{m,n} \log p_n \tag{5.5}$$

Note that this equation is identified in observable variables and thus estimable. Using the estimator for $\gamma_{m,n}$, partial price elasticities η can be obtained (Pindyck, 1979):

$$\eta_{m,m} = \frac{\gamma_{m,m} + s_m(s_m - 1)}{s_m} \tag{5.6}$$

$$\eta_{m,n} = \frac{\gamma_{m,n} + s_m s_n}{s_m} \tag{5.7}$$

Note that, due to the two-stage-structure, the partial price elasticities only account for the substitution between fuels (hence *partial*), i.e. under the constraint that total energy usage remains unchanged. In other words, it neglects substitution of aggregate energy by labour and capital as well as possible output changes, and measures relative changes in the energy mix only.

In addition, this section computes Uzawa-Allen and Morishima partial elasticities of substitution, which measure the extent to which the ratio (i.e. shares) of two particular energy types change in response to a change in their relative prices (Blackorby and Russell, 1989; Uzawa, 1962). Uzawa-Allen partial elasticities of substitution σ^{AES} can be written as

(Uzawa, 1962; Pindyck, 1979)

$$\sigma_{m,m}^{AES} = \frac{\gamma_{m,m} + s_m(s_m - 1)}{s_m^2} = \frac{\eta_{m,m}}{s_m} \qquad (5.8)$$

$$\sigma_{m,n}^{AES} = \sigma_{n,m}^{AES} = \frac{\gamma_{m,n} + s_m s_n}{s_m s_n} = \frac{\eta_{m,n}}{s_n} \qquad (5.9)$$

and Morishima partial elasticities of substitution σ^{MES} as (Blackorby and Russell, 1989; Frondel, 2010)

$$\sigma_{m,n}^{MES} = \eta_{m,n} - \eta_{n,n} \qquad (5.10)$$

$$\sigma_{n,m}^{MES} = \eta_{n,m} - \eta_{m,m}. \qquad (5.11)$$

Results

Estimated partial price elasticities for the whole sample are presented in Table 5.4 (for individual sectors see Appendix A.5). Most notably, the estimated **partial cross price elasticities** (off- diagonal entries) indicate that all pairs of energy types are substitutes, i.e. elasticities that are larger than 0, except petrol and LPG. This suggests that – when certain energy prices increase – firms can indeed replace most energy types for others. Kerosene and diesel are estimated to be the strongest substitutes, while petrol and LPG are the strongest complements.

Own price elasticities (diagonal entries) for all energy types are estimated to be negative, and hence are consistent with standard microeconomic theory. Demand for petrol is estimated to be most inelastic, while demand for kerosene and LPG is estimated to be most elastic.

According to the estimates in Table 5.4, electricity can be substituted by a mix of all other types of energy. In contrast, electricity plays a minor role in replacing any other energy types. Moreover, while being an important source of energy for most manufacturing firms, petrol is estimated to be the least substitutable one. This may be attributed to the fact that only three suitable substitutes exist, as LPG and petrol are complements. Instead, diesel and kerosene are the most important substitutes.

Quantitatively, kerosene is estimated to be an important substitute for all other main energy types. This does not necessarily imply that it is technologically superior to other alternatives, but rather that it is economically attractive given relative prices. However, the fact that it reacts most sharply to own price changes and is substituted easily by moderate quantities of other inputs emphasises economical attractiveness rather than technical significance.

Table 5.4 Partial own and cross price elasticities for the five main energy types. Asterisks indicate the confidence level (***0.1%; ** 1%; * 5%) of the underlying estimate for $\gamma_{m,n}$ and $\gamma_{m,m}$, respectively. Insignificant estimates of own-price elasticities are statistically indistinguishable from $s_m - 1$ (equation 5.6; in particular in the case of petrol, $s_{petrol} - 1 = -0.897$).

		Price change				
m\n		Electricity	Petrol	Diesel	Kerosene	LPG
	Electricity	−1.51***	0.17***	0.16**	0.09***	0.05**
Quantity	Petrol	0.24***	−0.93*	0.48***	0.11*	−0.29***
response	Diesel	0.18**	0.37***	−1.06***	0.32***	0.39***
	Kerosene	0.37***	0.30*	1.12***	−5.68***	1.17***
	LPG	0.09**	−0.38***	0.64***	0.45***	−2.90***

The estimates for Uzawa-Allen and Morishima elasticities of substitution are reported in Appendix A.6, and confirm the overall conclusions derived above from price elasticities.

5.5.3 Energy efficiency

Firms may also respond to energy cost increases by increasing energy efficiency, i.e. reducing the energy intensity of output. Formally, energy (or material) efficiency relates to the marginal product of energy (or material inputs), i.e. the output obtainable from the last unit of energy input given the current production technology. This implies that gains in energy efficiency require an adjustment to the production function, for instance by updating production processes or technology. Thus, from a policy-making perspective, improvements in energy efficiency are a desirable and welfare improving response to FFS reforms, as they are associated with modernisation, innovation, and reduction of negative externalities of inefficient energy usage such as air pollution (Flachenecker, Bleischwitz, and Rentschler, 2016).

Similar to the case of substitution, the ability of firms to increase energy efficiency depends on a variety of factors, all of which mandate dedicated policy measures: e.g. to improve the availability and affordability of modern technology, and to provide support programmes for identifying, financing, and implementing efficiency enhancing measures (Rentschler, Bleischwitz, and Flachenecker, 2016; Rohdin, Thollander, and Solding, 2007; Trianni, Cagno, Thollander, and Backlund, 2013).

Regression set-up

This section investigates whether firms do use energy efficiency improvements as a response to higher energy prices; i.e. whether firms facing higher energy prices, systematically display lower energy intensity of output compared to competitors in the same sector. For this purpose, a measure for the energy intensity of revenue is constructed in two steps:

First, for a given firm, the energy content of different energy inputs is computed (in MJ) based on the reported energy usage and the physical conversion factors summarised in Table 5.5. These figures for different energy types are then aggregated to yield the total energy content used by the firm. Second, the total energy content is divided by the firm's total revenues, in order to obtain a measure of the energy intensity of revenue (in MJ/IDR); i.e. an indicator of energy efficiency. Table 5.6 summarises the variation of energy efficiency across and within sectors.

Regression equation 5.2 is then modified by replacing the dependent variable with the firm-specific energy efficiency measure.

$$
ln\left(\frac{E_i}{R_i}\right) = \alpha_0 + \sum_{e=1}^{5} \alpha_e \left(ln(price_{e,i})\right)
$$

$$
+ \sum_{s=1}^{21} \sigma_s sector_{s,i} + \sum_{p=1}^{32} \pi_p province_{s,i} + \varepsilon_i \qquad (5.12)
$$

Table 5.5 Energy content of different fuels (in terms of energy density or specific energy), based on BP (2016), EIA (2016), and IPCC (2006).

	Energy content
Petrol	33.36 MJ/litre
Diesel	36.25 MJ/litre
Electricity	3.60 MJ/kWh
Kerosene	34.95 MJ/litre
LPG	47.30 MJ/kg
Coal	28.20 MJ/kg
Gas	35.00 MJ/m^3

Table 5.6 Energy efficiency: total energy content divided by revenues (in KJ/IDR). Mean, standard deviation, and percentiles.

	Sector	Mean	SD	1st	99th
Mining & quarrying	1. Coal, lignite, peat	0.31	2.79	0	2.62
	2. Crude oil, gas, uranium	0.26	2.68	0	1.64
	3. Metal ores & others	0.15	1.34	0	1.29
Manufacturing	4. Food & beverages	0.16	1.85	0	0.79
	5. Tobacco products	0.12	1.4	0	1.11
	6. Light consumption goods	0.23	1.4	0	2.5
	7. Coke & petroleum refineries	0.13	1.15	0	1.63
	8. Intermediate materials	0.22	3.01	0	1.35
	9. Technical products	0.26	4.25	0	1.24
	Total	0.2	2.35	0	1.73

This set-up can then capture the extent to which energy price levels determine the energy efficiency of firms; i.e. whether firms facing high energy prices have systematically adapted by reducing the energy intensity of revenue.

Results

Table 5.7 reports the estimated coefficients for the full sample. Overall, the negative signs of the estimates confirm the intuition that higher prices for all energy types are associated with lower energy intensity of revenue – i.e. higher energy efficiency. On average, increasing electricity prices by 1% prompt firms to use 60 KJ less energy from all fuel types per 10,000 IDR (about US $1) of revenue.

It should be noted that controlling for wages has no notable effect on the results reported in Table 5.7. The estimates indicate that wages have an insignificant positive impact on energy efficiency.

5.5.4 Pass-on

The net impact of energy prices on competitiveness also depends on whether firms can pass on high energy costs to end-users (see Chapter 4; Rentschler and Kornejew, 2016). Essentially, this channel refers to firms' ability to adjust the unit sales price of output in response to changing input costs (without incurring excessive reductions of sales quantities).

Table 5.7 Sensitivity of energy efficiency to fuel prices. Standard errors (in *italics*) are robust to heteroscedasticity, *** p<0.001; ** p<0.01; * p< 0.05.

	$\hat{\alpha}_e$
ln (electricity price)	−0.624***
	0.118
ln (kerosene price)	−0.196**
	0.072
ln (LPG price)	−0.138
	0.186
ln (petrol price)	−0.245
	0.214
ln (diesel price)	−0.155
	0.093
industry dummies	YES
province dummies	YES
N	36,758
Adjusted R^2	0.021

Regression set-up

This section investigates whether firms do pass on high energy prices; or more specifically, whether firms facing higher energy prices, systematically charge higher unit sales prices compared to competitors in the same sector. The sales prices and quantities required for this purpose are reported in the dataset. Since firms frequently sell multiple goods, an average unit sales price is computed for each firm, weighted by the goods' relative shares in overall sales.

Regression equation 5.2 is again modified by replacing the dependent variable with the natural logarithm of the firm-specific average sales price asp_i.

$$ln(asp_i) = \theta_0 + \sum_{e=1}^{5} \theta_e\big(ln(price_{e,i})\big) + \theta_c(ln(total\ cost_i)) + \theta_w(ln(wage_i))$$

$$+ \sum_{s=1}^{21} \tau_s sector_{s,i} + \sum_{p=1}^{32} \omega_p province_{s,i} + \varepsilon_i \qquad (5.13)$$

In this sample, larger firms tend to produce goods and services that are more valuable, e.g. due to either higher quality or simply larger scale.

Moreover, the IEA (2015a) suggest that larger firms are more likely to operate in areas with better energy infrastructure or to receive preferential supply of subsidised fuel in the event of shortages. To avoid an omitted variable bias, the regression controls for firm size, approximated by (the natural logarithm of) a firm's total cost.[8]

Additionally, the regression controls for wages as these can offer an important reference point: Labour costs typically exceed energy costs and may be passed on to consumers at a higher rate, since higher wages are typically associated with higher purchasing power *ceteris paribus*. Overall, this regression set-up can capture the extent to which energy price levels determine the average unit sales price charged by firms; i.e. whether firms facing high energy prices have adapted by systematically passing on these costs.

Results

Table 5.8 reports the estimated pass-on coefficients for the full sample. The positive signs of the estimates confirm that higher prices for all

Table 5.8 Sensitivity of unit sales prices to fuel prices. Standard errors (in *italics*) are robust to heteroscedasticity, *** $p < 0.001$; ** $p < 0.01$; * $p < 0.05$.

	Control for total costs	*Controls for total costs & wages*
ln (**electricity** price)	0.051*	0.052*
	0.02	*0.02*
ln (**kerosene** price)	0.166	0.184*
	0.09	*0.089*
ln (**LPG** price)	0.180*	0.186*
	0.086	*0.086*
ln (**petrol** price)	0.231*	0.185
	0.114	*0.114*
ln (**diesel** price)	−0.027	−0.016
	0.177	*0.177*
ln (total **costs**)	0.453***	0.445***
	0.01	*0.01*
ln (**wage**)	–	0.361***
		0.036
industry dummies	YES	YES
province dummies	YES	YES
N	36,742	36,742
Adjusted R^2	0.49	0.491

energy types are indeed associated with higher long-run sales prices – i.e. that firms pass on (direct and indirect) energy costs to consumers. Due to the sample's focus on certain economic sectors and on small firms, no concrete conclusion can be drawn about the effect on overall consumer price levels. However, significant pass-on estimates highlight that indirect transmission of energy costs along value chains can be significant, and must be taken into consideration for understanding the net effect of energy prices on firms.

It is noteworthy that on average the pass-on of wage costs occurs at a higher (and more significant) rate than for energy. This confirms the intuition that wages are more easily and thus more often passed on, since they are – contrary to energy costs – associated with higher purchasing power of consumers.

5.6   Robustness tests and limitations

The sensitivity of results has been tested with regards to following variations of the regression set-up:[9]

- Overall, estimates are robust to alternative approaches to account for missing labour cost data (Appendix A.3). Specifically, the tested approaches are: Constructing missing data by averaging peer wage bills (same province and employment), or obtaining out-of-sample predictions from a regression of existing labour costs (in natural logarithms) on dummies for numbers of employees, sector and province.
- Excluding the regionally concentrated food and beverages sector makes no statistically significant difference to the estimates (not least due to the small sub-sample size of this sector).
- Including outliers in the energy price distributions makes no significant difference to estimates.
- Excluding one or more energy types from the regression equations leaves standard errors and point estimates stable, thus suggesting that multi-collinearity is no issue. Moreover, regressing only one single price on cost shares at a time and restricting the sample to those firms for which individual prices are available yield similar coefficients for all five energy types. Applying a Heckman correction does not alter conclusions.[10]
- Including seasonally operating firms leads to a minor increase in the estimated coefficients of the cost share regression (Section 5.5.1) for all energy prices, except kerosene. Price impacts on energy efficiency (Section 5.5.3) stay the same apart from a doubling of the diesel coefficient, which becomes significant at the 5% level. Pass-on estimates (Section 5.5.4) remain qualitatively unchanged.

- Controlling for firm size – as measured by either total cost, employment, or total revenue – in the cost share (Section 5.5.1) and energy efficiency model (Section 5.5.3) has no considerable effect on energy price coefficients.
- Clustering structural errors at the province or industry level slightly inflates the coefficients' standard errors in all regression set-ups. However, p-values of formerly significant estimates again remain well below 5% in virtually all cases.

These sensitivity tests suggest that the results, and qualitative conclusions, are reasonably robust. Nevertheless, two caveats should be highlighted:

Estimates for sector 4 (food and beverages) need to be interpreted with caution. This sector represents the smallest sub-sample in terms of number of observations; moreover, almost 50% of firms in this sub-sample are concentrated in two provinces (over 80% in 5 provinces), thus the regional variations which this analysis relies on are not pronounced. This is likely to cause the negative (though insignificant) coefficients for kerosene, petrol, and diesel (Table 5.3). In all other sectors, the sampled firms are far more evenly distributed across provinces.

Interpretation in the context of FFS reforms: Regional price differences in this cross-section setting do not necessarily reflect the sudden and simultaneous energy price shocks due to a FFS reform. Firms and value chains require time to respond and adjust to energy price increases, e.g. by enabling energy substitution and efficiency increases through capital investments, technological updates, and reallocation of resources. Since regional price differences in Indonesia are persistent, firms in this sample will have adjusted to existing local energy prices. Thus, results in this chapter provide an estimate of the orders of magnitude of how FFS reforms affect the performance of firms in the long-term.

5.7   Conclusion and policy implications

This chapter analyses to what extent energy price variation – e.g. due to FFS reform – can affect the performance of firms. It considers cross section data for micro and small enterprises in the manufacturing and mining sectors in Indonesia. It provides a detailed analysis of the effect of energy prices on the long-term profitability of firms, and of the measures used by firms to adapt to higher prices. Overall, the analysis in this chapter yields following key results:

- **Competitiveness:** By computing a competitiveness proxy based on profits, this chapter shows that firms across all sectors have adapted to varying energy prices and availability, and are able to operate profitably across all provinces of Indonesia. Firms in provinces with relatively high energy prices are still able to compete nationally.

- **Energy intensity:** The considered data also shows that energy shares in total costs are low. Despite considering the relatively energy intensive manufacturing and mining sectors, this chapter finds that energy costs make up only between 1% and 6% of total costs in almost all sectors, thus suggesting limited exposure to energy price changes.
- **Energy prices and competitiveness:** Exploiting regional price differences, this chapter finds that higher energy prices have a small (but statistically significant) adverse effect on long-term competitiveness – approximated by profitability. This observation is valid for almost all considered sectors and energy types. Different energy types are found to matter in different sectors, with diesel showing the largest and most stable effect, presumably due to its importance for commercial freight and on-site power generation.
- **Response measures:** This chapter shows that firms use a mix of response measures to mitigate the adverse effect of high energy prices on profitability. In particular, firms are able to respond to higher energy prices by adjusting their energy mix, i.e. substituting certain energy types for others. Moreover, firms increase energy efficiency in response to higher energy prices, as well as passing on energy cost increases to end-users. The estimates suggest that these response measures play a significant role, but cannot fully mitigate the adverse effect of energy prices on long-term profitability.

By considering the effects on firms and competitiveness, this chapter provides an important contribution to the literature on FFS reform, which has focused predominantly on the effect on households and consumption. The observations made in this chapter allow several conclusions which are of immediate relevance for policy makers that design and implement energy pricing reforms, such as FFS reforms, or carbon and energy taxes. In particular:

- **Drastic competitiveness losses unlikely in the long-term:** Firms in this sample have adapted to large differences in energy prices. Energy price increases due to subsidy reform are unlikely to cause drastic long-run reductions of competitiveness for the considered sample; yet different fuels matter in different sectors.
- **Consider indirect effects:** Non-energy inputs (incl. materials, labour) account for far higher shares in firms' total costs. Energy price increases may (through indirect price effects) affect the price of these inputs, which may in turn have significant effects on competitiveness. While the total price effect (i.e. direct and indirect) has been estimated to be

small for the sample in this chapter, policy makers need to consider this possibility on a case-by-case basis.

- **Enabling substitution:** Ensuring the availability of alternative energy types is crucial to enable firms to substitute from subsidised fossil fuels to cleaner alternatives. Complementary policy measures are needed to ensure that (i) firms are able to substitute fuels, in order to cope with high energy prices, and (ii) fossil fuels are not substituted with other unsustainable fuels (including charcoal or firewood).
- **Enabling efficiency gains:** The ability of firms to implement efficiency enhancing measures can be obstructed by a variety of barriers (such as information or financial constraints). Dedicated policy measures may be needed to support firms in implementing efficiency enhancing measures, e.g. through modernisation and technological updates. If efficiency measures are successfully implemented, excessive pass-on of energy price increases to end-users can be avoided.
- **Strengthen other factors determining competitiveness:** The observation that energy prices only play a small role, confirms that other factors are far more significant in determining the competitiveness of firms and overall industries. Such factors include transport infrastructure, administrative capacity of authorities, corruption and red tape, access to credit, education and training, trade protectionism, and others (Dethier et al., 2011; WEF, 2016). Policy makers can strengthen competitiveness by addressing challenges in these areas.

All of these specific conclusions highlight that energy pricing reforms – such as the removal of fossil fuel subsidies – must be accompanied by a number of complementary policy measures. Policy measures that strengthen general conditions for the "ease of doing business", or that promote cleaner and more efficient production processes will not only mitigate potential adverse effects on competitiveness, but strengthen a reform's contribution towards sustainable development.

Notes

1 *An abridged version of this chapter has been published as* Rentschler, J. E., Kornejew, M. (2017). Energy price variation and competitiveness: Firm level evidence from Indonesia. *Energy Economics* 67, 242–254.
2 Following the official administrative classification, there are 34 provinces (provinsi) in Indonesia. As part of an administrative reform in 2012, Kalimantan Timur was split into two new provinces: Kalimantan Timur and Kalimantan Utara. The dataset does not distinguish these new provinces, but applies the old classification of 33 provinces instead.
3 Excluding firewood.
4 Robustness checks in Section 5.6 find results to be insensitive to alternative outlier treatment.

5 Appendix A.2 offers an analytical derivation of the regression equation to illustrate its theoretical foundation.

6 Note that the inclusion of sector dummies supersedes any sector-related normalisation for the dependent variable. It is easy to show that the log-linear setting brings about algebraic equivalence.

7 Note that this setup implies that expenditure shares for different energy types are independent of total energy expenditures, and of expenditure shares for other factors of production.

8 Using *employment* or *total revenue* instead yields very similar results.

9 For the sake of brevity, not all these results are reported (available upon request).

10 If there is a systematic reason why certain firms report energy usage while others do not, then the sample is non-random. This may lead to an omitted variable bias, and hence erroneous results. The Heckman correction procedure corrects this bias, by first estimating the probability of a given firm reporting energy usage. Then, this probability is included as an additional explanatory variable in the regression. As the Heckman correction does not alter results, the firm's reporting energy usage can be assumed to be randomly selected into the sample.

6 Illicit dealings

General equilibrium effects of fossil fuel subsidy reform, and the role of tax evasion and smuggling

Jun Rentschler and Nobuhiro Hosoe[1]

6.1 Introduction

Global subsidies to fossil fuel consumption amounted to $493 B in 2014 (IEA, 2015b) – i.e. exceeding the climate finance commitment of $100 B agreed under the Paris Agreement by a factor five. As Chapter 2 has outlined, the true economic and societal cost is bound to be far higher than this figure, since fossil fuel subsidies (FFS) cause countless adverse effects, including the lock-in of inefficient technology and behaviour, crowding out of funds for public spending such as education and health care, an erosion of competitiveness, exacerbating environmental pressures, and regressive wealth transfer to the rich (see Chapter 2; Rentschler and Bazilian, 2016). In addition to these adverse effects, FFS are also frequently argued to be associated with illicit activities, including corruption, fuel smuggling, and tax evasion. However, no systematic study exists exploring the role of such activities in determining the outcomes of FFS reforms.

Against this background, this study develops a dedicated computable general equilibrium (CGE) model to provide estimates of the orders of magnitude of the tax evasion and smuggling effects associated with FFS reform. More specifically, this study addresses the following interrelated questions: (i) What are the effects of FFS reform on key economic parameters, including income distribution, consumption, and output? (ii) How do effects differ when illicit market activities are taken into account, in particular tax evasion and rampant fuel smuggling? (iii) How do effects differ when FFS are not only removed, but replaced by fuel taxes? (iv) How do different methods of revenue re-distribution affect households?

To address these questions, this study develops a small open economy general equilibrium model, calibrated to reflect the characteristics of Nigeria. The model features six representative households (reflecting income quintiles and a smuggling household), a government which collects taxes, consumes, and provides cash transfers and fossil fuel subsidies, as well as four economic sectors. While building on the standard model outlined by Hosoe et al. (2010), this study introduces several innovative model features which distinguish this model from previous analyses (e.g. Plante, 2014). In particular, it introduces a large informal sector, evasion of labour and production taxes, and fuel smuggling.

The standard literature on FFS reforms has focussed on cash transfers as the main method of re-distributing FFS reform revenues (Chapters 2 and 3). Drawing on the environmental and carbon tax literature (in particular the "double dividend" field), this study also considers the role of labour tax reductions – in addition to cash transfers – as a way of revenue redistribution (Parry and Williams, 2010). Conceptually, as demonstrated by Parry and Williams (2010), these two approaches have different advantages: Reducing FFS and redistributing revenues using cash transfers has a strong progressive distributional effect. Reducing FFS and redistributing revenues by cutting labour taxes increases fiscal and economic efficiency, as distortive pre-existing taxes are reduced.

By introducing the novel model features on fuel smuggling and tax evasion, this study is able to analyse additional perspectives to these arguments:

- *The rationale for considering fuel smuggling:* FFS cause rampant fuel smuggling to neighbouring countries, meaning that a significant fraction of FFS benefits leaks out of the country. Replacing FFS with cash transfers is not only progressive, but terminates smuggling; i.e. the government can disburse the same aggregate benefit to the population at a lower cost.
- *The rationale for considering tax evasion:* Labour taxes not only distort incentives to work, but are associated with high evasion rates and incentivise informal economic activity. Reducing FFS and using revenues to lower labour tax rates not only mitigates labour market distortions, but reduces overall tax evasion; i.e. the government can earn the same level of tax revenues, while charging lower tax rates.

Overall, the study presented in this chapter finds that replacing FFS with cash transfers results in substantial progressive redistribution. While the top income quintile incurs a reduction in consumption, all other income quintiles gain, with the poorest income quintile benefitting from the largest relative consumption increase. Moreover, using revenues from FFS reform to cut labour taxes results in an improvement of fiscal efficiency. Crucially, this study finds that taking into account illicit activities can lower the social welfare costs of FFS reform by up to 40%. Moreover, by going beyond FFS reform and also considering the introduction of fuel taxes, this study finds that the above mentioned benefits can be extended further: A revenue neutral shift of the tax base from income to fuel taxes can significantly reduce illicit activities and their associated welfare costs. However, this move may also incentivise a reversal of the fuel smuggling direction from out- to inbound.

The remainder of this chapter is organised as follows: Section 6.2 discusses the relation of this study to prior literature on FFS, environmental tax reform, tax evasion, and smuggling. Section 6.3 provides a brief conceptual outline of the social welfare implications of tax evasion and fuel smuggling. Section 6.4 makes reference to the history of FFS in Nigeria, which are discussed in more detail in Section 3.2. Section 6.5 offers a detailed technical account of the CGE model set-up. Section 6.6 outlines data sources and calibration strategies for latent parameters. Section 6.7 outlines the three simulation scenarios considered in this study. Section 6.8 presents measures used for evaluating social welfare and fiscal efficiency in different simulation scenarios. Section 6.9 presents the results. Section 6.10 presents insights from key sensitivity analyses and robustness checks, and Section 6.11 concludes.

6.2 Relation to prior literature

6.2.1 Fossil fuel subsidies

A large body of literature and numerous case studies have helped to document the adverse effects of FFS. Often used as a political tool, FFS have been justified by objectives such as alleviating poverty, redistributing natural resource revenues to citizens, and promoting industrialisation and economic development (Strand, 2013).

However, the evidence is very clear in showing that FFS are a very ineffective way of achieving these objectives, and cause a wide range of adverse side effects pertaining to all dimensions of sustainable development: economic, social, and environmental (Rentschler and Bazilian, 2016). These side effects include economic and technological inefficiency, fiscal imbalances, crowding out of public funds for innovation and social services, pollution, climate change, fuel smuggling, and corruption (IMF, 2013c; Coady et al., 2015b; Coady, Flamini, and Sears, 2015a; ADB, 2015).

In addition to the fiscal pressure they place on national budgets, FFS are also particularly problematic because of their highly regressive nature. In reviewing FFS schemes in a range of developing countries, Arze del Granado et al. (2012) found that the top income quintile receives on average six times more in absolute subsidy benefits than the poorest income quintile. In this way, FFS continuously reinforce and exacerbate existing patterns of income and wealth inequality. A comprehensive overview of FFS definitions, adverse side effects, reform progress and barriers is provided by Rentschler and Bazilian (2016; and see Chapter 2).

In light of mounting evidence in favour of FFS reform, the key question for policy makers has been *how* to design and implement reforms in a way that ensures public support for reform and protects livelihoods of vulnerable households. In this context, ex-ante simulations of FFS reforms have been particularly important in understanding the potential socio-economic consequences of reforms. This in turn has been critical for designing effective social protection and compensation measures alongside FFS reforms.

Broadly speaking, such studies on FFS removal have used either econometric approaches or general equilibrium models.

6.2.2   Fossil fuel subsidy reform simulations

Econometric reform simulations typically focus on changes in household consumption, and are useful for understanding the welfare and distribution effects of FFS reform (Chapter 3). Various such empirical ex-ante impact assessments of FFS reforms have been conducted to provide useful guidance for policy makers seeking to estimate reform impacts. For example, several studies provide econometric analyses of the welfare impacts of FFS reforms, and highlight the need to provide adequate social protection (e.g. in the form of cash compensation) along with FFS reform (Anand, Coady, Mohommad, Thakoor, and Walsh, 2013; Araar et al., 2015; Zhang, 2011; Coady, Gillingham, Ossowski, Piotrowski, Tareq, and Tyson, 2010; Verme and El-Massnaoui, 2015).[2]

Both the IMF and World Bank provide analytical tool kits for the empirical simulation of FFS reforms using household expenditure surveys and input-output models (Verme and El-Massnaoui, 2015; IMF, 2016a). The approach taken by these models enables swift and consistent analyses with relatively few data requirements. See Chapters 2 and 3 for a more detailed discussion and further references.

However, as Plante (2014) points out, these models also strongly simplify complex interactions, as they overlook the fiscal policy and general equilibrium perspective on subsidies: These models focus exclusively on the fact that the removal of FFS leads to energy price shocks, which in turn reduce purchasing power and aggregate consumption of households. Thus, FFS removal necessarily and exclusively has negative consequences, while benefits such as reduced deadweight losses or increased economic efficiency are not taken into account. Similarly, general equilibrium effects on key macro-economic parameters cannot be captured in models based on household surveys, including changes in government expenditure, output, and tax revenues.

To address the above mentioned shortcomings, Plante (2014) developed a general equilibrium model aimed at capturing the fiscal policy aspect of FFS reform. It is a standard small open economy model with two sectors, and a single representative household. FFS reductions are balanced in the government's budget constraint through tax adjustments or lump-sum cash transfer provision. Using this model, it is shown that FFS cause distortions of relative prices, which are identified as the main reason for substantial aggregate welfare losses. Moreover, FFS are shown to aggravate fiscal imbalances, crowd out non-energy consumption, and cause inefficient allocation of labour across sectors, regardless of whether the country is an oil importer or exporter (Plante, 2014). The model also suggests that permanent cash transfers can be an efficient and equitable tool for redistributing resource revenues, consistent with overarching development objectives of reducing poverty and inequality.

At least two other general equilibrium models have followed: Durand-Lasserve et al. (2015) offer an analysis for Indonesia based on the OECD's ENV-Linkages model, a global CGE model. This study focusses in particular on distributional effects of FFS reform, considering redistribution of reform revenues through cash transfers or food subsidies. Siddig et al. (2014) use the CGE model by the Global Trade Analysis Project (GTAP) to analyse subsidy reform in Nigeria. They distinguish twelve households, each representing a region rather than an income group. Using this set-up they consider the impact of FFS reform on several standard macro-economic parameters, such as consumption and GDP.

While the above mentioned models differ in the complexity of their modelling set-ups, they coincide in their focus on key macro-economic parameters, in particular output, consumption, trade and fiscal balances, or income distribution. Hence, these studies must also be seen in the broader context of – not only FFS reform – but the environmental taxation literature.

6.2.3 The double dividend

In particular, there is a prominent strand in this literature suggesting that there is a "double dividend" – i.e. that if environmental taxes are increased, but other distortionary taxes are reduced (while maintaining revenue neutrality), then not only can environmental benefits be reaped, but also fiscal efficiency can be increased (Goulder, 1995a; Fullerton and Metcalf, 1997; Bovenberg, 1999). However, Parry and Williams (2010) also show that there is a considerable trade-off between efficiency and distributional effects. That is, income tax reductions are economically efficient, but regressive, while cash transfers are progressive, but less efficient.

Since FFS are (at least theoretically) equivalent to a negative carbon tax, the double dividend argument deserves thorough consideration in the context of FFS reforms. Especially given the significant economic efficiency costs of labour and consumption taxes (Bovenberg and Goulder, 1996; Parry, 1997; Goulder, 1995b), there may be a rationale for using FFS reform revenues to reduce these taxes. However, instead of reducing pre-existing taxes, past reforms and associated analyses have focussed almost exclusively on cash transfers for revenue redistribution. Nevertheless in practice, it must also be kept in mind that the practicality of using tax cuts to redistribute FFS reform revenues depends largely on country-specific characteristics. For instance, in economies with large informal sectors, tax cuts are unlikely to reach the entire population and may need to be complemented with other measures such as direct transfers.

6.2.4 Tax evasion and smuggling

More recent studies have contributed an additional perspective, which significantly strengthened the double dividend argument. Liu (2013) observes that energy (or carbon) taxes are more difficult to evade than labour or income taxes. Using a simple CGE model, the author shows that a revenue neutral shift from labour to carbon taxes can substantially reduce tax evasion and the welfare cost of climate change mitigation policy.[3] Especially when pre-existing tax evasion is high, this argument can significantly strengthen both the environmental and fiscal case for carbon taxes (Kuralbayeva, 2013; Liu, 2013; Bento, Jacobsen, and Liu, 2017; Carson, Jacobsen, and Liu, 2014; Vasilev, 2016).

Even though tax evasion tends to be particularly high in developing countries – large informal sectors are symptomatic for this – the "tax evasion effect" has not been studied in the context of FFS reform. Similarly, despite being a frequently cited side-effect of fossil fuel subsidies, smuggling has also received little attention from researchers (Mlachila et al., 2016; Rentschler and Bazilian, 2016). As subsidised fuels are smuggled out of a country, the government is directly subsidising fuel consumption in neighbouring countries; in other words public funds intended for domestic beneficiaries are continuously leaking out of the country (ADB, 2015). Mlachila et al. (2016) offer one of the few studies that systematically analyse the magnitude and implications of fuel subsidies on smuggling activities. They show that fuel smuggling can severely undermine the effectiveness of fuel price adjustment mechanisms and energy tax collection, when neighbouring countries subsidise their domestic fuel consumption.

The model presented in this chapter contributes to the literature on FFS reform and the double dividend, by providing a systematic account of tax evasion, the informal sector, and fuel smuggling in the case of Nigeria. These issues are of great significance in developing countries, especially when considering that the informal economy in Nigeria is estimated at 50% of GDP, and that 85% of fuel consumed in Benin is smuggled from (and thus subsidised by) Nigeria (Mlachila et al., 2016; Hassan and Schneider, 2016).

6.3 The societal cost of illicit activities

This section provides conceptual detail on the argument underlying this chapter. More specifically, it briefly discusses the welfare costs associated with tax evasion and smuggling activities.

A key assumption by Liu (2013) is that tax evasion (and legal tax avoidance) activities incur real cost. The reason for this is that tax evasion efforts require real resources, and thus compete for production factors with real productive activities (ADB, 2015). Bribes paid to tax officials, the employment of tax lawyers and advisors, or the complex shifting of profits between international subsidiaries are examples of costly tax avoidance or evasion activities. In addition, taxes may reduce economic efficiency by distorting business decisions and production processes. In practice, the increased need for fiscal audits and monitoring may also impose a costly burden on authorities. Overall, tax evasion imposes real costs on society, not only because productive resources are allocated to unproductive evasion activity, but also because of foregone tax revenues.

Analogously, fuel smuggling activities also represent a loss to society. Fuel subsidies that are intended for the benefit of a country's own citizens are smuggled abroad; in other words, the government is directly subsidising the energy consumption of foreign consumers. In addition, the smuggling activity itself is costly, as significant resources are used on transporting fuel, and avoiding and bribing border and customs controls (Mlachila et al., 2016). As in the case of tax evasion, these resources are lost and thus unavailable to productive economic activities.

A key argument considered in this chapter is that reducing FFS and using revenues to cut distortionary labour taxes can be welfare-enhancing, since welfare losses associated with smuggling and tax evasion are also reduced. In line with Parry and Williams (2010), this chapter contrasts such labour tax cuts with other ways of recycling reform revenues: increasing public expenditure, or the provision of uniform lump-sum transfers to citizens.

6.4 Fuel subsidies in Nigeria: background and overview

To avoid repetition, no further background information on the Nigerian FFS programme is provided here. Section 3.2 offers a detailed account, including the objectives and challenges of the programme, past reform attempts, and estimates.

6.5 Fuel subsidy reform, tax evasion, and smuggling: a Computable General Equilibrium model

This section formally presents the features of the CGE model used to analyse the welfare effects of fossil fuel subsidy reform. The model developed for this purpose is a static small open economy model, featuring multiple representative households, firms, and a government. It features taxes on production, factor usage, and imports, as well as direct taxes on households. The government is modelled to disburse fossil fuel subsidies, funded from tax revenues.

The basic structure of this model builds on Hosoe et al. (2010), who offer a small open economy CGE model featuring a representative household, two sectors, and a government. The model in this study distinguishes five income quintiles, introduces fossil fuel subsidies, and adds several non-standard features: A small group of households is modelled to engage in fuel smuggling

activities. The profits of smuggling depend on the price differential between
the domestic and international price of fuel, which is determined through the
level of subsidies paid. Moreover, the model allows for the evasion of production and factor taxes. In order to represent different policy options for
using reform revenues, the model considers (1) government expenditure,
(2) direct cash transfers, and (3) reductions of pre-existing taxes, such as
labour or production taxes.

6.5.1   Tax evasion: representation in the model

In this model it is assumed that firms choose to evade taxes on different
factors and on production, while incurring a real cost of evasion. Formally,
factor taxes $\tau^f_{h,j}$ on factor h and sector j are evaded at the rate $e^f_{h,j}$. Similarly,
production taxes τ^z_j are evaded at the rate e^z_j.

In line with Liu (2013), tax evasion activities incur real costs $F^{loss}_{h,j}$ and X^{loss}_j:

$$F^{loss}_{h,j} = c(e^f_{h,j})F_{h,j} \quad \text{with} \quad c(e^f_{h,j}) = \frac{A^f_{h,j}}{N^f_{h,j}+1}(e^f_{h,j})^{N^f_{h,j}+1} \tag{6.1}$$

$$X^{loss}_j = c(e^z_j)Z_j \quad \text{with} \quad c(e^z_j) = \frac{A^z_j}{N^z_j+1}(e^z_j)^{N^z_j+1} \tag{6.2}$$

This setting implies that the cost of tax evasion is measured as a share $c(e)$ of
either factor inputs $F_{h,j}$ (in the case of factor tax evasion) or production Z_j
(for production tax evasion). Parameters $A^f_{h,j}$, A^z_j, $N^f_{h,j}$, and N^z_j characterise
the relationship between the cost of evasion and the evasion rate, and are
determined during calibration (Section 6.6). The total net benefit to firm j
from evading factor taxes is $\sum_h F_{h,j}(\tau^f_{h,j}e^f_{h,j}p^f_h - c(e^f_{h,j}))$.

Evasion losses reflect the extra (unproductive) "self-input" due to
evasion efforts. Specifically, if a firm engages in evasion activities, a share
of its resources will be directed towards this evasion activity rather than
production (e.g. labour hours). This unproductive evasion activity means
that fewer resources are available for producing output, thus resulting in
the output loss X^{loss}_j.

Moreover, the marginal costs of evading taxes can be expressed as

$$\frac{\partial c(e^f_{h,j})}{\partial e^f_{h,j}} = A^f_{h,j}(e^f_{h,j})^{N^f_{h,j}} \quad \text{and} \quad \frac{\partial c(e^z_j)}{\partial e^z_j} = A^z_j(e^z_j)^{N^z_j}. \tag{6.3}$$

Since these marginal costs are increasing in $e^f_{h,j}$ or e^z_j, firms choose evasion
rates and factor input quantities as to maximise profits (Section 6.5.3).

6.5.2   Smuggling: representation in the model

In practice, fuel subsidies often incentivise smuggling, as subsidised domestic energy prices are significantly lower than in neighbouring countries,

where fuel prices are unregulated. This price gap presents a lucrative opportunity for smugglers, who buy energy at the subsidised domestic price and sell it abroad at the unregulated market price. However, in doing so smugglers are likely to incur real costs, e.g. in the form of bribes or transport costs (Mlachila et al., 2016).

For the sake of consistency, this model not only allows such *outbound* smuggling (smuggling "exports"); it also considers the possibility of *inbound* smuggling ("imports"), which may occur by the same logic when domestic fuel subsidies are removed and fuel taxes imposed.

In this model, smugglers are assumed to choose the smuggling quantity E_j^{SM} ("exports", i.e. *outbound* smuggling) or M_j^{SM} ("imports", i.e. *inbound*) as to maximise their profit. They purchase fuel for smuggling in the domestic market at the subsidised price $(1 - s_j^e)p_j^q$ (where s_j^e is the subsidisation rate), and sell it abroad at the export price p_j^e. In addition, smugglers incur smuggling costs E_j^{loss}, e.g. transportation costs. Analogously, they may also choose to conduct *inbound* smuggling M_j^{SM} ("imports"). In this case they will purchase fuel abroad at the import price p_j^m, and sell it domestically at the subsidised (or taxed) price $(1 - s_j^e)p_j^q$. Thus, the smuggler's optimisation problem is given by

$$\max_{E^{SM}, M^{SM}} \quad \pi^{SM} = (p_j^e - (1 - s_j^e)p_j^q)E_j^{SM} - (1 - s_j^e)p_j^q E_j^{loss}$$
$$+ ((1 - s_j^e)p_j^q - p_j^m)M_j^{SM} - p_j^m M_j^{loss} \tag{6.4}$$

$$\text{subject to} \quad E_j^{loss} = \frac{A_j^{SM}}{r}[E_j^{SM}]^r \tag{6.5}$$

$$M_j^{loss} = \frac{A_j^{SM}}{r}[M_j^{SM}]^r \tag{6.6}$$

E_j^{SM} (or M_j^{SM}) denotes the smuggled quantity from sector j, while the total cost of smuggling is denoted by E_j^{loss} (or M_j^{loss}) expressed as a share of the total smuggled quantity. The shape of the cost function is characterised by parameters A_j^{SM} and r, both of which are determined during calibration (Section 6.6).[4]

The smuggler's profit is maximised under following first order conditions:

$$\frac{\partial \pi_j^{SM}}{\partial E_j^{SM}} = p_j^e - (1 - s_j^e)p_j^q = (1 - s_j^e)p_j^q A_j^{SM}(E_j^{SM})^{r-1} \tag{FOC 1.1}$$

$$\frac{\partial \pi_j^{SM}}{\partial M_j^{SM}} = (1 - s_j^e)p_j^q - p_j^m = p_j^m A_j^{SM}(M_j^{SM})^{r-1} \tag{FOC 1.2}$$

For both FOC 1.1 and FOC 1.2, π_j^{SM} is maximised when the marginal benefit of smuggling (LHS) is equal to its marginal cost (RHS). Note that the sign of the subsidisation rate s_j^e plays a key role in determining whether the smuggler chooses inbound or outbound smuggling. Solving the first order conditions yields the profit maximising smuggling quantities E_j^{SM} and M_j^{SM}.

$$E_j^{SM} = \left[\frac{p_j^e - (1 - s_j^e)p_j^q}{(1 - s_j^e)p_j^q A_j^{SM}} \right]^{\frac{1}{r-1}} \tag{6.7}$$

$$M_j^{SM} = \left[\frac{(1 - s_j^e)p_j^q - p_j^m}{p_j^m A_j^{SM}} \right]^{\frac{1}{r-1}} \tag{6.8}$$

6.5.3 Domestic production

The comparably simplistic model by Liu (2013) is extended to include intermediate inputs. A neat way of modelling intermediate inputs is by distinguishing two stages of the production process. In the first stage, the firm uses primary factors (i.e. labour, capital) to produce a composite factor. In the second stage, the firm combines the composite factor with intermediate inputs to produce its output. This section formally describes the firm's profit maximisation problem.

First stage:

The firm's first production stage is described by a Cobb-Douglas production function, which is homogeneous of degree one and exhibits constant returns to scale. It maximises profits by choosing the quantity of its output (i.e. the composite factor Y_j), of its inputs (i.e. production factors $F_{h,j}$), and the factor tax evasion rate $e_{h,j}^f$.

$$\max_{F, e^f} \quad \pi_j^y = \left\{ p_j^y Y_j - \sum_h \left(1 + \tau_{h,j}^f \left(1 - e_{h,j}^f\right)\right) p_h^f F_{h,j} - p_h^f F_{h,j}^{loss} \right\} \tag{6.9}$$

$$s.t. \quad Y_j = b_j \prod_h F_{h,j}^{\beta_{h,j}} \tag{6.10}$$

The first term of the profit function reflects revenues from the sale of the composite factor Y_j at the price p_j^y. The second term is the sum of the post-tax costs of factor inputs (net of tax evasion), with $\tau_{h,j}^f$ representing factor taxes and $e_{h,j}^f$ the tax-specific evasion rate for factor h and sector j. Note that $F_{h,j}$ denotes factor inputs priced at p_h^f, out of which the amount $F_{h,j}^{loss}$ (the third term) is lost due to evasion activities.

Standard Lagrangian optimisation yields the following first order conditions:

$$\frac{\partial \pi_j^y}{\partial e_{b,j}^f} = A_{b,j}^f (e_{b,j}^f)^{N_{b,j}^f} = \tau_{b,j}^f \qquad \text{(FOC 2.1)}$$

$$\frac{\partial \pi_j^y}{\partial F_{b,j}} = p_b^f(1 + \tau_{b,j}^f(1 - e_{b,j}^f) + c(e_{b,j}^f)) = p_j^y \beta_{b,j} \frac{Y_j}{F_{b,j}} \qquad \text{(FOC 2.2)}$$

Note that FOC 2.1 states that at optimum the firm's marginal cost of evasion (LHS) is equal to the marginal benefit of evading tax (RHS). Similarly, FOC 2.2 states that the marginal cost of an additional unit of input (LHS) equals its marginal benefit (RHS).

Moreover, using FOC 2.1 the optimal evasion rate $e_{b,j}^f$ can be derived:

$$e_{b,j}^f = \left(\frac{\tau_{b,j}^f}{A_{b,j}^f}\right)^{\frac{1}{N_{b,j}^f}} \qquad (6.11)$$

Equation 6.11 shows that the optimal evasion rate is increasing in the factor tax rate ($\tau_{b,j}^f$).

By plugging $e_{b,j}^f$ into the original cost equation (6.1), the cost of evasion at optimum can be determined. This also allows solving for and calibrating parameter $A_{b,j}^f$, as all other parameters are known (Section 6.6.2). FOC 2.2 allows solving for the optimal factor demand $F_{b,j}$:

$$F_{b,j} = \beta_{b,j} \frac{p_j^y}{p_b^f(1 + \tau_{b,j}^f(1 - e_{b,j}^f) + c(e_{b,j}^f))} Y_j \qquad \forall b, j \qquad (6.12)$$

Second stage:

The firm's second production stage is described by a Leontief production function, which is homogeneous of degree one and exhibits constant returns to scale. Note that the Cobb-Douglas production function in the first stage can describe substitution between factors, while a Leontief function cannot. However, by applying a Leontief production function in the second stage the computational complexity of the model can be reduced considerably (Hosoe et al., 2010).

The firm maximises profits by choosing the quantity of output (Z_j), of intermediate inputs ($X_{i,j}$), of the composite factor (Y_j), and the production tax evasion rate e_j^z.

$$
\max_{Z,Y,X,e^z} \pi_j^z = \left\{ p_j^z Z_j + \tau_j^z e_j^z p_j^z Z_j - p_j^y Y_j \right.
$$
$$
\left. - \sum_i p_i^q (1 - s_i^e) X_{i,j} - p_j^q (1 - s_j^e) X_j^{loss} \right\} \tag{6.13}
$$

$$
s.t. \quad Z_j = \min \left[\frac{X_{i,j}}{ax_{i,j}}, \frac{Y_j}{ay_j} \right] \tag{6.14}
$$

The first term of the profit function denotes revenues from the sale of outputs, the second term denotes the benefit from tax evasion, the third and fourth terms denote the cost of composite and intermediate inputs, while the last term is the cost of evasion. Moreover, $ax_{i,j}$ (or ay_j) is the input requirement coefficient of the i-th intermediate input (or j-th composite factor) for one unit of the output j.

The production function (equation 6.14) can be used to replace $X_{i,j}$ and Y_j, and thus derive an unconstrained maximisation problem:

$$
\max_{Z,e^z} \pi_j^z = \left\{ p_j^z Z_j + \tau_j^z e_j^z p_j^z Z_j - p_j^y ay_j Z_j \right.
$$
$$
\left. - \sum_i (1 - s_i^e) p_i^q ax_{i,j} Z_j - (1 - s_j^e) p_j^q c(e_j^z) Z_j \right\} \tag{6.15}
$$

This yields the following first order conditions:

$$
\frac{\partial \pi_j^z}{\partial e_j^z} = p_j^z \tau_j^z = (1 - s_j^e) p_j^q A_j^z (e_j^z)^{N_j^z} \tag{FOC 3.1}
$$

$$
\frac{\partial \pi_j^z}{\partial Z_{h,j}} = (1 + \tau_j^z e_j^z - c(e_j^z)) p_j^z = p_j^y ay_j + \sum_i (1 - s_i^e) p_i^q ax_{i,j} \tag{FOC 3.2}
$$

As in the case with factor tax evasion, the firm chooses production tax evasion such that the marginal benefit of tax evasion (LHS of FOC 3.1) is equal to the marginal cost (RHS of FOC 3.1). This means that the firm's optimal level of production tax evasion e_j^z can be expressed as

$$
e_j^z = \left(\frac{p_j^z}{(1 - s_j^e) p_j^q A_j^z} \frac{\tau_j^z}{} \right)^{\frac{1}{N_j^z}}. \tag{6.16}
$$

Note that the optimal evasion rate is increasing in the production tax rate (τ_j^z).

To summarise, the following set of equations describes the firms' behaviour for optimising its two stage production process:

$$F_{h,j} = \beta_{h,j} \frac{p_j^y}{p_h^f(1 + \tau_{h,j}^f(1 - e_{h,j}^f) + c(e_j^f))} Y_j \qquad \forall h,j \tag{6.17}$$

$$X_{i,j} = ax_{i,j} Z_j \tag{6.18}$$

$$Y_j = ay_j Z_j \tag{6.19}$$

$$Y_j = b_j \prod_h F_{h,j}^{\beta_{h,j}} \tag{6.20}$$

$$Z_j = \min\left[\frac{X_{i,j}}{ax_{i,j}}, \frac{Y_j}{ay_j}\right] \tag{6.21}$$

$$e_{h,j}^f = \left(\frac{\tau_{h,j}^f}{A_{h,j}^f}\right)^{\frac{1}{N_{h,j}^f}} \quad \text{and} \quad e_j^z = \left(\frac{p_j^z}{(1 - s_j^e)p_j^q} \frac{\tau_j^z}{A_j^z}\right)^{\frac{1}{N_j^z}} \tag{6.22}$$

Last, note that the Leontief production function implies rectangular isoquants, which are prone to computational problems due to their kinks. Thus, as suggested by Hosoe et al. (2010), equation 6.21 is replaced with a unit cost function for computational purposes. This unit cost function can be obtained by transforming the zero profit condition $\pi_j^z = 0$ using functions 6.18 and 6.19:

$$p_j^z = ay_j p_j^y + \sum_i p_i^q (1 - s_j^e)ax_{i,j} + p_j^q (1 - s_j^e)c(e_j^z) \tag{6.23}$$

6.5.4 Government

The government in this model takes the role of levying taxes, consuming goods, and providing subsidies and direct cash transfers. Formally, government consumption X_i^g is a sum of its revenues from different tax sources, net of subsidy payments (S_j^e) and cash transfers (Ct_l^{tax}):

$$X_i^g = \frac{\mu_i}{p_i^q}\left(\sum_l T_l^d + \sum_b\sum_j T_{h,j}^f + \sum_j T_j^z + \sum_j T_j^m - \sum_j S_j^e - \sum_l Ct_l^{tax}\right) \tag{6.24}$$

The share of the i-th good in government expenditure is denoted μ_i. Prices are denoted p_i^q for the i-th composite good, p_h^f for production factors, p_j^z for output, and p_j^m for imports. Direct taxes T_l^d are levied on the factor endowment $F\,F_{b,l}$ of household l at the rate τ_l^d.

$$T_l^d = \tau_l^d \left(\sum_b p_b^f F F_{b,l} \right) \tag{6.25}$$

Factor taxes $T_{b,j}^f$ are levied on firms' factor inputs at the rate $\tau_{b,j}^f$ and are subject to evasion.

$$T_{b,j}^f = (1 - e_{b,j}^f) \tau_{b,j}^f p_b^f F_{b,j} \tag{6.26}$$

Production taxes T_j^z are levied on output Z_j by firm j at the effective tax rate $(1 - e_j^z) \tau_j^z$ after evasion.

$$T_j^z = (1 - e_j^z) \tau_j^z p_j^z Z_j \tag{6.27}$$

Import taxes are levied on imports M_j at the rate τ_j^m.

$$T_j^m = \tau_j^m p_j^m M_j \tag{6.28}$$

Besides public expenditure on goods (X_i^g), the government also provides energy subsidies S_j^e at the rate s_j^e.

$$S_j^e = s_j^e p_j^q \left(\sum_l X_{j,l}^p + \sum_i X_{j,i} + X_j^{loss} \right) \tag{6.29}$$

Note that the subsidy s_j^e is provided for household consumption ($X_{j,l}^p$) and for energy used by firms – either as an intermediate input ($X_{j,i}$), or as an ("unproductive" or lost) input to tax evasion activity (X_j^{loss}). Government and investment demand (X_i^g and X_i^v) are not subsidised. Cash transfers Ct_l^{tax} are defined in Section 6.5.6.

6.5.5   Investments and savings

Given the static setting of the model, dynamic aspects such as investment and savings cannot be reflected in their strict sense. However, recognising that these activities can constitute significant shares of final demand, a virtual investment account is incorporated (Hosoe et al., 2010). This account is modelled to use savings from households and abroad to invest these in investment goods. Formally, investment demand X_i^v is given by

$$X_i^v = \frac{\lambda_i}{p_i^q}\left(\sum_l Ss_l^p + \varepsilon Ss^f\right) \tag{6.30}$$

$$Ss_l^p = ss_l^p\left(\sum_b p_b^f FF_{b,l} + Ct_l^{tax} + Ct_l^z + \sum_b Ct_{l,b}^f\right) \tag{6.31}$$

To avoid confusion with subsidies (S_e), savings are denoted Ss^f for the foreign sector (at exchange rate ε), and Ss^p for households. Moreover, the parameter λ_i denotes the expenditure share of the i-th good in overall investment; the average propensity to save is denoted SS^g for the government and Ss^p for households. Household income from cash transfers (Ct_l) are detailed in the following subsection.

6.5.6 Households

This study distinguishes five households, each representing an income quintile, as well as an additional smuggler, representing a relatively small number of households engaged in fuel smuggling activities. Households are modelled to maximise their utility subject to a standard budget constraint. The optimised consumption choice $X_{i,l}^p$ can be expressed as

$$X_{i,l}^p = \frac{\alpha_{i,l}}{p_i^q(1-s_i^e)}\left(\sum_b p_b^f FF_{b,l} + Ct_l^{tax} + Ct_l^z + \sum_b Ct_{l,b}^f - Ss_l^p - T_l^d\right). \tag{6.32}$$

The first term in the round parentheses reflects income from factor income (e.g. wages); the second term reflects direct government transfers for redistributing tax revenues; and the third and fourth terms reflect the benefits of production (Ct_l^z) and factor ($Ct_{l,b}^f$) tax evasion which ultimately accrue to households. These income sources are balanced by savings (Ss_l^p), direct tax payments (T_l^d), and consumption ($X_{i,l}^p$) of good i which is determined by $\alpha_{i,l}$, the share parameter in the utility function.

Government cash transfers for redistributing tax revenues are implied by equation 6.24 and can be expressed as:

$$Ct_l^{tax} = R_l^{tax}\left(\sum_l T_l^d + \sum_b \sum_j T_{b,j}^f + \sum_j T_j^z + \sum_j T_j^m\right.$$
$$\left. - \sum_j S_j^e - \sum_i p_i^q X_i^g\right) \tag{6.33}$$

The overall budget for these redistribution transfers is given by tax revenues from four different tax types, from which subsidy payments and government consumption must be subtracted. The redistribution rule R_l^{tax} determines the share of the overall redistribution budget obtained by each household. Cash transfers Ct_l^{tax} will play a key role as a means for redistributing subsidy reforms revenues in the policy simulations of this study.

Moreover, household income from tax evasion activities are defined as

$$Ct_l^z = R_l^z \sum_j \tau_j^z e_j^z p_j^z Z_j \qquad (6.34)$$

for the evasion of production taxes, and

$$Ct_{l,h}^f = R_{l,h}^f \sum_j \tau_{h,j}^f e_{h,j}^f p_h^f F_{h,j} \qquad (6.35)$$

for factor tax evasion. The benefits of tax evasion are distributed across households according to redistribution rules R_l^z and R_l^f. The numerical values of these parameters are chosen to reflect the distribution of consumption and factor endowments.

In addition to the five households, this model considers a smuggler who consumes the same goods as all other households, but earns income from fuel smuggling activities. Thus, the smuggler's budget constraint prescribes that his consumption expenditure equals smuggling profits:

$$X_j^{SM} = \frac{\alpha_j}{p_j^q (1 - s_j^e)} \sum_j \pi_j^{SM} \qquad (6.36)$$

Based on anecdotal evidence that fuel smuggling is typically done by low income households, the smuggler's share parameter α_j is calibrated according to the share parameter of the 2nd income quintile household. Note that for consistency, the above notation allows smuggling in all sectors j, yet the empirical evidence suggests that it is a relevant consideration only in the petrol sector.

6.5.7 Exports, imports, and the balance of payments

For considering the implications of cross-border smuggling, the use of an open economy model is necessary. This section briefly sets out the interaction between the model economy and the rest of the world. For this purpose a small open economy set-up is used, which implies that import and export prices (denominated in foreign currency terms) are exogenously given. Formally, domestic import (p_i^m) and export prices (p_i^e), are linked to their corresponding world prices (p_i^{Wm} and p_i^{We}) through the exchange rate ε.

$$p_i^e = \varepsilon p_i^{We} \qquad (6.37)$$

$$p_i^m = \varepsilon p_i^{Wm} \qquad (6.38)$$

The balance of payments condition requires that monetary outflows (i.e. due to imports M_i, and inbound smuggling M_i^{SM} and M_i^{loss}) equal inflows.

$$\sum_i p_i^{Wm}(M_i + M_i^{SM} + M_i^{loss}) = \sum_i p_i^{We}E_i + Ss^f + \sum_i p_i^{We}E_i^{SM} \qquad (6.39)$$

Monetary inflows comprise exports (E_i), "foreign savings" or the current account deficit (Ss_f), and gross earnings from the foreign sale of smuggled fuel (E_i^{SM}).

Substitution between imports and domestic goods
Moreover, an "Armington composite good" is introduced to reflect the widely accepted notion that imports and domestic goods are imperfect substitutes (Armington, 1969). Thus, this reflects a modelling approach which allows endogenous market shares for imported goods, as opposed to a "cheapest takes all" setting.

In its essence, this approach introduces profit maximising firms which choose a combination of imported and domestic goods to produce the Armington composite – which is then consumed by households, firms, and the government. Thus, the solution of their profit maximisation determines the demand for imports and domestic goods (and is thus also directly influenced by the respective prices).

Using the constant elasticity of substitution (CES) production function

$$Q_i = \gamma_i(\delta m_i M_i^{\eta_i} + \delta d_i D_i^{\eta_i})^{\frac{1}{\eta_i}} \qquad (6.40)$$

a standard profit maximisation procedure yields demand functions for imports and the domestic good:

$$M_i = \left(\frac{\gamma_i^{\eta_i}\delta m_i p_i^q}{(1+\tau_i^m)p_i^m}\right)^{\frac{1}{1-\eta_i}} Q_i \qquad (6.41)$$

$$D_i = \left(\frac{\gamma_i^{\eta_i}\delta d_i p_i^q}{p_i^d}\right)^{\frac{1}{1-\eta_i}} Q_i \qquad (6.42)$$

In terms of notation, Q_i denotes the i-th Armington composite good, which is composed of imports (M_i) and domestic goods (D_i). The coefficients δm_i and δd_i denote the respective input shares of the composite good (fulfilling $0 \leq \delta m_i \leq 1$, $0 \leq \delta d_i \leq 1$, and $\delta m_i + \delta d_i = 1$); while γ_i is the scaling coefficient in the composite production function. Prices are defined for the Armington composite good (p_i^q), imports (p_i^m), and domestic goods (p_i^d). Lastly, η_i is a parameter defined by the elasticity of substitution σ_i ($\eta_i = (\sigma_i - 1)/\sigma_i$, with $\eta_i \leq 1$).

Transformation between exports and domestic goods

In direct analogy to the demand side, imperfect transformation on the supply side (i.e. between exports and domestic goods) is reflected using a constant elasticity of transformation (CET) production function. Similar to the CES function, this setting allows that the gross domestic output of a good comprises both exports and domestic supply, the ratio of which is determined by their relative prices.

Formally, this is modelled by introducing a "virtual" profit maximising firm, which transforms the gross domestic output (Z_i) into exports (E_i) and domestically supplied goods (D_i) according to following CET production function:

$$Z_i = \theta_i \left(\xi e_i E_i^{\phi_i} + \xi d_i D_i^{\phi_i} \right)^{\frac{1}{\phi_i}} \tag{6.43}$$

By solving a standard profit maximisation problem following supply rules for exports and domestic goods are obtained:

$$E_i = \left(\frac{\theta_i^{\phi_i} \xi e_i (1 + \tau_i^z (1 - e_j^z)) p_i^z}{p_i^e} \right)^{\frac{1}{1-\phi_i}} Z_i \tag{6.44}$$

$$D_i = \left(\frac{\theta_i^{\phi_i} \xi d_i (1 + \tau_i^z (1 - e_j^z)) p_i^z}{p_i^d} \right)^{\frac{1}{1-\phi_i}} Z_i \tag{6.45}$$

In terms of notation, Z_i denotes the gross domestic output of the *i*-th good, which can either be exported (E_i) or supplied domestically (D_i). The coefficients ξe_i and ξd_i are the share coefficient of the transformation process (fulfilling $0 \leq \xi e_i \leq 1$, $0 \leq \xi d_i \leq 1$, and $\xi e_i + \xi d_i = 1$). Moreover, θ_i is the scaling coefficient characterising the transformation. Prices are defined for gross domestic output (p_i^z), exports (p_i^e), and domestic goods (p_i^d). Lastly, ϕ_i is a parameter defined by the elasticity of transformation ψ_i ($\phi_i = (\psi_i + 1)/\psi_i$, with $\phi_i \leq 1$).

6.5.8 *Market clearing*

To reach an equilibrium, conditions need to be formulated that ensure the equivalence of demand and supply in goods and factor markets. The goods market equilibrium is achieved when following condition is met:

$$Q_i = \sum_l X_{i,l}^p + X_i^g + X_i^v + \sum_j X_{i,j} + X_i^{SM} + X_i^{loss} + E_i^{loss} \tag{6.46}$$

This condition implies that the supply of the *i*-th Armington composite good must equal its aggregate demand. Demand is composed of demand by households ($X_{i,l}^p$), the government (X_i^g), investment (X_i^v), firms ($X_{i,j}$), and the smuggler (X_i^{SM}); in addition some of the goods are lost as inputs to tax evasion (X_i^{loss}) and smuggling (E_i^{loss}) activities.

The second market clearing condition ensures an equilibrium in the factor market:

$$\sum_l FF_{h,l} = \sum_j \left(F_{h,j} + F_{h,j}^{loss} \right) \tag{6.47}$$

This implies that the sum of endowments of the h-th factor $(FF_{h,l})$ must equal the aggregate factor demand. Note that firms' total factor demand is the sum of standard factor demands for production $(F_{h,j})$ and factors used for the purpose of tax evasion activities (e.g. labour), denoted $F_{h,j}^{loss}$.

Note that the closure rules applied here follow standard neo-classical assumptions of full employment and zero profits for the sake of simplicity. Non-standard closure rules – e.g. on imperfect competition, non-clearing of factor markets (unemployment and resource inventories) – may be considered as useful extensions to this model.

6.6 Calibration and data

Section 6.6.1 describes data sources used for this study. Sections 6.6.2 and 6.6.3 provide detailed derivations for the calibration of latent parameters.

6.6.1 Data

Economic variables

The baseline values for macro-economic parameters have been obtained from the GTAP 9 database – in particular, Nigeria's social accounting matrix (SAM) for the 2011 reference year. These macro-economic parameters are the size of economic sectors (i.e. output), intermediate inputs, capital and labour inputs, taxes, government expenditure, household consumption, imports, exports, and the current account balance. Four sectors are distinguished: (i) the (subsidised) petrol sector, (ii) the (unsubsidised) energy sector, which excludes petrol, (iii) the formal (non-energy) sector, and (iv) the informal (non-energy) sector. The parameters and coefficients $\alpha_{i,l}$, $\beta_{h,j}$, b_i, γ_i, μ_i, λ_i, θ_i, $ax_{i,j}$, ay_j, δm_i, δd_i, ξe_i, ξd_i, $sspl$ and ssg have been calibrated on the basis of the 2011 baseline data, and the model equations set out in Section 6.5.

Since the GTAP 9 SAM does not provide information on the distribution of income and consumption, overall household consumption figures have been split into income quintiles according to expenditure shares contained in the Harmonised Nigeria Living Standards Survey 2010. Across income quintiles, this household expenditure survey provides details on the level of spending on petrol, other energy, and non-energy consumption goods. It is thus essential for the distributional aspects considered in this study.

Data on FFS in Nigeria have been obtained from the International Energy Agency's World Energy Outlook 2015 Fossil Fuel Subsidies database (IEA, 2015b). Based on the *price gap* definition (Chapter 2.2), the IEA provides an estimate of $7.1 bn of fossil fuel consumption subsidies in 2011, of which over $6.5 bn are paid to subsidise oil (primarily petrol). This figure, in combination with the estimated size of the petrol sector, translates to a baseline subsidisation rate of 17.8%.[5] Finally, population data has been obtained from the World Bank's World Development Indicators database.

Tax evasion

For the purpose of comparing sectors with high and low tax evasion, Liu (2013) uses the self-employment rate of an economy to approximate the size of the high-evasion sector. This approach works particularly well in developed and emerging economies, for which reasonably reliable estimates of self-employment are available from sources such as the International Labour Organization (ILO). However, the ILO's Labour Statistics database offers no estimate of the self-employment rate in Nigeria.

Instead of relying on uncertain alternative estimates for self-employment, this study uses the size of the informal sector as a proxy for the high-evasion sector. The advantage of this approach is that estimates of informal economic sectors exist for a wide range of countries – including developing countries – and are based on a consistent estimation procedure. Specifically, the formal economy estimates from the GTAP 9 database are supplemented by including an informal sector, which in 2011 measured 50% of GDP in Nigeria according to the comprehensive analysis by Hassan and Schneider (2016).

This study uses a very conservative estimate of 2% for the tax evasion rate in the formal economy. For comparison, Liu (2013) uses a 5% evasion rate in a selection of 27 developed and emerging economies, based on estimates by Slemrod (2007). The Swedish National Tax Agency (2008) reports a 4.8% evasion rate for income taxes in its jurisdiction. In line with the notion of informality, this study assumes that the informal sector does not pay any taxes. Moreover, this study uses the conservative assumption by Liu (2013), that 10% of evaded taxes are spent on non-productive evasion activities (see Section 6.3). The net benefits of tax evasion are assumed to ultimately accrue to households; in line with the distribution shares of regular income, the top income quintile is assumed to benefit disproportionately more than lower quintiles.

Based on these numbers, the evasion parameters $A_{h,j}^f$, $N_{h,j}^f$, A_j^z, and N_j^z can be calibrated to characterise the evasion cost functions (Eq. 6.1 and 6.2). Section 6.6.2 provides detailed derivations associated with the calibration of these parameters.

Smuggling

This section outlines the steps taken to estimate the baseline magnitude of fuel smuggling out of Nigeria.

The first step is to focus on smuggling activity from Nigeria to Benin (and from there to Togo), as detailed estimates are available from the IMF (Mlachila et al., 2016). While Togo does not share a border with Nigeria, its distance to the Nigerian border is under 120 km, and thus extensive smuggling occurs via Benin. The IEA (2016) reports total gasoline consumption for Benin (616 k tonnes) and Togo (175 k tonnes) in 2011. The IMF outlines that in both Benin and Togo respectively, gasoline is sold on two separate markets (Mlachila et al., 2016): an official market for the sale of legal and regulated gasoline, as well as an informal market for the sale of gasoline smuggled from Nigeria. Mlachila et al. (2016) estimate that the informal market constituted about 85% of total gasoline consumption in Benin in 2011, and 70.7% in Togo. This allows the computation of the absolute size of the informal markets (in physical units), which reflects the quantity of smuggled fuel.

The revenues earned by smugglers are then estimated by multiplying the total smuggled quantity of gasoline with the respective price differential between Nigeria's official subsidised market price and Benin's (or Togo's) informal market price. These informal market prices are also reported by Mlachila et al. (2016).

The second step is to extrapolate the smuggling estimates for Benin (and Togo) to Nigeria's remaining neighbouring countries Niger and Cameroon.[6] Using the border length between Benin and Nigeria (773 km), and by assuming that the smuggled quantity is proportional to the length of the external border, a rough estimate of total smuggling can be obtained. In other words, the longer the border between Nigeria and a neighbouring country, the more smuggling activity takes place towards this country. For instance, Nigeria shares a 773 km border with Benin and 1,497 km with Niger, thus the quantity of fuel smuggled to Niger should be roughly twice as large.

Table 6.1 Parameters used for refining extrapolated smuggling estimates.

	Nigeria	Benin	Togo	Niger	Cameroon	Chad
Border with Nigeria (km)	–	773	–	1,497	1,690	89
Gasoline price (N/litre)	97.4	162.8	182.9	167.4	186.8	204.6
Pop. in bordering Nigerian states (m)	–	27.9	–	23.6	16.5	6.1
Av. fuel consumption in bordering Nigerian states (N/month)	–	286	–	100	175	insig.

The third step is to refine this extrapolation by making two further adjustments:

- *Population:* Since the states bordering Benin are particularly populous (and states in Northern Nigeria are sparsely populated), the smuggling estimate is further adjusted proportional to the population size in Nigerian border states. This reflects the presumption that a larger population means that more smugglers are present and that more smuggling takes place. Moreover, this accounts for the fact that population densities on two sides of a border tend to be correlated; thus taking into account the number of foreign consumers demanding smuggled fuel.
- *Availability of energy:* Furthermore, the availability of gasoline varies significantly across Nigeria, and directly affects the quantity of gasoline available for smuggling: The states bordering Benin are more developed and urbanised, and offer better access to energy goods. This is not least due to proximity to harbours, where imported gasoline is landed, and better distribution infrastructure. In more remote states gasoline tends to be less widely available and more expensive (reflecting domestic transport costs), thus reducing smugglers' profit margins. To reflect these factors, smuggling estimates are further adjusted in line with the average per capita expenditure on gasoline in each of the relevant bordering states (Figure 6.1).

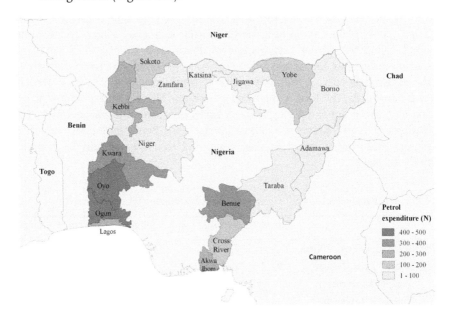

Figure 6.1 Monthly per capita petrol expenditure in Nigerian border states (in Naira).

To summarise the three estimation steps outlined above, the total quantity of smuggled fuel is estimated as

$$
\begin{aligned}
E^{SM}_{Petrol} &= \sum_c SQ_c \\
&= \sum_c \left[\frac{BL_c}{BL_{Benin}} \frac{AFC_c}{AFC_{Benin}} \frac{Pop_c}{Pop_{Benin}} SQ_{Benin} \right]
\end{aligned}
\tag{6.48}
$$

where:

- SQ_{Benin} = Petrol quantity smuggled to Benin (and from there also to Togo)
- SQ_c = Estimated petrol quantity smuggled to neighbouring country c
- BL_c = Length of external border shared by Nigerian states and country c
- AFC_c = Average petrol consumption per capita in Nigerian states sharing a border with country c
- Pop_c = Population in Nigerian states sharing a border with country c.

Based on this method a total petrol smuggling estimate of \$ 641 m is obtained, about 43% of which is smuggled to Benin and Togo, 33% to Cameroon, 24% to Niger, and less than 1% to Chad.

Mlachila et al. (2016) report that petrol smuggled from Nigeria is sold in Benin with an average mark-up ranging between approximately 20% and 40%. They note that informal prices in Benin are lower (i.e. the mark-up smaller) closer to the Nigerian border. This mark-up contains the cost of smuggling (including transport costs), but also profits by smugglers and middlemen. This study makes the assumption that the cost of smuggling corresponds to 10% of the smuggling value.[7]

6.6.2 *Calibration of evasion parameters* $A^f_{h,j}$, $N^f_{h,j}$, A^z_j, *and* N^z_j

Following parameter calibrations are based on the SAM, constructed for the purpose of this CGE model using the data described above. Appendix B.1 provides the full SAM, along with explanations of the variable names and subscripts used in this subsection.

The benefit of factor tax evasion is recorded in the SAM as the entry $SAM_{EV\_h,j}$, which is equivalent to $\tau^f_{h,j} e^{f0}_{h,j} p^{f0}_{h,j} F^0_{h,j}$ in the model's notation. Superscripts 0 denote baseline (i.e. observed) values. By replacing $e^{f0}_{h,j}$ with equation 6.11, $A^f_{h,j}$ can be expressed and calibrated as

$$
A^f_{h,j} = \frac{\left(\tau^f_{h,j}\right)^{N^f_{h,j}+1} \left(F^0_{h,j}\right)^{N^f_{h,j}}}{SAM^{N^f_{h,j}}_{EV\_h,j}} .
\tag{6.49}
$$

The cost of factor tax evasion is recorded in the SAM as $SAM_{EC\_h,j} = p_h^{f0} c(e_{h,j}^{f0}) F_{h,j}^0$. This can be re-written as

$$SAM_{EC\_h,j} = p_h^{f0} \frac{A_{h,j}^f}{N_{h,j}^f + 1} \left(e_{h,j}^{f0} \right)^{N_{h,j}^f + 1} F_{h,j}^0.$$

By replacing $e_{h,j}^{f0}$ this can be written as

$$SAM_{EC\_h,j} = p_h^{f0} \frac{A_{h,j}^f}{N_{h,j}^f + 1} \left(\frac{\tau_{h,j}^f}{A_{h,j}^f} \right)^{\frac{N_{h,j}^f + 1}{N_{h,j}^f}} F_{h,j}^0.$$

Since at the baseline equilibrium $p_h^{f0} = 1$, the expression can be re-written further:

$$SAM_{EC\_h,j} = \frac{\left(\tau_{h,j}^f \right)^{\frac{N_{h,j}^f + 1}{N_{h,j}^f}} F_{h,j}^0}{\left(A_{h,j}^f \right)^{\frac{1}{N_{h,j}^f}} (N_{h,j}^f + 1)}.$$

Furthermore, by using equation 6.49 the term $\left(A_{h,j}^f \right)^{\frac{1}{N_{h,j}^f}}$ can be replaced:

$$SAM_{EC\_h,j} = \frac{SAM_{EV\_h,j}}{\left(\tau_{h,j}^f \right)^{\frac{N_{h,j}^f + 1}{N_{h,j}^f}} F_{h,j}^0} \frac{\left(\tau_{h,j}^f \right)^{\frac{N_{h,j}^f + 1}{N_{h,j}^f}} F_{h,j}^0}{N_{h,j}^f + 1}.$$

Thus, $N_{h,j}^f$ can be expressed and calibrated as:

$$N_{h,j}^f = \frac{SAM_{EV\_h,j}}{SAM_{EC\_h,j}} - 1 \tag{6.50}$$

Analogously, the same procedure is used to calibrate parameters A_j^z and N_j^z associated with the production tax evasion function:

$$A_j^z = \frac{(\tau_j^z)^{N_j^z + 1} (Z_j^0)^{N_j^z}}{SAM_{EV\_ENE,j}^{N_j^z}} \tag{6.51}$$

$$N_j^z = \frac{SAM_{EV\_ENE,j}}{SAM_{EC\_ENE,j}} - 1 \tag{6.52}$$

6.6.3 Calibration of smuggling parameters A_j^{SM}

The smuggling parameter A_j^{SM} can be calibrated based on the smuggler's profit maximisation expression in Section 6.5.2 (in particular FOC 1.1):

$$A_j^{SM} = \frac{p_j^e - (1 - s_j^e)p_j^q}{(1 - s_j^e)p_j^q(E_j^{0SM})^{r-1}} \tag{6.53}$$

E_j^{0SM} is recorded in the SAM as the baseline value of smuggled goods.

6.7 Simulation scenarios

Scenario 1: Baseline

This scenario reproduces the baseline economy observed in the data. It serves as a reference point for evaluating the results in the subsequent simulation scenarios. It also enables a baseline evaluation of the regressivity of fossil fuel subsidies.

Scenario 2: Uncompensated subsidy reform

This scenario simulates an uncompensated petrol subsidy reduction and petrol tax increase (from $s_{Petrol}^e = 0.22$ to $s_{Petrol}^e = -0.22$).[8] The government uses reform revenues to increase government spending. Households receive no compensation.

Scenario 3: Subsidy reform with cash transfers

This scenario simulates a petrol subsidy reduction and petrol tax increase, in which reform revenues are redistributed to households uniformly in the form of direct cash transfers. Each household – no matter the income level – receives the same amount.

Scenario 4: Subsidy reform with labour tax reduction

This scenario simulates a petrol subsidy reduction and petrol tax increase, in which reform revenues are used to reduce labour taxes (i.e. a double dividend style fiscal reform). Labour taxes across all sectors are reduced.

Counter-factual scenario: Revenue neutral subsidy reform
ignoring tax evasion and smuggling

This scenario repeats the simulation of a double dividend style fiscal reform (Scenario 4), but disregards tax evasion and smuggling activities. This enables an assessment of the size of the evasion and smuggling effects on estimated reform benefits.

6.8   Assessing welfare effects

6.8.1   *Fiscal efficiency and social welfare*

As Liu (2013) shows, a "double dividend" style tax reform – i.e. using environmental tax revenue to reduce pre-existing taxes – can reduce, but not fully eliminate, the social welfare cost of environmental taxes (Bovenberg and Goulder, 1996; Goulder, 1995b). The same welfare costs must be expected when FFS reform revenue is used to reduce pre-existing taxes (simulation scenario 4).

To confirm this, this study estimates the social welfare cost of a double dividend style FFS reform (i.e. scenario 4) by evaluating changes at the tax base.[9] For this purpose, this study adopts the approach taken by Williams (2002), Bento and Jacobsen (2007), and Liu (2013), who use the following expression to measure the welfare effect of a change in the environmental tax rate – in this case the subsidisation rate s_j^e:[10]

$$\text{Welfare impact} =$$

Tax base effects
$$\begin{cases} \sum_j \sum_h \tau_{h,j}^f (1 - e_{h,j}^f) p_h^f \dfrac{\partial F_{h,j}}{\partial s_j^e} \\[2ex] + \sum_j \tau_j^z (1 - e_j^z) p_j^z \dfrac{\partial Z_j}{\partial s_j^e} \\[2ex] - \sum_j s_j^e p_j^q \dfrac{\partial \left(\sum_l X_{j,l}^p + \sum_i X_{j,i} + X_j^{loss} + X_j^{SM} \right)}{\partial s_j^e} \end{cases}$$

Tax evasion effects
$$\begin{cases} - \sum_j \sum_h \dfrac{\partial c(e_{h,j}^f)}{\partial s_j^e} p_h^f F_{h,j} \\[2ex] - \sum_j \dfrac{\partial c(e_j^z)}{\partial s_j^e} p_j^z Z_j \end{cases}$$

Smuggling effects
$$\begin{cases} - \sum_j p_j^q \dfrac{\partial E_j^{loss}}{\partial s_j^e} \\[2ex] - \sum_j p_j^m \dfrac{\partial M_j^{loss}}{\partial s_j^e} \end{cases} \tag{6.54}$$

The first line represents the marginal change in factor tax revenues following a change in the subsidisation rate. The second line represents the marginal change in production tax revenues. The third line represents the marginal change in subsidy payments (or petrol tax receipts, in the case of a negative subsidisation rate). The fourth line represents the marginal change in real factor losses associated with factor tax evasion. Similarly, the fifth line represents the marginal change in real output losses due to production tax evasion. Last, lines six and seven represent the marginal change in smuggling losses associated with outbound (E_j^{loss}) and inbound smuggling (M_j^{loss}). Note that Liu (2013) does not consider subsidies, production tax evasion, and smuggling; likewise, this study does not consider the environmental benefits due to emission reduction.

6.8.2 Distribution and household welfare

In addition to the effects on fiscal efficiency and social welfare, this study considers the reform's effects on household welfare, i.e. utility. However, utility, being an ordinal measure, is not a practical measure for the purpose of quantitative policy evaluation. This is especially the case when welfare effects on heterogeneous households are to be quantified and compared.

Nevertheless, changes in utility levels can be monetised and thus consistently evaluated and compared by computing *Hicksian equivalent variations* (Mas-Colell, Whinston, and Green, 1995; Hosoe et al., 2010; Durand-Lasserve et al., 2015). Equivalent variation measures by how much households' income would need to change (at original price levels) to induce the same welfare change as caused by the policy reform. As the original price levels are used to monetise both baseline and counterfactual utility, the equivalent variation measure allows consistent evaluation of fiscal reforms which directly affect prices.

The Hicksian equivalent variation for household l is obtained by minimising expenditure for a given level of utility U_l:

$$\min_{X_{i,l}^p} \quad exp_l = \sum_i p_i^q X_{i,l}^p \tag{6.55}$$

$$\text{subject to} \quad U_l = \prod_i (X_i^p)^{\alpha_i} \tag{6.56}$$

Simple optimisation yields following expenditure function:

$$exp_l = \frac{\prod_i \left(X_{i,l}^p\right)^{\alpha_i}}{\prod_i \alpha_i^{\alpha_i}} \tag{6.57}$$

Note that at the baseline prices are normalised to unity. Hicksian equivalent variation is defined as the difference between the baseline and counter-factual expenditure:

$$HEV_l = exp_l(p_i^{q0}, U_l) - exp_l(p_i^{q0}, U_l^0) \tag{6.58}$$

$$= \frac{\prod_i (X_{i,l}^p)^{\alpha_i}}{\prod_i \alpha_i^{\alpha_i}} - \frac{\prod_i (X_{i,l}^{p0})^{\alpha_i}}{\prod_i \alpha_i^{\alpha_i}} \tag{6.59}$$

6.9   Results

This section presents the key results from the simulations, while distinguishing the different simulation scenarios wherever relevant or useful.

6.9.1   *Effect on the distribution of petrol consumption*

In Nigeria FFS are predominantly provided for petrol consumption, thus this section presents evidence on the inequality of petrol consumption across income groups – and how this pattern changes as FFS are removed. The results show that removing fuel subsidies (from a baseline subsidisation rate of 18%) will cause a 21% reduction in national petrol consumption. Increasing a petrol tax to 22% will cause an additional 36% reduction in consumption. Figure 6.2 (top) shows that – in absolute terms – the reduction in petrol consumption mainly occurs in the top income quintile.

6.9.2   *Effect on subsidy (or tax) incidence*

From a distributional perspective the key criticism of FFS is their highly regressive nature (Arze del Granado et al., 2012). Figure 6.2 (bottom) shows that in the baseline scenario ($s_{Petrol}^e = 18\%$) most of the subsidy benefits are indeed received by the top income quintile. Thus, in absolute terms, removing FFS and moving to fuel taxation predominantly affects the top income quintile. Likewise in absolute terms, imposing a fuel tax will also affect the top income quintile most heavily. This illustrates why FFS reform is considered to be a progressive tax reform – and why rich people and powerful political interest groups are often vocal opponents to reform.

6.9.3   *Effect on consumption*

This section presents the estimated effects of subsidy reduction and energy tax increase on the consumption expenditure of different income groups. For this purpose distinguishing the different revenue redistribution mechanisms (i.e. simulation scenarios) is essential. All results in this section are presented as consumption gains (or losses) relative to income, as this also

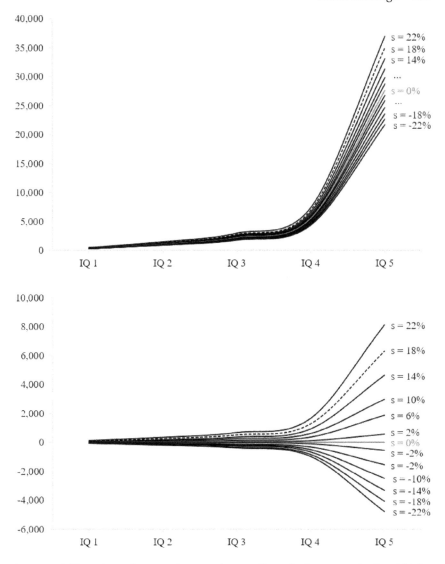

Figure 6.2 **Top:** Annual per capita petrol expenditure by income quintiles (IQ) for different subsidisation rates (in Naira). **Bottom:** Annual receipt (or payment) of fossil fuel subsidies (or taxes) in N per capita for different income quintiles (IQ).[11]

enables an insight into the vulnerability and exposure of different income groups.

Figure 6.3 (top) presents relative consumption losses for an uncompensated subsidy reform and tax increase (Scenario 2). Reform revenues are used by the government to increase public spending. The estimates show that reform induced consumption losses are relatively consistent at

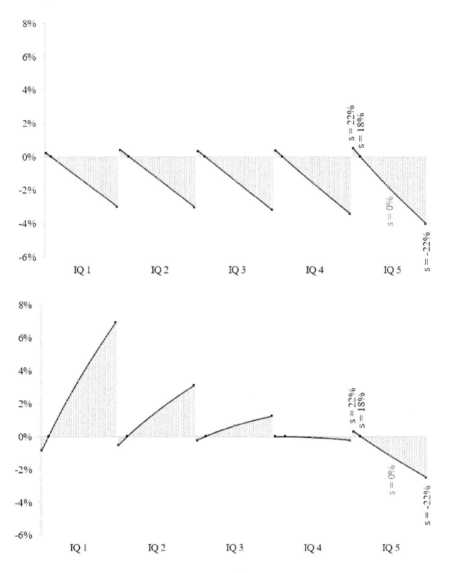

Figure 6.3 Relative change in consumption for each income quintile in Scenario 2
(**top**), Scenario 3 (**middle**), and Scenario 4 (**bottom**).

around 3-4% of income across the whole income distribution. The reason
for this is that in the case of Nigeria, energy shares in total consumption
expenditure are relatively even across income groups (ranging from about
4% to 7%; see Figure 3.2) – thus uncompensated FFS removal affects different income quintiles to similar extents (relative to income).

Figure 6.3 (middle) presents relative consumption losses for a subsidy
reform and tax increase, with reform revenues redistributed uniformly to

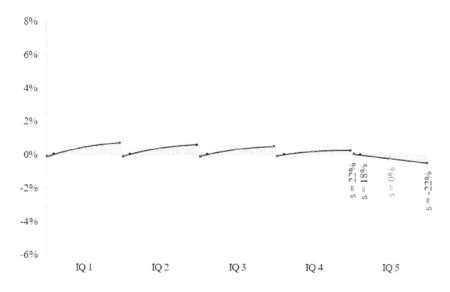

Figure 6.3 (Continued)

all households using cash transfers (scenario 3). Note that this scenario does not simulate *targeted* cash transfers (i.e. to specific income or population groups), but *universal* transfers. While the highest income quintile (IQ 5) is estimated to incur consumption losses despite thecash compensation, the first, second, and third income quintiles experience significant consumption increases. A full FFS removal ($s^e_{Petrol} = 0$) is estimated to increase consumption of the bottom income quintile by 3.4%, while the introduction of a fuel tax ($s^e_{Petrol} = -0.22$) increases this to 7%.

The reason for this progressive effect is that the highly regressive distribution of benefits via FFS is replaced by a uniform distribution, such that post-reform benefits received by low-income households significantly exceed their receipts through FFS (vice versa for high-income households). Overall, this illustrates that replacing (highly regressive) fuel subsidies with uniform cash compensation is a progressive fiscal reform. This observation applies analogously to the imposition of petrol taxes, if the revenues are redistributed using uniform cash transfers.

Figure 6.3 (bottom) presents relative consumption losses for a subsidy reform, in which reform revenues are used to reduce pre-existing labour taxes in all sectors (scenario 4). Falling in a range between 0.7% (IQ1) and -0.5% (IQ5), the estimated consumption changes are small compared to the other scenarios. The reason is that no significant redistribution of resources takes place across income groups, as in the case with cash trans-fers. Instead, households benefit from labour tax rate reductions proportional to their pre-reform consumption spending. However, not visible in Figure 6.3 (bottom), a significant shift takes place within households' consumption bundles: As the tax base shifts, the aggregate consumption of petrol falls by 35.5%, while consumption of formal sector goods increases by 1.3%. The net change resulting from shifting consumption bundles is depicted in Figure 6.3 (bottom).

6.9.4   Effect on household welfare

This section presents the estimated welfare effects of subsidy removal and fuel tax increases for each of the redistribution scenarios. As discussed in Section 6.8.2 welfare effects are measured as Hicksian equivalent variation.

Figure 6.4 (top) shows that households across the entire income distribution incur welfare losses as subsidies are reduced (and fuel taxes increased) without compensation (Scenario 2). A marginal welfare gain can be observed for all income quintiles for a subsidisation rate of 22%, as it is higher than the baseline subsidisation rate of 18%. Welfare losses are presented in absolute terms, and are thus largest for the top income quintile.

Figure 6.4 (middle) illustrated the redistribution of wealth associated with the uniform, universal cash compensation scheme (Scenario 3). Compared to the baseline scenario, the bottom 60% (i.e. bottom three income quintiles) experience significant welfare gains, at the expense of the richest 20%. The fourth income quintile is barely affected in this scenario, as cash compensation offsets welfare losses due to energy price increases.

Welfare effects in Scenario 4 (presented in Figure 6.4, bottom) are less pronounced than in the first two scenarios, as previous results have also suggested (see Figure 6.3, bottom). The reason is that revenue redistribution using tax rate reductions benefits households proportionally to their pre-reform consumption expenditure – thus no significant redistribution across income groups takes place, and the reduction of disposable income due to FFS removal is mostly offset.

6.9.5   Effect on government expenditure

Figure 6.5 presents the estimated changes in government expenditure. The observed effect depends crucially on the redistribution mechanism for reform revenues. In scenario 2 the government uses revenues directly to increase public spending. In scenarios 3 and 4 government spending remains mostly constant, as reform revenues are used to finance either cash transfer schemes or tax reductions.

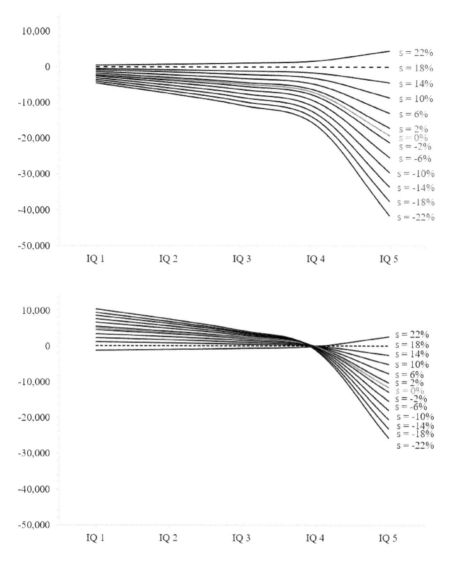

Figure 6.4 Change in welfare, measured by Hicksian equivalent variation, for Scenario 2 (**top**), Scenario 3 (**middle**), and Scenario 4 (**bottom**) (all in N).

6.9.6   Effect on output

Figure 6.6(a) presents the estimated change in output for all sectors considered in scenario 4. Full subsidy removal is estimated to result in a 10% reduction of the petrol sector, while increasing petrol taxes to 22% would reduce this sector by 20%. Estimated output changes are very similar in scenario 3, thus not reported separately.

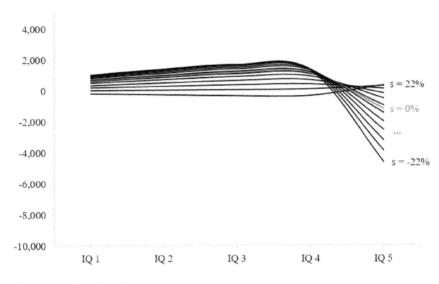

Figure 6.4 (Continued)

Figure 6.6(b) shows further that the largest absolute growth would occur in the formal sector of the economy. This illustrates that FFS result in grave misallocation of resources in favour of the petrol and energy sectors, crowding out consumption from all other sectors.

6.9.7 *Effect on labour tax evasion*

This section presents the estimated changes in tax evasion activities for different scenarios. As factor and production taxes remain unchanged in Scenarios 2 and 3, tax evasion is not reduced significantly in most sectors (Figure 6.7, top). A notable exception is the petrol sector. A significant reduction in the size (i.e. output) of the petrol sector means that its tax burden decreases, and thus necessarily also the amount of evaded taxes. As this observation is valid for Scenarios 2 and 3, only results for the latter are presented here (Figure 6.7, top). In Scenario 4 reform revenues are used exclusively to reduce labour taxes in all sectors. Accordingly, Figure 6.7 (bottom) shows a significant reduction in labour tax evasion throughout the economy.

6.9.8 *Effect on fuel smuggling*

This section presents the estimated changes in fuel smuggling as fuel subsidies are decreased and taxes increased (Figure 6.8).

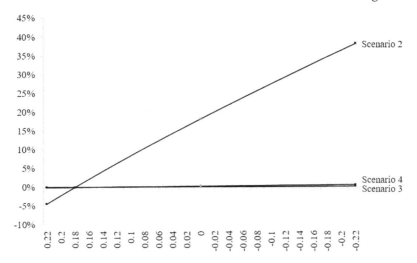

Figure 6.5 Change in government expenditure, relative to baseline expenditure, for different rates of subsidisation (baseline $s^e_{Petrol} = 0.18$).

Note that smuggling is positive for the baseline subsidisation rate, i.e. fuel is being smuggled out of the country. As the subsidy is reduced, and eventually turned into an energy tax, the energy price differential between domestic and foreign fuel is reversed. Without measures to prevent smuggling, in-bound smuggling takes place, thus undermining the energy tax. It should be noted that smuggling is not necessarily zero when the subsidisation (or tax) rate s^e_{Petrol} is zero; the smuggling quantity depends not only on s^e_{Petrol}, but also on the ratio between prices p^e_j and p^q_j (see equations 6.7 and 6.8).

Figure 6.8 (bottom) presents the total value of fuel subsidy leakage (or fuel tax undermining) due to smuggling. Out-bound smuggling implies that fuel subsidies provided by the home government are smuggled (i.e. leaked) out of the country. In-bound smuggling implies that domestic energy taxes are being evaded, as cheaper un-taxed fuel is smuggled in, thus reducing the government's fuel tax revenue.

6.9.9 Fiscal efficiency and social welfare: the role of tax evasion and smuggling

Figure 6.9 (top) presents the social welfare cost of reform, which is used to evaluate double dividend style reforms (see Section 6.8.1) – i.e. scenario 4. For reference the figure presents welfare costs for a counterfactual simulation which omits tax evasion and smuggling (line (a) in

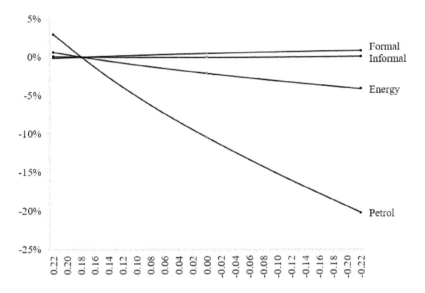

(a) Relative output change (%) for different subsidisation rates

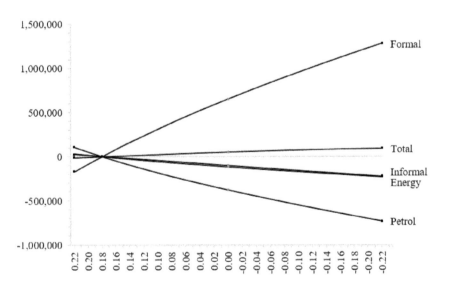

(b) Absolute output change (mil. Naira) for different subsidisation rates

Figure 6.6 Scenario 4: relative and absolute change in output in different sectors. (a) presents the change relative to baseline output, while (b) presents absolute change in mil. Naira.

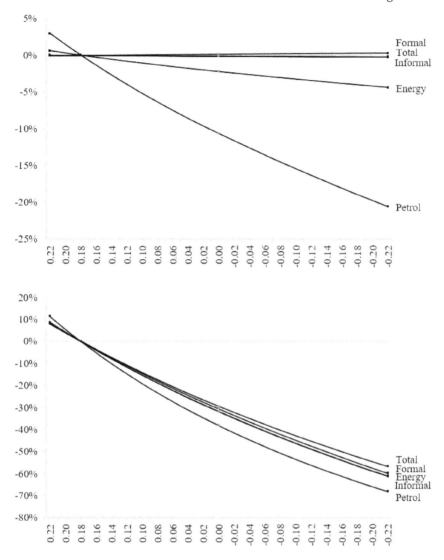

Figure 6.7 Change in labour tax evasion for different subsidisation rates in Scenario 3 (**top**), and Scenario 4 (**bottom**).

Figure 6.9, top), and the model which takes these illicit activities into account (b).

The results show that taking into account illicit activities lowers the estimated welfare costs of full FFS removal (i.e. $s^e_{Petrol} = 0$) by 34% relative to the counter-factual simulation (omitting tax evasion and smuggling). When fuel taxes are further increased to 22% (i.e. $s^e_{Petrol} = -0.22$), taking into

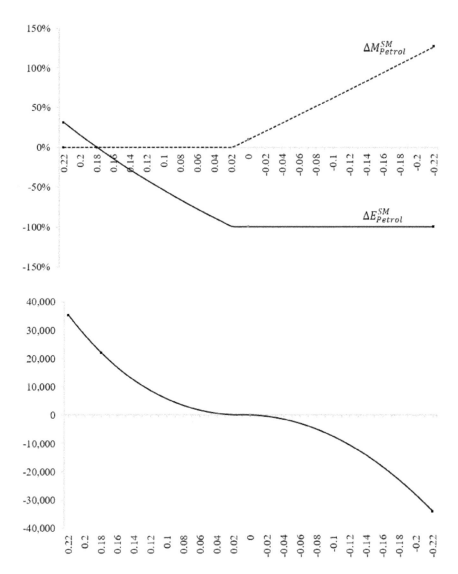

Figure 6.8 **Top:** Percentage change in petrol smuggled out of (ΔE^{SM}_{Petrol}) or into (ΔM^{SM}_{Petrol}) Nigeria in Scenario 2. **Bottom:** Total net subsidy value smuggled out (for $s^e_{Petrol} > 0$), or fuel tax undermined through inbound smuggling (for $s^e_{Petrol} < 0$). In mil Naira.

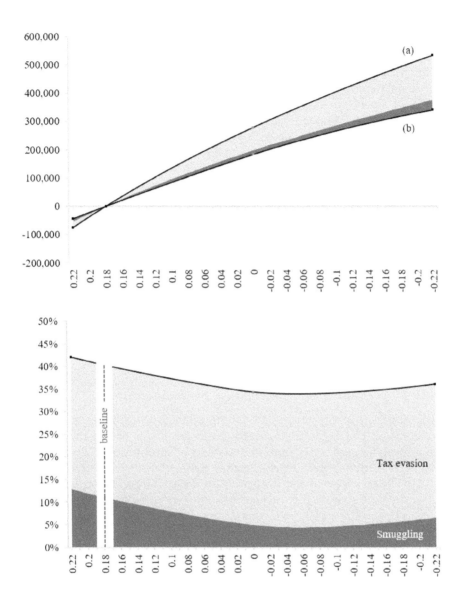

Figure 6.9 Smuggling in Scenario 4. **Top:** Welfare cost of FFS reform (a) without, (b) and with tax evasion and smuggling taken into account (in mil N) for different subsidisation rates. The reduction of welfare costs due to tax evasion effects (grey) is larger than the reduction due to smuggling effects (blue). **Bottom:** Percentage reduction of welfare cost of FFS reform when illicit activities are taken into account (relative to counter-factual scenario). The tax evasion effect (grey) accounts for a larger share of the reduction than the smuggling effect (blue).

account illicit activities lowers the welfare cost by 36% relative to the counter-factual. Figure 6.9 (bottom) summarises these results: In the simulated range for the subsidisation rate, the effect of tax evasion and smuggling reduces welfare costs by between 34% to 42%. The larger portion of this difference is due to the tax evasion effect (accounting for 69% to 86% of the welfare cost reduction).

Overall, these results highlight that accounting for illicit activities, such as tax evasion and fuel smuggling, can make a crucial difference when determining the costs and benefits of FFS reform. Omitting these aspects may cause studies to significantly under-estimate the benefits (or over-estimate the costs) of FFS reform.

6.10   Sensitivity and robustness

This section provides the results from sensitivity analyses around parameters that may influence the key results: In particular it considers variations of + and – 25% around the elasticities of substitution (σ_i) and transformation (ψ_i), the parameter r in the smuggler's loss function, and parameters $N_{b,j}^f$ and N_j^z in the tax evasion loss functions. More detailed results are provided by Rentschler and Hosoe (2017).

6.10.1   *The elasticities of substitution and transformation*

To test the sensitivity of sectoral output estimates to variation in elasticity values, low and high value cases for the elasticities of substitution and transformation are considered. The elasticity of substitution in the CES production function is given by σ_i (Equation 6.40, where $\eta_i = (\sigma_i - 1)/\sigma_i$, with $\eta_i \leq 1$). The elasticity of transformation in the CET production function is given by ψ_i (Equation 6.43, where $\phi_i = (\psi_i + 1)/\psi_i$, with $\phi_i \leq 1$). The low case is defined as a 25% reduction of the elasticity value compared to the base run calibration (see Section 6.6); the high case is defined as a 25% increase over the base run value. Table 6.2 shows that the variation in elasticities has minimal impact on the estimates.

6.10.2   *Parameter r in the smuggling function*

The smuggler is modelled to maximise their profits, by choosing the inbound and outbound smuggling quantities (E_j^{SM} and M_j^{SM}). His optimisation problem is constrained by the cost of smuggling (e.g. transportation costs, bribes), which primarily depends on the smuggled quantity, as well as parameters r and A_j^{SM}. In the base run analysis the parameter value is set at $r = 2$, which assumes linear smuggling behaviour.

Table 6.2 Sensitivity of sectoral output to variation in the elasticities of substitution (σ_i) and transformation (ψ_i). Absolute values represent the total value of output (in mil Naira) for each sector in each case. Percentage values represent the deviation of the low and high case estimates from the base run results.

$\sigma_i; \phi_i$		Base run	Low case		High case	
Petrol	$s^e_{Petrol} = 0.22$	3,736,698	3,728,096	-0.23%	3,744,630	0.21%
	$s^e_{Petrol} = 0$	3,252,824	3,288,715	1.10%	3,217,423	-1.09%
	$s^e_{Petrol} = -0.22$	2,898,255	2,970,800	2.50%	2,827,282	-2.45%
Energy	$s^e_{Petrol} = 0.22$	5,870,983	5,870,212	-0.01%	5,873,555	0.04%
	$s^e_{Petrol} = 0$	5,720,992	5,735,723	0.26%	5,709,553	-0.20%
	$s^e_{Petrol} = -0.22$	5,607,641	5,635,414	0.50%	5,584,303	-0.42%
Formal	$s^e_{Petrol} = 0.22$	142,209,300	142,341,800	0.09%	142,257,400	0.03%
	$s^e_{Petrol} = 0$	143,031,500	143,116,800	0.06%	143,157,200	0.09%
	$s^e_{Petrol} = -0.22$	143,661,100	143,701,300	0.03%	143,849,000	0.13%
Informal	$s^e_{Petrol} = 0.22$	114,992,600	115,065,200	0.06%	115,144,100	0.13%
	$s^e_{Petrol} = 0$	114,866,800	114,996,800	0.11%	115,004,900	0.12%
	$s^e_{Petrol} = -0.22$	114,745,200	114,924,800	0.16%	114,868,500	0.11%

This section demonstrates the sensitivity of smuggling estimates and the overall results to a variation in parameter r. It presents model results for a low value case of r (25% lower than the base run value), and a high value case (25% higher). Note that the parameter A_j^{SM} is calibrated on the basis of r, thus no separate sensitivity analysis is required (Section 6.6.3). Table 6.3 presents the deviation of the estimated smuggling quantities for these low and high value cases of r.

The percentage deviations in Table 6.3 appear large, in particular for subsidisation rates close to zero. However, it should be noted that the absolute values are small in all cases. This is illustrated by Figure 6.10, which demonstrates that the variation in r mainly affects the curvature of the smuggling estimates. In both the low and high cases of r the smuggling quantity can be below or above the base run estimate, depending on the value of s_{Petrol}^e. Due to the relatively small contribution of smuggling to the welfare difference (see Figure 6.9), the impact on the overall results is minor.

6.10.3 Tax evasion parameters $N_{h,j}^f$ and N_j^z

As part of its optimisation problem, the firm chooses the optimal level of factor and production tax evasion (see equations 6.11 and 6.16). Besides the effective tax rates ($\tau_{h,j}^f$ and τ_j^z), the choice of the optimal evasion rate is determined by the parameters $N_{h,j}^f$ and N_j^z, which characterise the cost of evasion activities (equations 6.1 and 6.2). The values of $N_{h,j}^f$ and N_j^z in the base run calibration range between 8.01 and 9.02; thus the elasticities of tax evasion with respect to the tax rate (expressed as $1/N_j$) are between 0.11 and 0.13. These values are in line with the elasticities used by Liu (2013).

As before, the low case considers 25% lower values for $N_{h,j}^f$ and N_j^z, while the high case considers 25% higher values. Note that the parameters $A_{h,j}^f$ and A_j^z are calibrated on the basis of $N_{h,j}^f$ and N_j^z (Section 6.6.2). Thus no separate sensitivity analysis is required for these. Table 6.4 reports the sensitivity of tax evasion estimates with respect to variation in parameters and N_j^z. Note that base run parameter values for illicit activities have been chosen conservatively; i.e. the base run is likely to underestimate the role of tax evasion.

With respect to the social welfare cost of FFS reform, the difference between the illicit activities model and the counter-factual remains large regardless of the value of $N_{h,j}^f$ and N_j^z. In the high value case, the social welfare cost of reform is nearly 50% lower in the illicit activities model compared to the counter-factual. Even in the low value case, the welfare cost is at least 30% lower compared to the counter-factual. Thus, the overall conclusion remains unchanged that illicit activities play a significant role in determining the welfare costs of reform.

Table 6.3 Sensitivity analysis for smuggling parameter r. Absolute values represent the total value of smuggled fuel (in mil Naira) in each case. Percentage values represent the deviation of the low and high case estimates from the base run results.

r		Base run	Low case		High case	
	$s^e_{Petrol} = 0.22$	160,376	212,556	+32.54%	145,940	-9.00%
Value of smuggling	$s^e_{Petrol} = 0.1$	55,919	25,869	-53.74%	72,264	+29.23%
outbound (+)	$s^e_{Petrol} = 0$	-12,048	-1,203	-90.02%	-27,116	+125.06%
and inbound (-)	$s^e_{Petrol} = -0.1$	-76,158	-48,018	-36.95%	-94,089	+23.54%
	$s^e_{Petrol} = -0.22$	-154,739	-197,849	+27.86%	-135,590	-12.38%

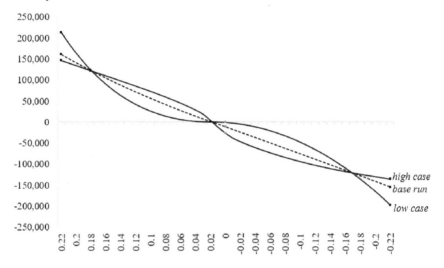

Figure 6.10 Sensitivity to variation in *r*: Estimated change in the outbound (+) and inbound (-) smuggling estimates (in mil Naira) at different subsidisation rates s^e_{Petrol}.

6.11 Conclusion

It is widely accepted that FFS incentivise rampant fuel smuggling to neighbouring countries, meaning that a significant fraction of FFS benefits leaks out of the country. In addition, labour taxes not only distort incentives to work, but are associated with high evasion rates and incentivise informal economic activity.

This study makes the case that such illicit activities can play a key role in determining the welfare costs and benefits of fiscal reform, in particular FFS reform. It develops a CGE model for Nigeria to study the impact of FFS reform – and energy taxes – on key economic parameters, including consumption, income distribution, tax incidence, and fiscal efficiency. Throughout this analysis, the study examines the role of tax evasion and fuel smuggling, and shows that these factors can substantially strengthen the argument in favour of subsidy removal.

First, the study confirms several key observations made by the existing literature on FFS reform and energy taxation (also see Chapters 2 and 3):

- FFS are highly regressive, with the bottom income quintile receiving 1% of total FFS payments and the top income quintile 75%.
- Removing FFS without compensation measures results in significant disposable income shocks to households across all income levels.
- Removing FFS and redistributing revenues using uniform cash transfers has a strong progressive (i.e. pro-poor) distributional effect. This

Table 6.4 Deviation from the base run estimates for low and high value cases for the tax evasion parameters $N^f_{h,j}$ and N^z_j.

$N^f_{b,j}$		Base run	Low case		High case	
Total factor tax evasion	$s^e_{Petrol} = 0.22 = 0.22$	2,416,237	2,343,597	-3.01%	2,463,199	+1.94%
	$s^e_{Petrol} = 0$	1,577,961	1,494,444	-5.29%	1,631,069	+3.37%
	$s^e_{Petrol} = -0.22$	966,775	895,413	-7.38%	1,012,810	+4.76%

N^z_i		Base run	Low case		High case	
Total production tax evasion	$s^e_{Petrol} = 0.22$	2,078,998	2,078,724	-0.01%	2,079,238	+0.01%
	$s^e_{Petrol} = 0 = 0$	1,978,902	1,977,739	-0.06%	1,979,653	+0.04%
	$s^e_{Petrol} = -0.22$	1,906,655	1,905,962	-0.04%	1,907,141	+0.03%

progressive distribution becomes even more pronounced when FFS are replaced by fuel taxes.

- Removing FFS and using revenues to cut pre-existing labour taxes reduces fiscal distortions and the associated welfare losses.
- Removing FFS causes significant structural shifts in consumption bundles, with overall petrol consumption by households decreasing by over 19%. The simulated fuel tax can extend this reduction to over 35%. In turn, households increase their formal market consumption accordingly.

In addition, by considering the role of illicit activities, this study shows that conventional analyses may be overlooking a significant part of the picture:

- Regardless of the method of revenue redistribution, reducing subsidies diminishes the incentives for fuel smuggling, and hence the welfare losses associated with it. The reduction of these welfare losses must be considered when evaluating FFS reforms.
- In the case when revenues of FFS reform are redistributed using cash transfers, avoided smuggling means that the cash transfer scheme is disbursing the same aggregate benefit to the population as in the FFS scheme, but at a lower cost.
- Reducing FFS and using revenues to lower pre-existing labour tax rates not only mitigates labour market distortions, but reduces tax evasion; i.e. the government can earn the same level of tax revenues, while charging lower tax rates.
- A conservative estimate for Nigeria is that taking into account illicit activities can lower the welfare cost of FFS reform by up to 40%. The tax evasion effect accounts for (on average) 75% of this difference, with smuggling effects accounting for the remainder.
- The above mentioned benefits of FFS removal (i.e. in terms of income distribution, consumption, fiscal efficiency) can be increased when subsidies are not only removed, but replaced by fuel taxes. Such fuel taxes may reverse the direction of smuggling activities, though this is not enough to undermine the overall benefits.

Even though tax evasion tends to be particularly high in developing countries – large informal sectors are symptomatic for this – the "tax evasion effect" has not been studied before in the context of FFS reform. Similarly, despite being a frequently cited side-effect of FFS, smuggling has also received virtually no attention in the literature so far. This study demonstrates that such illicit activities can make a significant difference to the argument in favour of FFS reform; and should be considered when designing and implementing such reforms. Moreover, evidence from Luxembourg demonstrates significant cross-border fuel demand due to large price differentials with neighbouring countries – and thus illustrates that the relevance of such activities is by no means limited to resource-rich developing countries (IMF, 2015). A better understanding of such activities can be vital for designing functioning energy and carbon pricing schemes.

Notes

1 *An abridged version of this chapter is under review for publication as* Rentschler, J. E., N. Hosoe (2017). Illicit dealings: Fossil fuel subsidy reform and the role of tax evasion and smuggling. *GRIPS Discussion Paper DP17-05.* Tokyo: National Graduate Institute for Policy Studies.
2 For additional empirical impact assessments of FFS reforms, see Jiang, Ouyang, and Huang (2015) and Ouyang and Lin (2014) for China, and Solaymani and Kari (2014) for Malaysia.
3 Liu (2013) shows that costs can be lowered by 89% in China and 97% in India.
4 A sensitivity analysis for these parameters is provided in Section 6.10.
5 For clarity, the baseline subsidisation rate is indicated in the results (rounded to 18%).
6 Chad shares a 89 km border with Nigeria. This implies that smuggling quantities to Chad are negligible for the purpose of this study.
7 The overall results of this study are not found to be influenced significantly by increasing the cost of smuggling to 20% or 30%.
8 Note that, as mentioned previously, the baseline subsidisation rate observed in the data is $s^e_{Petrol} = 0.18$. This means that the simulation range mainly focusses on the FFS reduction (0.18 to -0.22), but also provides estimates for the effects of an increase in FFS (from 0.18 to 0.22).
9 Note that the term "welfare" here is used – in line with the literature – to refer to the fiscal efficiency benefits of subsidy reform, and thus the associated increase in societal well-being. It does not refer to household level consumption, which is covered by Section 6.8.2.
10 See Liu (2013) for a full analytical derivation.
11 N10,000 correspond to roughly US $62 at the 2011 exchange rate.

7 Limits to green fiscal reform
How market distortions undermine price signals and create barriers to efficiency and clean energy

Jun Rentschler, Raimund Bleischwitz, and Florian Flachenecker[1]

7.1 Introduction

7.1.1 Fossil fuel subsidy reform and externality taxes in the presence of market distortions

Overconsumption of resources (i.e. energy and materials), as well as their inefficient use, are a key source of negative externalities, such as carbon emissions, pollution and the associated impacts on health. Pigou (1920) proposed to impose a tax on those activities that cause negative externalities, and argued that a tax which corresponds to the external social cost of certain activities will change behaviours and maximise social welfare (Aldy, Krupnick, Newell, Parry, and Pizer, 2010). The introduction of carbon taxes, fuel taxes, pollution taxes, congestion charges, or waste tariffs all follow the Pigouvian principle and will result in higher factor prices and production costs particularly for material and energy intensive firms.

Also the removal of subsidies for fossil fuel consumption are Pigouvian in the sense that they internalise social and environmental costs to some (albeit not full) extent. For instance, there is evidence from Yemen, Egypt, and India that FFS reform could play a central role in curbing the inefficient usage of other scarce resources, especially water (Commander et al., 2015). The ADB (2013) argues that FFS reform could be a key driver of energy efficiency investments in the Asia Pacific region. Thus, overall, the removal FFS is argued to trigger investments in efficiency, alternative energy sources, and innovation, and thus reduce negative environmental and economic externalities.

In an ideal setting, Pigouvian tax reform (be it FFS reform, or introduction of externality taxes) is the most efficient way of incentivising firms to increase factor productivity, i.e. improving energy efficiency, lowering resource use, and reducing carbon emissions, by modernising production processes and infrastructure, investing in other efficiency enhancing measures, and switching to cleaner fuel types (see Chapter 4; Requate, 1998). In short, firms are expected to implement exactly those measures which reduce social costs and environmental impacts. In addition, there is evidence for a double dividend from externality taxes, as tax revenues can be used to reduce other distortionary taxes (e.g. on labour) and mitigate associated economic inefficiencies (see Chapter 6; Bovenberg, 1999; Goulder, 2013). In theory, this makes externality taxes preferable to command & control instruments (such as efficiency standards) – and yet the political challenges of Pigouvian tax reform have overshadowed the economic arguments in favour of reform. The progress on FFS reform is slow, and fuel efficiency standards (or even inaction) remain attractive alternatives to externality taxes (Parry, Evans, and Oates, 2014).

Indeed, experience shows that Pigouvian tax reform can be unpopular and ineffective without complementary policies. For instance, in an urban setting, Avner, Rentschler, and Hallegatte (2014) show that the effectiveness of carbon and fuel taxes is significantly lower when they are not complemented by investments in public transport infrastructure. In practice, knowledge spill-overs, imperfect foresight and lacking credibility of a long-term carbon or fuel pricing regime can undermine effectiveness (Acemoglu, Aghion, Bursztyn, and Hemous, 2012; Hallegatte et al., 2013; Vogt-Schilb and Hallegatte, 2014). Moreover, the negative impact on existing polluting capital and stranded assets come at political costs which hamper implementation (Rozenberg, Vogt-Schilb, and Hallegatte, 2014).

This chapter argues that such market failures and distortions can undermine the effectiveness of FFS reforms in delivering economic, environmental, and social benefits, unless complementary measures are implemented. In particular, at the firm level the effectiveness of FFS reform depends crucially on whether and how firms are able to respond to changing price incentives (e.g. by increasing energy and resource efficiency; see Chapter 4). Evidence from Indonesia (Chapter 5) has shown that firms are not able to implement such response measures to the extent to fully mitigate reductions of their profit margin – thus suggesting the presence of barriers. In fact, for modernising production processes and realising efficiency gains, firms rely on a wide range of enabling factors, such as access to technology and information, technical capacity, and financial infrastructure. The absence of any of these factors, as well as constrained competition, trade protectionism, and fiscal mismanagement are likely to create barriers for firms to respond to FFS reforms by increasing energy and resource efficiency. These barriers can prevent the "first-best outcomes" of FFS reforms (and environmental tax reform more generally) to be achieved, and have been often overlooked in the literature on environmental policy and clean investments (Requate and Unold, 2003; Requate, 2005; Domenech, Bleischwitz, Ekins, O'Keeffe, and Drummond, 2014; Dijk and Kemp, 2016).

This chapter also shows that these barriers form a complex 'web of constraints', which obstructs corporate investments in efficiency, and hence diminishes the effectiveness of "green price instruments" such as FFS reform. The complexity and interconnectedness of these barriers is difficult to capture in theoretical analyses on the effectiveness of externality taxes. Some General Equilibrium models account for pre-existing distortionary taxes, or for imperfect information when analysing the impacts of carbon taxes (Parry, Williams III, and Goulder, 1999; Bovenberg and Goulder, 1996) – however, they typically yield an incomplete account of challenges in the wider political economy and investment environment. In fact, theoretical studies of policy optimality tend to be based on the assumption of perfect competition, while far fewer studies consider the real need for second best policy solutions (Montero, 2002; Lipsey and Lancaster, 1956).

Overall, this chapter provides a systematic review of the barriers which may prevent firms from responding to the incentives set through environmental pricing instruments. The relevance of these barriers extends beyond FFS reform, and affects pollution taxes or environmental regulation more generally. As a benchmark, this chapter refers to the fundamental theorems of welfare economics and the hypothetical characteristics of perfectly competitive markets (Section 7.1.2). It analyses how the hypothetical conditions which underlie perfectly competitive markets are violated in practice due to market failures and distortions, thus preventing firms from improving efficiency (Section 7.2). It argues that these distortions create investment barriers, which are exacerbated by systemic risks and uncertainty. It concludes that environmental taxes and FFS reforms are likely to be ineffective without complementary policies which mitigate market distortions (Section 7.3).

7.1.2 Competitive markets, distortions, and the rationale for complementary policies

Barriers and market distortions can diminish the effectiveness of Pigouvian tax reform, as they prevent firms from improving material or energy efficiency in response to price signals. In order to understand and categorise these barriers this chapter refers to the two *Fundamental Theorems of Welfare Economics*: The First Fundamental Welfare Theorem suggests perfectly competitive markets as a hypothetical benchmark for investigating the efficiency of actual market outcomes. Such perfectly competitive markets are based on several assumptions (Blaug, 2007), including:

- Perfect information
- No oligo- or monopolies
- No barriers to market entry (or exit)
- Perfect factor mobility
- Zero transaction costs
- Absence of externalities.

The violation of any of these assumptions leads to market failures, which hamper the effectiveness of externality taxes.

Also in the context of firms' energy and material efficiency, violations of these assumptions are ubiquitous in practice: Information or capacity constraints can lead to inefficient decision making in the face of environmental taxes. Missing or inefficient markets (e.g. for credit) can constrain the implementation of efficiency enhancing measures. Other missing markets (e.g. for carbon) can lead to severe externalities and excess waste. Large firms and protected industries face little competitive pressures to invest in efficiency gains, especially if protectionist trade policies are in place. This may also mean that energy price increases due to FFS reform are simply passed on to consumers, while firms take no further efficiency enhancing measures. Physical production infrastructure tends to be difficult and expensive to adjust to frequently changing market conditions, leading to long-term technology lock-in. Overall, all such factors will limit the ability of firms to respond to price based environmental policies (FFS reforms in particular) by improving energy or resource efficiency.

If no additional measures are undertaken to alleviate these barriers, firms may be unable to implement resource efficiency or fuel substitution measures in response to FFS reform. This will possibly reduce firms' competitiveness – while the actual policy objective of reducing economic and environmental externalities remains unaccomplished. Moreover, without complementary measures to reduce investment barriers, the accumulation of new productive capital is likely to be characterised by inefficiency. This infrastructure then pre-determines and possibly restricts investment and innovation options available in the future. Such so called 'path dependence' can even result in a lock-in situation, in which costs associated with pre-existing inefficiency prevent any future investments into efficiency and green innovation (Hallegatte et al., 2013).

In practice, the assumptions underlying perfectly competitive markets are violated in many ways; not rarely due to inadequate policy making and regulation. However on the flipside, the Second Welfare Theorem assigns an important role to market interventions (e.g. by governments), stating that they may improve Pareto efficiency of a given economic allocation by redistributing resources. In practice, however, the government's role can also be negative if public policy provides perverse incentives (e.g. by subsidising inefficient behaviour), thus perpetuating inefficiencies. Within this framing, the subsequent sections will discuss specific barriers which may prevent firms from implementing energy and resource efficiency, and green innovation measures. This chapter will thus suggest entry points for measures to complement FFS reforms and other price based environmental policies.

7.2   Barriers to resource efficiency investments

Ideally, the removal of distortive FFS will increase the cost of polluting consumption and production practices, and thus cause households and firms to

Table 7.1 Barriers to efficiency investments: underinvestment in energy and resource efficiency can be due to various market or government failures (Rentschler et al., 2016).[2]

Barriers to Investments in Energy & Resource Efficiency					
Investment barriers at the firm or government level	Information constraints	Capacity constraints	Financial constraints	Market structures	Fiscal mis-management
	• Limited information on scale and type of inefficiencies (monitoring & disclosure) • Limited information on modern technology and methods (access & dissemination)	• Technical capacity • Managerial capacity • Institutional capacity • Lacking awareness & individual biases	• Uncertain payoffs hamper financing (e.g. due to lacking information) • Competing investment opportunities • Inadequate credit markets	• Lack of competition (e.g. mono-/ oligopolies) • Protected industries • Trade protectionism	• Subsidies to inefficient, polluting industries • Lacking enforcement (e.g. carbon taxes & landfill tariffs)
Systemic risks & uncertainty	Resource price volatility Economic, political, and social instability ⎫ Lacking long-term credibility of policies ⎭		Can exacerbate existing barriers.		

adjust their behaviour, and invest into cleaner, more efficient, low-carbon technology. Such responses measures are key for determining the overall adverse effect of FFS removal on households (Chapter 3) and firms (Chapter 4), as well as the effect on environmental externalities. However in practice, barriers may mean that such response measures are not effective; i.e. that investments do not deliver the anticipated efficiency gains,or that they are not undertaken at all.

Based on Rentschler et al. (2016), this chapter outlines the key barriers as summarised in Table 7.1, and presents a framework for systematically assessing the environment within which efficiency investments take place. Each of the columns corresponds to a violation of one (or more) of the basic hypothetical conditions for perfectly competitive and efficient markets. This extends the discussion on market failures by Gillingham, Newell, and Palmer (2009) by providing empirical evidence at the firm level. While the focus in this chapter is on firms, it should be noted that many of the discussed barriers are of equal relevance in the context of households; for instance information and financial constraints, behavioural biases, and distorted market structures are likely to influence households' choices in purchasing more energy efficient household appliances or vehicles, in retro-fitting dwellings, or switching to cleaner fuel types.

7.2.1 Information constraints

Monitoring and disclosure: limited information
on the scale and nature of inefficiencies

'Imperfect' information violates one of the key assumptions underlying efficient markets. Which are the most inefficient processes in a specific firm (or industry)? How inefficient are they? Without this knowledge firms may be unable to undertake targeted efficiency enhancing investments in response to FFS reform; and governments may be unable to design adequately targeted policies to complement FFS reforms.

Specifically, there are two major issues: (i) Insufficient firm level monitoring of energy and resource efficiency and environmental performance (possibly due to insufficient legal disclosure requirements): This may prevent firms from identifying whether and where within their operations efficiency enhancing investments can help to mitigate energy price shocks due to FFS reform; and (ii) insufficient information disclosure of environmental performance and lacking industry level monitoring of efficiency: This may prevent governments from designing targeted policies to complement FFS reforms. These challenges add to the inherent difficulty of identifying an "optimal" environmental tax rate (see Chapter 7.1), and illustrate why a robust and practical tax system may differ from an optimal one.

The lack of comprehensive, regular monitoring and disclosure at the firm and household level makes it difficult to track potential improvements, and identify particularly successful investments. The Principles of Corporate Governance by the Organisation for Economic Cooperation and Development (OECD, 2004) argue that an effective legal framework is critical for ensuring an industry wide practice of information disclosure. When enforced effectively, this will entail better performance monitoring at the firm level, thus facilitating efficiency enhancing investments and modernisation measures (OECD, 2004; World Bank, 2006). Furthermore, Onischka, Liedtke, and Jordan (2012) argue that reporting requirements on corporate resource and energy efficiency performance and investments are critical for increasing the acceptance by firms (and banks) of resource efficiency projects. They also suggest that in the longer term such disclosure practices can play an important role in making commercial financing of energy and resource efficiency more accessible and affordable.

Energy price shocks due to FFS reform may put the access to and affordability of vital inputs at risk. This not only includes energy inputs, but all energy-intensive intermediate materials. In order to mitigate such cost shocks, firms will need to improve the efficiency with which such inputs are used. However, the monitoring and disclosure of such resource input related risks remain limited. A series of assessments has shown that e.g. in Eastern Europe, Central Asia, Middle East, and North Africa, disclosure of corporate information (e.g. on technological or environmental risks to operations) remains insufficient in terms of coverage and quality (World Bank, 2006, 2004b,a). In a model of technology adoption and policy timing, D'Amato and Dijkstra (2015) show that resulting information asymmetries can result in corporate under-investment in efficient technology.

If implemented comprehensively, the benefits of performance monitoring and disclosure can mitigate information constraints at the macro level: As policy makers gain a better understanding of inefficiencies in the energy and resource use of the private sector, they are able to design targeted measures and regulation for complementing Pigouvian tax reform, including FFS reform. In the European Union (EU) for instance, firm level surveys have managed to identify the key barriers which prevent firms from improving their resource and energy efficiency (European Commission, 2013). The "Roadmap to a Resource Efficient Europe" (European Commission, 2011) and the EU Energy Efficiency Directive (European Commission, 2012), which outline goals and policy measures for increasing efficiency at a large scale, critically rely on such information. This confirms studies by Baron (1985) and Laffont (1994) who highlight the important role of information for designing effective environmental policy.

Dissemination, access, and management:
limited information on the solutions

Firms are necessarily unable to implement clean, efficient, low-carbon technology, when markets (or governments) fail to provide adequate information on the costs, benefits, and methods of increasing the efficiency of resource and energy use in their production processes. The Asian Development Bank (ADB, 2013) notes that the lack of information considerably increases the transaction costs (in terms of time and effort) of implementing energy and resource efficiency measures, as well as of modernisation and green innovation more generally. Evidence for small and medium-sized enterprises (SMEs) in China shows that information constraints are one of the key barriers to energy efficiency investments (Kostka, Moslener, and Andreas, 2013).

Corporate management of information. Various studies show that the management of information is a key determinant of innovation and technological change in firms. Technological change however is crucial in order to modernise old, polluting, inefficient production machinery, and thus respond to environmental regulation and taxes (Bast et al., 2014). Frishammar and Åke Hörte (2005) find that the way in which firms manage information determines innovation and efficiency gains to a significant extent. Anderson and Newell (2004) and Sutherland (1991) too highlight the critical role of information in promoting energy efficiency gains. Disseminating the knowledge about the existence and functionality of new technology requires effective information infrastructure (Howarth and Andersson, 1993).

Figure 7.1 Whether latest technologies (and related information) are available and accessible to firms, determines to a significant extent whether firms adopt such technologies into their operations. This figure shows availability and absorption scores (standardised, where 7 represents the maximum). In global comparison, the USA rank 6th and Kyrgyzstan 138th (WEF, 2013)

Access to information. Firms will fail to improve energy efficiency in response to FFS reform, if they lack access to relevant information and technologies (Figure 7.1). For instance, almost 50% of small and medium-sized enterprises (SMEs) in the EU perceive information constraints as a key obstacle to improving resource efficiency (European Commission, 2013). Struggling to access adequate information, they state that some of the most useful support mechanisms for improving resource efficiency would be either (i) firm specific technical assistance (i.e. consultancy), or (ii) detailed information on technologies and processes for resource efficiency. Firms in lower income economies struggle with access to information to an even larger extent (Figure 7.2). Rohdin et al. (2007) confirm similar issues in the Swedish foundry industry, as they show that information access constraints are a key obstacle to improving energy efficiency.

The need for efficiency audits and information programmes. Furthermore, Rohdin et al. (2007) find that technical consultants and auditors can play a critical role in overcoming information constraints. In the USA for instance, government financed information services aimed to increase awareness for resource efficiency and offer technical assistance. These programmes included educational workshops, training programmes, advertising, or on-site efficiency audits. Anderson and Newell (2004) show that these information programmes were very successful in alerting firms of cost-effective efficiency investments, and providing technical information, thus reducing the uncertainty related to adopting new technology. They show that as a consequence of such information programmes, manufacturing firms adopted at least half of the recommended energy efficiency

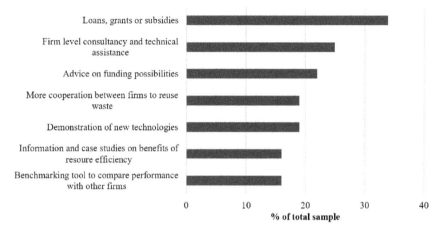

Figure 7.2 Most effective measures to promote investments in efficiency: percentage of firms identifying which measures are most effective in helping them adopt energy and resource efficient technologies. Technical assistance, and different types of information programmes prove to be critical (European Commission, 2013).

projects. Also in the EU information programmes and technical assistance have been shown to be critical (Figure 7.2). The reason behind this is that 17% of (11,000 surveyed) firms state that the difficulty of identifying cost-effective resource efficiency projects is a key obstacle to improving resource efficiency; another 20% state a "lack of specific expertise" as the main obstacle (European Commission, 2013). These figures are likely to be higher in countries, where technical information and advisory services are less widely available.

DeCanio (1993) emphasises the crucial importance of providing informational services as a complement to standard regulatory instruments and technology investments. Resource and energy efficiency targets, standards, and environmental taxation and regulation more generally cannot trigger the desired effects, if information on alternative, more efficient and cleaner technology is not available. Firms, without the knowledge of effective ways to increase efficiency, will continue to operate within existing information constraints – thus being unable to realise the efficiency gains envisaged byregulators. Overall, this suggests that information programmes and advisory services may be crucial complementary measures alongside FFS reforms.

7.2.2　Capacity constraints

This section discusses how capacity constraints can prevent firms from implementing efficiency enhancing investments in response to energy price increases following a FFS reform. It distinguishes capacity constraints at government, firm, and individual level, all of which can compromise the effectiveness of a FFS reform in mitigating economic and environmental externalities.

Efficiency investments: Do the characteristics of firms matter?

Capacity constraints at the individual, firm, or government level may mean that even if information exists (e.g. about the cost-efficiency of resource efficiency solutions), decision makers may not be able or willing to act upon it.[3] All investments with a positive net present value (NPV) will be implemented by profit maximising firms – at least so claims standard neoclassical theory. In practice however countless examples show that not all such profitable projects are implemented by firms (including simple measures such as energy efficient light bulbs; DeCanio and Watkins, 1998). Bastein, Koers, Dittrich, Becker, and Lopez (2014) show for a sample of firms from the EU-27 that this lack of investment in efficiency can be explained by various barriers internal to firms. Also the European Commission (2013) identifies firms' technical capacity as a key constraint to the implementation of cost-effective investments in resource and energy efficiency.

In a discrete choice model, DeCanio and Watkins (1998) show that the characteristics of firms play a key role in determining whether they implement profitable efficiency projects or not. They identify characteristics such as the number of employees, company earnings, or the type of economic sector to influence decision making. This shows that the simple availability of a positive NPV project will not ensure its implementation, if the firm is unable or unwilling to do so. This suggests that under certain firm-specific circumstances, price signals (due to FFS reform) may not be enough to trigger efficiency investments. In another study DeCanio, Dibble, and Amir-Atefi (2000) show that organisational structure is a key determinant for the effective adoption of innovations, and thus of efficiency gains. They emphasise that certain organisations are better adapted than others in terms of technical and managerial capacity, thus enabling them to implement efficiency investments more effectively.

At the firm level: technical expertise and management capacity

Technical capacity. Technical capacity is essential, in order to effectively assess, install, operate and maintain modern, efficient, and clean technology (Durbin, 2004). Complementing FFS reform with financial support mechanisms for firms to acquire such technology, may not be sufficient if firms lack the technical expertise to identify, install, operate, and maintain it. This implies that investments in physical infrastructure (e.g. production machinery), which aim at improving energy and material efficiency, should be accompanied by measures to build technical expertise within firms.

Especially in manufacturing firms improving energy and resource efficiency typically requires technological change. For instance, more modern and efficient machinery, advanced monitoring techniques, and adequate installation and maintenance of machinery are critical to achieving a higher degree of resource productivity. Basic technical knowledge can help managers appreciate the importance of efficiency related investments, and the opportunities associated with them.

Regional evidence. In the EU, 20% of SMEs state the 'lack of specific expertise' to be the biggest obstacle to resource efficiency investments (European Commission, 2013). Another 17% state that 'difficulties in identifying suitable actions' (i.e. investment opportunities) as the main reason for not being able to invest in resource efficiency. While such specific data is scarce for developing and emerging countries, there is evidence suggesting that technical capacity is a major constraint for firms, even more than for their EU counterparts. In Eastern Europe and Central Asia the majority of manufacturing firms consider technical capacity and an inadequately educated workforce to be a major impediment to their firms' operations (Figure 7.3; EBRD, 2010).

Management capacity. Resource efficiency investments are typically subject to the process of developing or identifying technological innovations, and then implementing them within operating production and

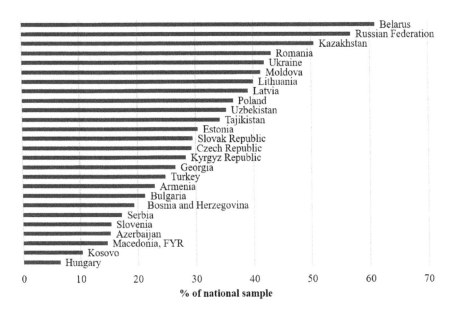

Figure 7.3 Technical capacity constraints: percentage of manufacturing firms which state technical capacity to be a major obstacle to their operations (EBRD, 2010).

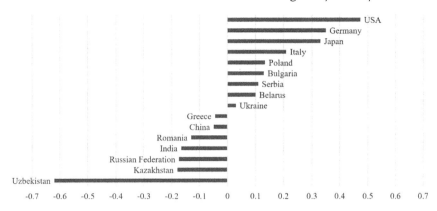

Figure 7.4 Indicators of managerial capacity (EBRD, 2010).

consumption systems. Such a process requires forward-looking management which is able to identify opportunities for efficiency gains (DeCanio and Watkins, 1998). Indeed the ADB (2013) notes that firms typically perceive 'greening' of their businesses to cause potentially severe disruptions to on-going operations. A regional firm survey conducted in Eastern Europe and Central Asia by the European Bank for Reconstruction and Development (EBRD, 2010) uses the methodology by Bloom and Van Reenen (2007) for investigating management practices in manufacturing firms. The survey shows that firms perform poorly compared to their counterparts in developed economies (Figure 7.4). While the survey does not focus on resource efficiency directly, such lack of managerial capacity is likely to hamper the effective implementation of efficiency investments, which are a crucial response measure to energy price shocks associated with FFS reform (see Chapter 4).

Institutional capacity

The external environment for implementing resource and energy efficiency investments and green innovation is determined by the quality of government and administrative capacity. Inadequate government capacity can create major obstacles to firms: corruption, politicised planning, ineffective enforcement, cumbersome bureaucratic processes, and the lack of competitive market regulation can make it difficult for firms to undertake efficiency enhancing investments in practice (Acemoglu and Robinson, 2010; Bontems and Bourgeon, 2005). Certainly, these issues are relevant beyond environmental considerations and affect corporate investments and operational efficiency more generally. Nevertheless, they can create significant obstacles to the effective functioning of environmental tax reform, and thus require policy makers' attention (Bastein et al., 2014).

The fact that the administrative environment can obstruct efficiency enhancing investments, can even be observed in the EU, where administrative capacity is considered comparably high: 26% of SMEs indicated complex legal or administrative procedures to be a key obstacle to implementing energy and resource efficiency measures (European Commission, 2013). In countries, where government effectiveness, regulatory quality, transparency, and the rule of law are weaker, this percentage can be thought to be considerably higher.

Emerging and developing countries and resource rich countries in particular tend to perform poorly with respect to various governance indicators (e.g. corruption, or regulatory quality Gill et al., 2014). Data by the (EBRD, 2010) shows that between 20% and 50% of firms in Eastern Europe and Central Asia perceive lacking administrative capacity to be the single most severe obstacle to their operations. Institutional reforms aimed at increasing the "ease of doing business" and facilitating efficiency enhancing investments may thus be crucial complementary measures alongside FFS reform.

Biases at the individual level

Awareness. Lacking awareness and understanding of the benefits of energy and resource efficiency and green innovation can lead decision makers to underestimate opportunities. Lacking awareness can typically be attributed to information deficits, though Morris and Venkatesh (2000) show that age can also influence decisions to adopt technology. Studying a sample of SMEs in Germany, Jordan, Lemken, and Liedtke (2014) identify lacking awareness to be one of the key barriers to investments in resource efficiency. These cases provide a direct rationale for implementing targeted information programs to build awareness as a complement to FFS reforms.

Behavioural biases. It must also be acknowledged that behavioural biases at the individual level strongly influence decision making, and can prevent the implementation of efficiency measures which would make economic sense. Such factors can partly root in the cultural and socio-economic context. Partly, they can be due to information constraints. Most fundamentally, the failure to act upon information may also reflect behavioural biases which are simply linked to human nature. DeCanio (1993) for instance notes that 'bounded rationality' can create substantial hurdles within firms to the implementation of energy efficiency measures. Kammerlander (2014) also shows that behavioural biases of individual users can pose significant barriers to the implementation of resource efficiency measures.

7.2.3 Financial market constraints

Especially energy-intensive manufacturing firms may need to implement substantial investments in modernising technology, once FFS are reduced and energy prices increase. For SMEs in low and medium income economies, cash flows may not permit major investments in efficiency and modernisation, without relying on external credit sources (Ghisetti, Mancinelli, Mazzanti, and Zoli, 2016). Allwood et al. (2011) note that businesses, which previously invested heavily in production systems, may face lock-ins due to constrained liquidity, preventing them from investing in modernisation and efficiency gains. In such a situation removing FFS or imposing an environmental tax may have little effect, if firms cannot afford to update or adjust their technology. Also in the EU, 34% of firms perceive high up-front investments costs to be the most significant obstacle to improving efficiency and environmental performance European Commission, 2013). Notably, this is despite various financial support mechanisms available from the EU and its member governments (e.g. the material efficiency programme in Germany; KfW, 2013). In emerging and developing countries such support for efficiency enhancing innovation and modernisation is typically more scarce, and financial constraints more substantial.

Uncertain investment payoffs hamper financing

Once firms face an increased financial burden due to deregulated energy prices, they may be cautious of taking on the financial risk of investing in expensive, new (and unknown) technology, and banks cautious of financing it. When resource and energy efficiency investments are not widely recognised as a way of cutting operating costs and increasing competitiveness, the commercial viability of such investments may not be perceived positively. Various studies show that lacking information and proliferation may lead firms (and local banks) to perceive the benefits of energy and resource efficiency investments as uncertain (European Commission, 2013; Anderson and Newell, 2004; Rohdin et al., 2007). Moreover, banks are likely to perceive investments in efficiency and "greening" as risky, especially if there is no larger scale reporting on the performance of similar projects (Onischka et al., 2012). Similarly, unknown technology is associated with risks, as information on reliability and durability may not exist (Anderson and Newell, 2004). The viability and profitability of resource related investments also critically depend on commodity prices. For instance, highly volatile energy and material prices make it difficult for firms to plan investments related to energy or resource efficiency, and reduce the availability and affordability of credit (see Section 7.2.6).

Alternative investments and opportunity costs

Firms face a broad range of possible investment opportunities, out of which energy or resource efficiency investments are not necessarily the most profitable ones – even if energy prices increase following FFS removal. Bleischwitz (2012) for instance notes that labour costs typically constitute a major element of production costs, and shows that firms in the EU have invested heavily in labour productivity. Indeed, when green technology or efficiency investments compete with other investment opportunities for limited funds, the presence of barriers (e.g. capacity or information constraints) may mean that Pigouvian tax reforms remain relatively ineffective in achieving intended efficiency gains and environmental objectives. More conventional investments (e.g. in labour productivity) may be associated with lower risks and higher returns, thus crowding out funds from investments in clean, low-carbon, efficient (but unknown) technology (Bleischwitz, 2010; Bleischwitz and Hennicke, 2004). Evidence for the European foundry industry shows that the presence of alternative investment and business priorities is a key barrier – especially in an environment of limited financial resources (Trianni et al., 2013).

Structural issues in the banking sector

Credit markets, particularly in developing and emerging countries, have undergone significant turbulences in the past decade. In Eurasia for instance, turbulences have resulted in a general loss of credibility of local banks, making credit less available and more expensive (Figure 7.5; Gill et al., 2014). As efficiency enhancing investments in physical infrastructure are typically associated with payback periods of several years, turbulences in financial markets may make such forward looking investments difficult.

As a consequence of structural problems in the banking sector, firms experience difficulties in gaining access to credit for financing efficiency

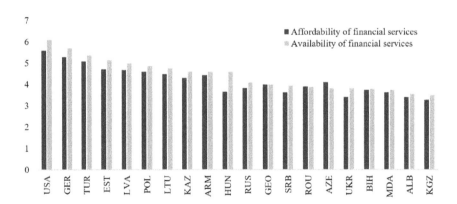

Figure 7.5 Throughout Eastern Europe and Central Asia, financial services are not only less commonly available, but also more expensive than in high-income countries. Countries scores are standardised to a scale from 0 to 7, where 7 is the best. In global comparison, the USA rank 10th and 7th (affordability and availability), while Kyrgyzstan ranks 130th and 131th (WEF, 2013).

investments and green innovation. Evidence from the EU underscores the importance of financial support mechanisms and availability of credit for funding green investments: In the EU, 20% of firms undertake energy and resource efficiency investments because financial public support is available (European Commission, 2013). 24% of all firms perceive the up-front costs of investments to be the main obstacle to energy and resource efficiency investments.

Even in high-income economies like Sweden, with well-developed credit markets, research has shown that access to capital is the biggest obstacle to efficiency improvements in industrial sectors (Rohdin et al., 2007). Similarly, Jordan et al., (2014) show that in Germany restricted access to financing is a key barrier to investments in resource efficiency. Moreover, the extent to which banks recognise the profitability of energy and resource efficiency projects will also depend on monitoring and reporting practices by firms (Onischka et al., 2012).

Some insight can also be gained from the literature on innovation more generally: Hyytinen and Toivanen (2005) for instance provide empirical evidence that financial constraints can play a significant role in holding back innovation in industries and firms which are dependent on external financing. They thus argue that in order to promote innovation (and efficiency gains likewise), public interventions ought to complement incomplete or inefficient credit markets.

Overall, this evidence suggests that FFS reforms may require complementary measures aimed at improving the affordability of efficient technology. Chapter 8 presents evidence from past FFS reform case studies, where governments indeed provided financial support to certain industries to encourage and facilitate efficiency enhancing technological updates.

7.2.4 Uncompetitive market structures

In well-functioning markets, competitive pressures are the key driver of innovation and efficiency gains. Firms can gain a competitive advantage by cutting costs and offering the same product at a lower price than competitors. However, if market structures do not allow free competition, some of the key assumptions of perfectly efficient markets are violated. Thus, if competition is suppressed or certain incumbent firms protected, competitive pressures may not suffice to incentivise investments in energy and resource efficiency, modernisation, or low-carbon innovation (for a comprehensive review see Requate, 2006). In such a setting, the removal of FFS or the introduction of environmental taxes is likely to be ineffective without complementary policies to foster competition.

Lack of competition. Monopolies and oligopolies may face lesser incentives to cut costs and increase the efficiency of their resource or energy use. The importance of competitive pressures in motivating and driving energy and resource efficiency can be seen in the EU (European Commission, 2013):

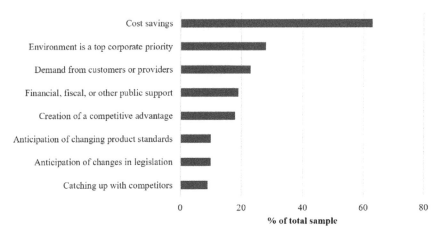

Figure 7.6 Main motivation for investments in resource and energy efficiency. Competitiveness is a key concern for firms investing in resource and energy efficiency (European Commission, 2013).

Out of 11,000 surveyed firms 63% state that their main motivation for improving energy and resource efficiency are "cost savings" in order to improve competitiveness. Further 18% of firms directly state "creating a competitive advantage" as their main reason to invest in resource efficiency. Another 9% state that improving resource efficiency is necessary for "catching up with main competitors" who have already invested in resource efficiency – this also implies that competition plays an important role in disseminating resource efficiency from a first mover to the entire sector (Figure 7.6).

Emerging and developing countries have a mixed record of actively promoting market competition, indicating shortcomings in regulation and enforcement (The World Bank, 2013). Barriers to market entry and exit (e.g. protectionist regulation) can prevent more efficient firms from entering a market, and outperforming less productive incumbents. Firms which are more efficient at complying with environmental standards can operate more cost-effectively under high energy prices or in the presence of environmental taxes, but may still be unable to compete with protected incumbents. Markets dominated by oligopolists or large state run (or formerly state run) monopolists may provide fewer incentives for investments towards efficiency gains, as there are fewer or no competitive pressures. Aghion, Bloom, Blundell, Griffith, and Howitt (2005) develop a model on competition and innovation, and find a strong relationship between the two. By showing that competition may increase the incremental profits from innovating, they implicitly emphasise the importance of competitive markets to foster resource related innovations and efficiency gains. Shleifer (1998) also argues that private ownership of firms is more conducive to innovation and efficiency gains than public ownership which also reduces competitive pressures.

In an uncompetitive market the removal of FFS or introduction of environmental taxes may simply mean that firms pass on cost shocks to consumers in the form of price increases, without improving technology (Castagneto-Gissey, 2014). Consumers may then choose to reduce their demand in response, thus indirectly reducing absolute environmental impacts. However, it would be preferable in terms of aggregate welfare if firms reduced their environmental impacts per unit of output instead, e.g. by investing in efficient and clean production technology.

Trade protectionism. Furthermore, pre-existing market structures and certain industries may be protected from foreign competition through protective trade policies. This can reduce competition from more efficient foreign firms, which reduces competitive pressures and incentives to innovate and increase resource efficiency. It may also obstruct access to foreign technologies and services, which may be crucial for improving resource efficiency – especially when technologies and expertise are not available domestically. Trade restrictions may make it even easier for firms to simply pass on price increases without adjusting technology, as they are shielded from more efficient competitors from abroad.

While direct empirical evidence on the role of trade restrictions in the context of resource efficiency is scarce, the literature on innovation and productivity offers some insights. The relationship between trade liberalisation measures and industrial productivity gains, has been explored in an early theoretical study by Rodrik (1988), and subsequently confirmed by various empirical studies. These studies argue that by being able to import modern technology from abroad, firms are able to realise efficiency gains: For instance, firm-level evidence from Turkey suggests that following a number of trade liberalisation measures in the 1980s, innovation among Turkish manufacturing firms increased significantly (Pamukcu, 2003). Most notably, improvements in innovation took the form of imported machinery, enabling increases in firm productivity. Similar results are presented by Krishna and Mitra (1998), who show that trade liberalisation measures in India increased competition and the growth rate of productivity across various industrial sectors.

FFS schemes are prone to artificially increase the competitiveness of domestic firms. FFS reforms thus require careful consideration with respect to complementary trade policies which ensure that domestic firms can benefit from and thrive in international competition.

7.2.5   Fiscal mismanagement

Corrective taxation and FFS reform can account for negative externalities, and direct firms and households towards desired economic outcomes by providing financial incentives, which the market per se may fail to provide.

However, fiscal mismanagement can extend beyond FFS, and aggravate the problems by providing conflicting and perverse incentives. While the removal of FFS addresses one fiscal distortion, other inefficient fiscal policies may continue to exist, which directly undermine the effectiveness of FFS reform in delivering economic, environmental, and social benefits. In particular, even if subsidies for fossil fuel consumption are removed, other inefficient activities or industries may continue to receive preferential tax rates, subsidies, or other monetary and in-kind benefits, which perpetuate negative externalities. In fact, many countries (including G20 economies) have parallel fiscal systems in place, which both subsidise the use or extraction of polluting fuels (especially fossils) and simultaneously impose environmental taxes upon them (Whitley, 2013; OECD, 2015b,a).

As Allwood et al. (2011) note lower energy prices (e.g. due to subsidies) may increase the overall demand for energy intensive materials.[4] In fact, FFS can directly impact on the resource efficiency of firms, since energy and resource efficiency are closely linked. Essentially, this means that if energy is cheap due to FFS, the processing of materials is cheap, and thus energy prices play a lesser role in motivating resource efficiency improvements. Particularly in energy intensive industries, FFS can thus reduce the incentives to improve resource efficiency. Likewise, subsidies and regulatory support to non-energy materials can perpetuate inefficient technology even once FFS are reformed.[5]

Besides subsidies for fossil fuel consumption, governments may also choose to subsidise specific resource and energy intensive industries or fossil fuel producers. Such industry subsidies (i.e. paid to producers) are far less documented, partly because of the many non-transparent forms they can take. Nevertheless, Legeida (2002) argues that by granting subsidies to inefficient industries, and thus artificially increasing their competitiveness, governments prolong existing resource inefficiencies. The steel industry, for instance in Russia, Ukraine and Poland, has been documented to receive substantial preferential treatment by the state, for instance through low interest loans, tax privileges, or write-offs of tax arrears (Legeida, 2002). Such advantages may not come as a surprise as the steel sectors in these countries faced substantial structural problems such as over-capacity, over-employment, and inefficient, obsolete machinery.

The specific example of Russia can illustrate this issue: For each ton of output, the Russian foundry industry is estimated to use 3 times more energy, 3.6 times more sand, and 161 times more water than comparable EU plants (IFC, 2011). Thus, if Russian plants were to match the level of resource efficiency in European plants, they would be able to save close to 20,000 GWh of energy, 5.7m tons of sand, and 879m cubic meter of water – corresponding to $3.3bn of savings per annum (IFC, 2011). Russia subsidises energy more than any other high-income high-emitting country (E11[6]) at $31.3bn in 2010 (Whitley, 2013). These subsidies play a significant role in lowering energy costs, which are 54% lower than for instance in Germany (IFC, 2011). However, removing these subsidies for fossil fuel consumption alone will not necessarily incentivise the foundry sector to invest in resource efficiency, as long as above mentioned producer and industry subsidies remain in place.

At the same time, it must also be noted that prudent subsidy schemes, targeted at improving competitiveness (rather than preserving inefficiencies), can play a substantial positive role e.g. by modernising inefficient industries, or supporting low-carbon technology (Fischer, M., and Rosendahl, 2015). Following the same rationale the Chinese government for instance announced $6 bn in investments in the steel sector in 2000, in order to introduce modern technologies, and improve efficiency (US Dept. of Commerce, 2001). Similarly, the fuel subsidy reform in Iran (in Dec. 2010) was accompanied by targeted financial assistance to firms to help them restructure and modernise in response to increase energy costs (Salehi-Isfahani et al., 2015; IMF, 2013c).

7.2.6 Uncertainty, volatility, and instability

Commodity price volatility. While uncertainty per se does not necessarily cause market failures and inefficiencies, it may exacerbate existing ones. Even if FFS reform increases average resource prices (including energy), firms may refrain from large capital investments (e.g. in energy efficient technology) if prices are volatile. The reason is that volatile energy prices can make the payoffs from efficiency investments uncertain, thus affecting the expected profitability of investments and the ability to finance them. On the one hand, if energy and resource prices are high, investments in the conservation and efficient usage of energy and resources prove more attractive, as payback periods on investments are shorter. On the other hand, low prices prolong payback periods, making investments less attractive. Furthermore, decreasing commodity prices can pose risks for firms, if efficiency investments have already been made: annual payoffs from the investment will be reduced, while high interest rates remain. Overall, uncertain prices will make obtaining credit for efficiency enhancing investments even more difficult and expensive than is already the case.

This issue has been explored by Pindyck (1990), who showed that irreversible investments (e.g. in physical infrastructure with large sunk costs) are particularly sensitive to cash flow risks and uncertainty. Pindyck (2007) relates this issue explicitly to environmental policies and emphasises the ubiquity of uncertainty surrounding environment related investments (including those in energy efficiency). Zhao (2003) too shows that the incentives for firms to make irreversible investments in efficient technologies is reduced when cost uncertainties increase.

At the same time it must be noted that increasing resource and energy efficiency is an important way to reduce the dependency on resources and the exposure to volatile prices, i.e. to hedge against price uncertainty (e.g. Ebrahim, Inderwildi, and King (2014) in the context of oil; Bleischwitz, Johnson, and Dozler, 2013). This implies that the implementation of energy and resource efficiency measures can act as a hedging measure against energy price volatility, and at the same time be obstructed by price volatility.

Policy credibility. A lack of policy credibility is typically a consequence of frequent changes or time-inconsistency in policy making (The World Bank, 2013). For instance, the implementation of green subsidies (e.g. for the installation of clean and efficient technology) may be a right step per se in favour of resource and energy efficiency. However, it may prove ineffective if markets lack confidence in the long-term reliability of such policies. A typical example in the energy sector are feed-in tariffs, which aim to incentivise investments in renewable energy. If such tariffs lack long term credibility, investors may not take up the offer. Similarly, if firms do not expect carbon taxes to persist in the long term, they are less likely to invest in low carbon infrastructure (Brunner, Flachsland, and Marschinski, 2012). Farzin and Kort (2000) show that such uncertainty surrounding environmental regulation raises firms' discount rate and results in underinvestment in clean technology. Moreover, Krysiak (2008) shows that firms not only invest less (i.e. lower quantity) in efficient technologies, but also select socially sub-optimal technology (i.e. lower quality).

Overall this suggests that governments implementing FFS reforms must signal strong commitment to reform, e.g. by taking measures to institutionalise and de-politicise energy price regulation.

Economic, political, and corporate context. Besides the above types of uncertainty, which are directly associated with green investments (e.g. resource prices, or reliability of relevant regulation), more general uncertainties will also affect investment decisions (incl. political conflict, economic crises, etc.). This is not least due to their impact on discount rates (Gollier, 2002). If uncertainties are perceived to be more significant, future benefits from efficiency investments may need to be discounted more (Pindyck, 1990). This negatively affects the cost-benefit ratio of green investments, since benefits are typically spread throughout the future, while costs are mostly up-front. This means that in an environment of short planning horizons and uncertainty firms are less likely to commit to efficiency enhancing investments with high up-front costs and long payback periods.

7.3 Policy instruments for improving resource efficiency

7.3.1 Need for complementary policies

Overall, if barriers are strong, the absence of complementary policies may mean that FFS reforms (and environmental taxes more generally) fail to trigger significant improvements of energy and resource efficiency, and overall environmental performance. Evidence from Indonesia (Chapter 5) has shown that higher energy prices only result in limited improvements of energy efficiency and inter-fuel substitution – thus suggesting that firms face barriers to implementing such response measures, and instead are forced to accept reductions of their profit margins. A better understanding of these barriers can inform the design of targeted complementary measures to facilitate the implementation of 'green' response measures (including energy efficiency, and fuel switching). In fact, this argument extends to environmental policies more broadly (including command & control regulation, quotas, and trading schemes):

Avner et al. (2014) demonstrate the synergies between carbon or fuel taxes and complementary infrastructure investments: If investments in public transport infrastructure are made, commuters are more likely to respond to increasing fuel prices by switching from cars to low-carbon public transport (thus improving the fuel efficiency of their commute). In a hypothetical scenario, in which no public infrastructure is provided, the authors estimate that carbon taxes would need to be 115€/tCo2 to achieve a 6% reduction in carbon emissions from commuting. However, if public transport infrastructure is made available as a complement to carbon taxes, the same emission reduction can be achieved at 65€/tCo2.

In the UK, landfill taxes have been one of the key instruments for implementing the European Union's Landfill Directive (European Commission, 2008, 1999). By increasing the cost of disposal, waste treatment and recycling technologies become commercially more attractive, and less waste is produced in the first place (Morris, Phillips, and Read, 1998). However, for these taxes to be effective, the EU Waste Framework Directive defines complementary targets which pertain to institutional context (incl. accountabilities and enforcement) and capacity building, and are complemented by financial support mechanisms (European Commission, 2008, 1999).

Various studies emphasise the importance and potential of complementary measures alongside environmental policies. Fay et al. (2015) argue that complementary policies for supporting environmental taxes cover a wide range and include government support for research, development and innovation, performance standards, fiscal incentives for green investments, and social policies. Grubb and Ulph (2002) also argue that there can be significant synergies between environmental, technological, and innovation policies. These policy types should be regarded as complements rather than substitutes (Fischer, 2008). Lecuyer and Quirion (2013) show that it can be socially optimal to implement complementary policies to carbon pricing in order to mitigate uncertainty.

This chapter has provided further evidence in support of complementary policies, as FFS reform may be less effective at achieving efficiency gains and environmental objectives, if end-users and firms have restricted options to respond to energy price increases. While FFS reform may address the market failure of under-priced fossil fuel usage and associated externalities, other market failures remain – such as the public goods nature of R&D and technological innovation. Popp (2006) shows that this combination of market failures requires a combination of policy measures. Addressing complementary policies can thus help to mitigate such barriers and reduce the welfare costs of FFS reform (and thus increase public acceptability).

7.3.2   Addressing distortions and complementing FFS reform

The wide variety of investment barriers suggests the need for a comprehensive and carefully designed package of complementary policy measures, including efficiency audits, training, hard infrastructure investments, waste management and recycling schemes, as well as more structural regulatory reforms. Short and medium term measures may be critical for assisting economic agents to respond to energy price shocks by increasing efficiency.

At the same time, systemic market and government failures exist which have led to investment barriers in the first place. These must be addressed using long-term measures, as they will create new inefficiencies and perpetuate existing ones (Reddy, 2013; Cagno, Worrell, Trianni, and Pugliese, 2013). This is important in order to achieve a larger scale enhancement of resource and energy efficiency, as well as to sustain efficiency gains and sustainable development over time (Bleischwitz, 2012). Sorrell and Sijm (2003) argue that carbon pricing (hence FFS reform) can be at the heart of such a policy mix, though trade-offs due to policy interactions may exist. For instance, Fankhauser, Hepburn, and Park (2010) suggest that combining multiple climate policy instruments bears risks to efficiency – though they mainly focus on combining different carbon pricing instruments, rather than complementary policies more broadly.

Essentially, this suggests two possible approaches for complementing FFS reforms (i.e. environmental pricing instruments), and tackling investment barriers that prevent the improvement of economic and resource efficiency: (i) Addressing the immediate 'Symptoms' of investment barriers, i.e. help firms to deal with and overcome the adverse effects of pre-existing investment barriers (e.g. supply specific technical information needed for increasing energy efficiency in a firm/sector); and (ii) addressing the underlying 'Causes' of investment barriers, i.e. resolving the pre-existing market failures and structural inefficiencies, which cause the barriers in the first place (e.g. fix overall information infrastructure and technology dissemination systems). These approaches are not mutually exclusive, and both need to be part of a comprehensive strategy for resource efficiency.

7.3.3   Complementary measures: intervention levels and types

Measures for complementing FFS reforms can broadly be distinguished into micro and macro level interventions: i.e. firm level measures which support firms in overcoming the above mentioned investment barriers, and more comprehensive macro level measures which reform structural deficiencies and inefficiencies of the overall system (see Table 7.2).

Complementing FFS reforms at the micro level means to support specific firms with the implementation of efficiency projects, modernisation and green innovation – especially when firms may otherwise struggle to implement necessary changes. Such support comprises both technical assistance (especially for building capacity), as well as financial assistance which can enable concrete efficiency enhancing measures at the firm level in the presence of financial barriers (DeCanio, 1993; Anderson and Newell, 2004).

Table 7.2 This typology presents a toolbox for micro and macro interventions, which can complement price based environmental policy instruments. The categorisation is indicative and not definite; for instance, micro level measures may eventually lead to more structural macro improvements (Author's illustration, adapted from Rentschler et al., 2016).

Complementary policy measures & interventions				
	Firm level		**Macro level**	
	Technical assistance	Project finance	Technical assistance & Policy reform	Development finance
Addressing the symptoms of market distortions	• Efficiency audits & advisory • Identification of specific projects	• Installation of efficient & clean infrastructure and machinery • Modernisation of production processes • Retro-fitting	• Cut red-tape • Information & technical advisory programmes	
Addressing the structural causes of investment barriers	• Building technical & managerial capacity • Establish systems for monitoring performance & info. disclosure • Awareness building • Disseminate information & technology • Foster R& D and innovations	• Infrastructure for information sharing and training • Infrastructure to link markets (e.g. transport infrastructure linking supply & demand for recycled materials)	• Institution building • Fiscal policy reforms (e.g. producer subsidies, waste tariffs) • Legal requirements for monitoring & disclosure of efficiency performance • Strengthening the financial sector • Create dedicated lending facilities for resource efficiency projects • Foster competition	• Developing markets & infrastructure • Strengthen macro-economy • Institution building • Direct support to research & innovation • Green growth strategies

Overall, micro level measures can be effective in facilitating quick efficiency gains in targeted industries, and may (eventually) lead to a bottom-up improvement of sector-wide efficiency and environmental performance. Firm level measures are however less suitable for resolving the structural causes of barriers to green investment.

Complementing FFS reforms at the macro level means to implement policy and regulatory reforms, which address incentive structures, and improve the investment environment within which firms operate (Reddy, 2013). As at the firm level, macro measures can comprise non-monetary and monetary ones likewise.

7.4   Conclusion: what it means for policy makers

Following the principle "getting the price right", environmental taxes are the policy instruments favoured by economists to address negative externalities. Such taxes are an efficient way of imposing the social and environmental costs of certain activities on those responsible. FFS, which reduce the price of fossil fuels, have the polar opposite effect, as incentivise the over-consumption and inefficient use of carbon-intensive energy. By the same token, removing FFS follows the principle of "getting the price right" as it increases the cost of polluting or inefficient activities.

However, as this chapter has argued, removing FFS per se does not necessarily cause firms (or end-users) to reduce inefficient practices. It is critical to recognize that various other market inefficiencies and distortions create barriers, which mean that firms and other economic agents may be unable (or unwilling) to improve efficiency and environmental performance. For instance, firms may fail to invest in cleaner, more efficient technology, if such technology is unaffordable (financial barrier) or unknown (information constraints).

As a consequence well intentioned FFS reforms (and in fact environmental policies more generally) may fall short of their objective of triggering efficiency enhancing investments, strengthening competitiveness, or mitigating adverse environmental impacts. This chapter presents evidence suggesting that these barriers can be substantial, inter-linked, and widespread in practice. To successfully overcome this 'web' of barriers[7], it is critical to complement FFS reforms, with measures for mitigating such investment barriers (Dijk and Kemp, 2016).

Overall, this chapter presents a comprehensive overview of the most common reasons why firms may respond less to FFS reforms than policy makers envisage. It can be concluded that in order for FFS reforms to yield long-term contributions to sustainable development, they need to be designed and implemented with additional measures, which address the adverse role of investment barriers. For this purpose, this chapter suggests a two-tiered multi-level policy toolbox: micro (i.e. firm level) and macro level measures, which include financial and technical support measures, short-term measures for immediate mitigation of investment barriers, as well as longer-term measures for addressing structural causes. Overall, by identifying and addressing investment barriers, policy makers can increase the prospects for FFS reforms to successfully mitigate adverse economic and environmental externalities and raise revenue in the long-term.

Notes

1 *An abridged version of this chapter has been published as* Rentschler, J. E., Bleischwitz, R., Flachenecker, F. (2016). On imperfect competition and market distortions: The causes of corporate under-investment in energy and material efficiency. *Journal of International Economics and Economic Policy.* doi:10.1007/s10368-016-0370-2.
   Rentschler, J. (2015). Barriers to resource efficiency investments. In: Flachenecker, F., Rentschler, J. (Eds.), *Investments in Resource Efficiency – Costs and Benefits, Investment Barriers, and Intervention Measures.* A report commissioned by the European Bank for Reconstruction & Development (EBRD). London: University College London.
2 This categorisation of barriers is adapted from Chapter 2 of the World Bank's World Development Report 2014 (Typology of obstacles to risk management) by Stéphane Hallegatte.
3 This violates the hypothetical condition of perfectly competitive markets that economic agents can make rational decisions based on available information, without incurring transaction costs (such as having to hire external technical consultants).
4 For other less energy intensive materials other factors, such as labour costs, can play an important role too.
5 See Yeo (2010) for a discussion of resource subsidies more generally.
6 The E11 country grouping is defined as Australia, Canada, France, Germany, Japan, Italy, Poland, Russia, Spain, United Kingdom, and United States.
7 This has been referred to as a 'web of constraints' in the Policy Options for a Resource Efficient Economy (POLFREE) article by Dijk and Kemp (2016).

8 Principles for designing effective fossil fuel subsidy reforms

Jun Rentschler and Morgan Bazilian[1]

8.1 Introduction

There is a strong consensus emerging within the international community that fossil fuel subsidies (FFS) are fundamentally unsustainable: that the economic, environmental, and social side-effects are severe, and include market distortions, escalating fiscal burdens, increased greenhouse gas emissions, poverty, and income inequality (see Chapter 2; IMF, 2013c). As the momentum for FFS reforms continues to build, policy practitioners can draw on the experiences and lessons of past reforms (both failed and successful) to guide the design and implementation of future reforms.

Reviews of past FFS reforms indicate that the most common driver of reforms has been mounting fiscal pressures, which make subsidy reform an attractive fiscal rescue measure (Vagliasindi, 2012b,a). Environmental and other socio-economic objectives have at most played a secondary role. As a result, past FFS reform efforts (and evaluations of them) have focussed primarily on their ability to manage downside risks (i.e. avoid public opposition and major shocks to livelihoods), for instance through communication and compensation. While such measures are indeed indispensable, they do not necessarily guarantee that the development potential and environmental benefits of a subsidy reform are maximised. For instance, Chapter 5 has shown that higher energy prices may simply reduce profit margins of firms, rather than increasing energy efficiency and incentivising a shift to cleaner energy sources.

This chapter distils key principles for designing effective FFS reforms, based on evidence from the previous chapters, as well as from past FFS reforms, and the environmental taxation and development planning literature. Thus, it provides an overview of the state-of-the-art on FFS reform design, as well as suggesting how FFS reforms can not only serve as a fiscal emergency measure, but also be more fully integrated into a country's long-term development strategy. The chapter emphasises that FFS reform is not only about removing subsidies; it requires an integrated strategy comprising a range of carefully designed and sequenced policy measures.

The remainder of this chapter is organised as follows. Section 8.2 provides a brief background on FFS. In Section 8.3 the key principles for designing and implementing effective FFS reforms are discussed, and illustrated with evidence from the previous chapters and past reform efforts. In particular, this includes: (i) Measures that must be taken in advance of reform implementation (including impact assessments and public communication); (ii) measures that are critical to mitigate immediate adverse effects on vulnerable population groups (including social protection and compensation); and (iii) measures that are critical to ensure the long-term sustainability of the post-FFS system (including transparent resource revenue management, reinvestment and institutional reform). Section 8.4 concludes with a summary of the key insights and policy recommendations.

8.2 Background: fossil fuel subsidies and their reform

Summarising the insights from Chapter 2, this section offers a brief overview of FFS, including definitions, adverse effects, and recent reform efforts.

Kojima and Koplow (2015) define FFS as any policy action that targets fossil fuels or fossil fuel based electricity or heat, and causes one or more of the following effects: (i) a reduction in net energy costs; (ii) a reduction in energy production or distribution costs; (iii) an increase in the revenues of energy suppliers. FFS can take various forms, but it can be divided into two main categories: consumer and producer subsidies (Whitley, 2013; IEA, 2014c).

Consumer subsidies refer to fiscal measures that lower the price of fossil fuel products below their market price (e.g. the international market price or the cost-recovery threshold), thus making such products more affordable to end-users. Producer subsidies are more difficult to observe and accurately quantify, as they refer to different kinds of preferential treatment of energy intensive companies, industries, or products (GSI, 2010a). Producer subsidies may be explicit, such as direct payments or tax exemptions, or they may be implicit (i.e. in-kind) such as government guarantees to protect investment (UNEP, 2003; Whitley, 2013; OECD, 2011). Overall, producer subsidies are estimated to be in the range of $80 billion to $285 billion annually in emerging and developing countries, and $452 billion in G20 countries (Bast et al., 2015; OECD, 2013), while consumer subsidies in 2013 amounted to $548 billion (IEA, 2014c).

In addition to the two main categories of subsidies, the IMF (2013c) provides the measure of "post-tax subsidies", which it estimates at $5.3 trillion per year (also see Coady et al., 2017). This not only accounts for consumer and producer subsidies, but also for government failure to price the negative externalities from fossil fuel use (including the social cost of carbon emissions, local pollution, and road congestion). This definition is particularly relevant from an environmental perspective because it highlights the substantial external costs which result from FFS. However, it should not be interpreted as an exact and fully robust quantification of externalities. Thus, for the purpose of this chapter the focus lies on consumer and producer subsidies.

The remainder of this section provides a brief overview of the adverse effects of FFS and ongoing reform efforts.

8.2.1 Adverse effects

Subsidies are typically implemented with the stated intention of alleviating poverty, redistributing national wealth, or promoting economic development by supporting energy-consuming industries (Strand, 2013; Commander, 2012). However, the evidence suggests that FFS both perform poorly at achieving these objectives and are generally detrimental to the economic, social, and environmental dimensions of sustainable development (Rentschler and Bazilian, 2016). In particular, by eliminating incentives for innovation and investment, FFS perpetuate inefficient technology and behaviour, thus reducing the competitiveness of the private sector (IMF, 2013c). FFS have also been shown to aggravate fiscal imbalances, to crowd out other productive public investments (e.g. in health, education or transport infrastructure), to lead to significant energy shortages, and to encourage fuel adulteration and smuggling (Victor, 2009; IEA, 2014c; IMF, 2013c; Calvo-Gonzales et al., 2015; Mlachila et al., 2016).

In addition, FFS have been shown to be highly inequitable because they reinforce existing patterns of poverty and inequality (Rao, 2012). For instance, empirical evidence from 20 developing countries indicates that subsidies on most energy goods are highly regressive, with an average 43% of the total subsidy amount reaching the richest 20%, but only 7% reaching the bottom 20% (Arze del Granado et al., 2012). Nevertheless, although the subsidies reaching poor households may be small in absolute terms, subsidy removal is likely to have the greatest proportional adverse impact on the poor (IEA et al., 2010a; Ruggeri Laderchi et al., 2013; Dickinson, 2015; Clements, Jung, and Gupta, 2007).

Finally, FFS are associated with severe environmental externalities, which in turn can have adverse impacts on human and economic development in the long run. By reducing energy prices, FFS encourage overconsumption and remove incentives for investing in energy efficiency, modern electricity infrastructure, and low-carbon energy sources (including renewables). The IEA (2014c) identifies FFS reform as one of the key measures for stabilising global warming at 2 degrees C above pre-industrial levels, and estimates that even a partial removal of FFS could reduce global GHG emissions by 360 million tons. At the local level, removing subsidies can help to curb traffic congestion and local pollution, and associated health threats (Davis, 2013; Commander et al., 2015; Coady et al., 2015a; del Granado, Coady, and Gillingham, 2012).

8.2.2   Recent reform efforts

FFS reform has become an increasingly high priority on the international policy agenda. For example, FFS removal is a 'sub-goal' (12.c) under the United Nations Sustainable Development Goals (UN, 2015b, 2016). Moreover, according to the IEA (2014c), in 2014, some 27 governments were actively pursuing FFS, including some of the countries with the largest subsidy schemes (e.g. India, Indonesia, Russia, Ukraine, Egypt, Iran).

Although rising fossil fuel prices in the early 2000s made the continuation of FFS increasingly unaffordable, especially for developing countries that have high subsidy rates, the track record of reforms has been mixed. For example, Nigeria's attempt to remove FFS in 2012 triggered extensive strikes and public protests, prompting the government to immediately reintroduce subsidies (Bazilian and Onyeji, 2012; Siddig et al., 2014). The governments of Bolivia (2010), Cameroon (2008), Venezuela (1989), and Yemen (2005 and 2014) were all forced to abandon their reform attempts following strong public protests, particularly by low-income population groups (Segal, 2011; IEA, 2014c). On the other hand, recent reforms in India and Indonesia (2014) are regarded as having been more successful (Benes et al., 2015). Overall, the successes and failures of past subsidy reforms illustrate the economic and political complexities, and underscore the need for tailored and effectively designed reforms.

8.3   The effective design and implementation of fossil fuel subsidy reform

As discussed earlier, there is clear evidence that FFS have detrimental effects. Thus the question for policy makers is not *whether* to reform subsidies, but *how*. The lessons learned from past reform efforts converge towards several guiding principles for the design and implementation of successful future FFS reforms. For this purpose, a minimum notion of "reform success" may be defined as the *permanent* removal of subsidies, which mitigates major economic and social disruption and ensures affordability and social protection. A more extensive notion of "success" includes not only successful subsidy removal, but also a comprehensive set of reform measures, which ensure that a FFS reform contributes to a country's long-term economic development objectives, rather than simply offering fiscal relief.

This section describes the design and sequencing of the main elements necessary for effective FFS reforms, and illustrates these elements with evidence from the previous chapters and past reform experiences. In particular, as summarised in Table 8.1, it is shown that FFS reform is not merely about removing subsidies. Rather, to ensure effectiveness and long-term sustainability, it must follow a comprehensive strategy that includes social protection measures, transparent systems for long-term

Table 8.1 Key elements of an integrated FFS reform (Author's illustration).

Assessment of subsidies & pricing mechanisms	Building public acceptance	Social protection & compensation	Revenue redistribution & reinvestment	Complementary measures	Timing & price smoothing
Definition	Communication strategies	Compensate vulnerable households (e.g. cash transfers)	Infrastructure investments	Support for energy/material efficiency & innovation	Sequencing reforms for different fuels
Identification			Public spending (e.g. health, education)	Infrastructure investments	Gradual subsidy reductions
Measurement & estimation	Mapping of interest groups	Support firms (energy access & efficiency programs)	Institutional reforms	Training & capacity building	Phase out ad-hoc pricing
Assess social costs, incl. illicit activities		Social safety nets	Tax cuts (e.g. labour taxes)	Reform market structures	Automatic fuel pricing & price smoothing mechanisms
Assess potential reform impacts	Stakeholder identification & engagement	Anti-inflationary policies	Direct transfers ("resource dividend")	Complementary fiscal reforms	

revenue redistribution and reinvestment, and additional complementary policies. The following subsections discuss each of these elements in turn.

8.3.1 Assessment of subsidies and pricing mechanisms

As outlined in Chapter 2, it can be difficult for policy makers to identify and quantify domestic energy subsidies, as reflected by the wide range of definitions and subsidy estimates discussed earlier. However, conflating different types of government interventions into the same subsidy "basket" can result in generic and inadequate reform attempts. For instance, Chapter 3 has shown that the removal of subsidies on different fuel types (e.g. petrol and kerosene) can have significantly different welfare effects. Thus, before designing a specific reform, policy makers must first conduct a thorough assessment in order to understand (1) the types and magnitude of energy subsidies, (2) whether and to what extent these subsidies are harmful and inefficient, and (3) what effects subsidy removal is likely to have, particularly on low-income households.

Definition, quantification, and evaluation

To help guide such an assessment, the Global Subsidies Initiative (GSI, 2010a) proposes a three-stage process, which allows policy makers to prioritise their FFS reform efforts (see also Lang, 2011). The first stage comprises the definition and identification of all existing subsidies in a given economy or sector – including both "beneficial" and "harmful" subsidies. The second stage is a quantitative measurement or estimation of the subsidies. In the third stage, the policy maker assesses whether existing subsidies are the most effective and efficient way to achieve policy objectives or reforms are required.

Kojima and Koplow (2015) provide an overview of existing definitions of FFS, as well as valuation and quantification methods, which can assist governments in conducting this three-stage assessment of domestic FFS. Throughout the assessment process, policy makers must be careful not to examine subsidies in isolation from the more general issues concerning domestic energy pricing, which include:

- **Pass-through:** the degree to which domestic and international price fluctuations coincide.
- **Transparency:** The degree to which the composition and regulation of energy pricing is open and transparent.
- **Enforcement:** The degree to which actual fuel pricing follows officially adopted energy pricing arrangements (GSI, 2013).

Once domestic energy subsidies have been identified and quantified, policy makers need to determine whether existing subsidies meet the criteria of sustainable fiscal policy or are, in fact, harmful from an economic, social or environmental perspective. UNEP (2003) presents criteria for assessing whether energy subsidies are sustainable:

- **Well-targeted:** Subsidies should reach only those who are meant and deserve to receive them.
- **Efficient:** Subsidies should not undermine incentives for suppliers or consumers to provide or use a service efficiently.
- **Soundly based:** Subsidies should be justified by a thorough analysis of the associated costs and benefits.
- **Practical:** The amount of subsidy should be affordable and it must be possible to administer the subsidy in a low-cost way.
- **Transparent:** The public should be able to see how much a subsidy program costs and who benefits from it.
- **Limited in time:** Subsidy programs should be of limited duration and defined at the outset, to avoid end-users getting "hooked" on subsidies and the cost of the program spiralling out of control.

While some renewable energy subsidies (e.g. feed-in tariffs) arguably meet these criteria, FFS virtually never do because they are often highly politicised, and do not achieve policy objectives effectively and efficiently (Plante, 2014). If subsidies are found to be unsustainable and harmful, then there is a case for governments to undertake reforms, which can yield substantial economic, social, and environmental dividends (GSI, 2010a). However, in the past, governments have underestimated the importance of careful advance planning, and have rushed (under mounting fiscal pressure) to remove subsidies, which has resulted in ineffective and thus unsuccessful FFS reform.

Assessing likely reform effects

A central element of advance planning of FFS reforms is a thorough assessment of the likely effects of such reforms. Ellis (2010) reviews analytical approaches for evaluating the effects of FFS reform and shows that general and partial equilibrium models can be used to conduct economic and social impact assessments. The objective of such impact assessments is to inform policy makers of the potential consequences of energy price increases on the income and livelihoods of various population groups, and to identify effective strategies for protecting poor and vulnerable groups from energy price shocks. The impacts to examine should include both those that are direct (e.g. a decline in households' purchasing power) and those that are indirect (e.g. increased cost of non-energy consumption).

Previous chapters have demonstrated various approaches for conducting such ex-ante impact assessments of FFS reforms, and illustrated that they can provide practical guidance for policy makers seeking to estimate reform impacts. Chapters 3 and 5 have shown that econometric approaches based on household or firm survey data are suitable for obtaining a disaggregated and granular picture of micro-level effects. Chapter 6 has shown how CGE models are powerful tools for conducting policy simulations and understanding the systemic interlinkages at the macro-level – and for understanding the role illicit activities, such as tax evasion and fuel smuggling.

Other studies – predominantly econometric simulations – have estimated the fiscal and welfare impacts of fuel subsidy reforms in India, Libya, and Turkey, and highlight the need to provide adequate social protection (e.g. in the form of cash compensation) along with FFS reform (Anand et al., 2013; Araar et al., 2015; Zhang, 2011). Verme and El-Massnaoui (2015) evaluate the impacts of Morocco's 2014 energy and food subsidy reform on household welfare, poverty, and the government budget, and also simulate the likely effects of further reforms; they conclude that subsidy reforms have been well designed and adverse effects managed well.[2]

More generally, to facilitate such empirical ex-ante impact assessments, Araar and Verme (2012) and the IMF (2016a) provide analytical toolkits, which enable policy analysts to simulate the effects of subsidy reforms using a single cross-section dataset. Moreover, the IMF (2008b) provides a practical but more general guide to conducting comprehensive poverty and social impacts analyses for macroeconomic and fiscal policy reforms. Ultimately, the purpose of such impact analyses is to identify vulnerable population groups and design adequate compensation schemes.

Last, it should also be emphasised that the political economy analysis in Chapter 7 has highlighted that empirical and theoretical simulations may rely on optimality assumptions that deviate from reality. Hence, when conducting and interpreting analytical impact assessments, it is important to keep in mind the political economy challenges which may complicate and alter the estimated effects.

8.3.2 Public acceptance and social protection – mitigating short-term price shocks

In order to build public support for FFS reforms, it is essential to communicate and implement effective compensation and social protection schemes. Although the poor account for a relatively small fraction of total energy demand, FFS may constitute a significant share of this group's overall income (Arze del Granado et al., 2012). Thus, removing subsidies may have detrimental effects on the livelihoods of the poor, especially if they rely on energy-intensive income generating activities. Moreover, the degree of energy dependence can vary significantly, even for households in the same bottom income quintile, depending on energy access and regional circumstances, including urban versus rural (see Chapter 3; Rentschler, 2015, 2016).

Energy subsidies and poor households: lessons from Nigeria

The case study on Nigeria – presented in Chapter 3 – has illustrated how some low-income households' reliance on FFS may be far greater than the average for their income group, suggesting that these households may be far more vulnerable to experiencing a substantial income shock when FFS are removed. As shown in Figure 3.5, while in most states the poorest households do indeed consume very little kerosene, in several southern states kerosene consumption by the poorest is significantly above the average for their income group. These regional differences may reflect issues such as differences in employment types, access to energy, and availability and affordability of alternative fuels.

This highlights the importance of focusing on the implications of FFS reform for different energy goods, income groups, and regions, and tailoring reforms and social protection measures to the needs of specific population groups. If policy makers focus only on national averages, and use income levels as the sole indicator of vulnerability, they may underestimate the vulnerability of certain population groups and provide inadequate social protection measures for the poor. For instance, Chapter 3 has also shown that "blanket" compensation (i.e. uniformly covering a large share of the population) may provide adequate compensation on average, but is likely to fail to protect particularly vulnerable households.

Communication

The main obstacles to FFS reform tend to be political challenges rather than fiscal complexity (Calvo-Gonzales et al., 2015; Rentschler and Bazilian, 2016). Thus, in order to generate public support for FFS reforms, transparent, credible, and clear communication and public outreach campaigns play a central role (GSI, 2013). Such campaigns must detail the reasons for and benefits of reforms, and address the public's concerns with realistic plans for mitigating adverse effects on energy affordability and poverty. If communication is not credible, or is not followed by actions, past experience shows that public opposition to FFS reform is likely (Segal, 2011).

Cash transfers

Ruggeri Laderchi et al. (2013) provide an in-depth account of the challenges associated with reconciling the need for subsidy reforms with the imperative of ensuring social protection and maintaining affordability. In particular, direct cash transfers have been an important component of numerous successful FFS reforms in the past (Vagliasindi, 2012b; Salehi-Isfahani et al., 2015; IMF, 2013a,b). For instance, Sdralevich et al. (2014) note that out of a series of FFS reform attempts in the Middle East and North Africa, all reforms that used cash and in-kind transfers were successful, while only 17 % of the FFS reforms that did not include cash transfers were successful.[3]

For this reason, Chapters 3 and 6 have focussed on cash transfers as central social protection and revenue redistribution mechanisms. Overall, these analyses have shown that cash transfers are a flexible, effective, and progressive alternative to FFS, which can increase aggregate welfare and protect livelihoods. However, Chapter 3 in particular has also shown that trade-offs may occur, when balancing the need for securing public support (by compensating heavy users of energy, i.e. the rich) with the imperative of protecting the livelihoods of the poor. In addition, it has shown that significant sub-national heterogeneity exists in the need for compensatory cash transfers.

Besides the case studies presented in the previous chapters, various examples of cash compensation exist. For instance, Iran implemented subsidy reforms in December 2010, increasing the price of petroleum products by between 230% and 840%. However, prior to the removal of subsidies, the government started making monthly cash payments to 70% to 80% of all citizens. The government later increased its targeting to the poor and vulnerable, facilitating transfers by opening bank accounts for heads of households. Overall, this structured cash transfer scheme and its timely implementation are argued to be two reasons for public support of Iran's 2010 FFS reform (Salehi-Isfahani et al., 2015). Recent subsidy reforms in Indonesia (2005, 2014), Mauritania (2012), and Armenia (2000) also relied on cash transfers.

The effectiveness with which cash transfers can be disbursed also depends on the existing social protection infrastructure. For instance, if a government maintains systematic records of the beneficiaries of existing social protection schemes, then compensatory cash transfers can be administered more easily. In fact, large-scale cash transfer systems already exist in several countries (e.g. Brazil's Bolsa Familia, Mexico's Prospera), which could be used as compensation vehicles for subsidy reforms. However, in certain circumstances, in-kind transfers and compensation measures may be easier and quicker to administer than cash transfers (e.g. if the banking infrastructure is inadequate). The IMF (2013c) discusses past FFS reforms that have relied on such in-kind compensation measures targeted to the most vulnerable households. These include the provision of gas vouchers (Brazil, 2002), college scholarships and rice subsidies (Philippines, 1998), and the strengthening of social safety nets (Armenia, 1995-1999), all of which can assist in coping with price shocks. In addition, governments can mitigate price shocks by implementing reforms in phases (Section 8.3.4).

Ensuring social stability and public support

Compensating vulnerable households is also critical for ensuring social stability and public support for reforms. Especially in countries where low-income and vulnerable households account for a large share of the population, disregarding their needs and endangering their livelihoods can result in nationwide unrest. In Nigeria, for example, inadequate attention to the needs of low-income households in 2012 resulted in public protests and fierce opposition (Bazilian and Onyeji, 2012; Siddig et al., 2014). Chapter 3 has shown that public protests were concentrated in urban regions (e.g. Lagos, Abuja), where low-income households are particularly fuel dependent (Figure 3.5).

Private sector compensation

The need for compensation and support measures applies not only to households, but also to the private sector. Chapter 4 has shown that firms rely on a variety of response measures (including energy efficiency, inter-fuel substitution, and pass-on), which can mitigate the energy cost shocks associated with FFS removal. However, as Chapter 7 has argued, various barriers may exist that prevent firms from implementing such response measures. Without policy actions to address these barriers, firms may incur substantial competitiveness losses; moreover, the potential of a FFS reform to deliver environmental benefits (through energy efficiency gains, and shift towards clean fuels) may be diminished significantly. Indeed, Chapter 5 has provided concrete evidence that higher energy prices alone do not necessarily result in higher efficiency levels and cleaner fuel mixes – i.e. that active support measures to firms are likely to be necessary. In particular, when pre-reform profit margins are small, firms may struggle to implement costly modernisation measures to adapt to high energy prices, which in turn can have adverse effects on economic activity and jobs.

In addition to the general policy recommendations given in Chapter 7, past FFS reforms provide some examples for such support measures: The Iranian government complemented its 2010 fuel subsidy reform with financial and technical support to help enterprises cope with higher energy prices, for example by restructuring and reducing their energy intensity (IMF, 2013c). Similarly, transport businesses in Niger were offered temporary subsidies (in 2010) to cope with the higher energy prices resulting from the reduction in diesel and petrol subsidies, while the governments of Indonesia (1997) and the Philippines (1998) provided support to small businesses to help them convert to more efficient and cheaper energy sources (mainly LNG; IMF, 2013c,a).

Short-term versus long-term measures

Broadly speaking, by compensating for sudden energy price increases, compensation measures (such as cash transfers) help to manage the downside risks of FFS reforms for vulnerable households and firms, and can increase public acceptance of reforms in the short-term (Chapters 3 and 6). However, it is important to note that these short-term compensation measures cannot replace longer-term measures for reinvesting reform revenues, such as infrastructure investments and public spending. Compensation measures do not guarantee that a FFS reform will be implemented in a way that optimises post-reform fiscal governance and equitable redistribution. Thus, whether a FFS reform is successful in the long-term – i.e. is an efficient and equitable alternative to FFS – depends on mechanisms for efficient energy pricing, prudent overall fiscal policy, and sustainable reinvestment of revenues.

8.3.3   Revenue redistribution and reinvestment in the long-term

FFS are often substantial relative to GDP. Thus it is crucial for policy makers to make transparent their plans for allocating the revenues from a FFS reform in a way that is consistent with a long-term development and public finance strategy. Depending on a country's specific needs, the use of FFS reform revenues for prudent and sustainable development financing can take many forms, including investments in infrastructure, social safety nets, health, and education.

Investing revenues domestically or abroad

Resource revenues which are no longer devoted to FFS could be invested abroad, with the objective of generating a future revenue stream (Gelb, Tordo, Halland, Arfaa, and Smith, 2014). However, there is also a strong rationale for developing countries to invest natural resource revenues domestically, despite several macroeconomic risks (e.g. exacerbating boom-bust spending cycles; Gelb et al., 2014). By using transparent public tenders and international partnerships, public domestic investments have the potential to yield significant development benefits, and are generally preferable to using resource revenues for FFS (Halland, Beardsworth, Land, and Schmidt, 2014). For instance, investments in education systems in Indonesia in 2008, in health care Nigeria in 2011, and in social protection programs in Mauritania in 2011 are measures which aimed at reinvesting the funds unlocked from subsidy reforms, and thus contribute to the longer-term development of an economy (IMF, 2013c,b).

Particularly in resource rich developing countries, where FFS are often financed by resource exports, subsidy reform is also an opportunity to create institutional and regulatory frameworks for transparent management and reinvestment of natural resource revenues.

Permanent cash transfers

As discussed earlier, cash transfers are a crucial tool for compensating vulnerable households. However, cash transfers are often gradually phased out once they have helped to smooth short-term energy price shocks. Recently, the notion of institutionalised long-term programs of universal cash transfers (i.e. uniform lump-sum payments to every citizen) has been gaining traction in debates about how to redistribute funds in resource rich developing countries (Devarajan et al., 2011; Standing, 2014; Plante, 2014). In line with this argument, Chapter 6 has shown that permanent cash transfers can be an efficient and equitable tool for redistributing resource revenues, consistent with overarching development objectives of reducing poverty and inequality.

Other concrete proposals to institutionalise universal cash transfers exist for Ghana, Uganda, and Nigeria (Moss and Young, 2009; Standing, 2014; Ploeg, Stefanski, and Wills, 2011; Gelb and Majerowicz, 2011; Sala-i Martin and Subramanian, 2012). These proposals extend the role of cash transfers from short-term compensation towards long-term redistribution, with the underlying notion that lump-sum transfers, which are paid uniformly to the entire population and funded by resource or FFS reform revenues, are a significantly more equitable and efficient way of stimulating development than FFS (Segal, 2011; Fay et al., 2015). Besides reducing poverty rates, universal transfer schemes (or "resource dividends") have also been argued to enhance the efficiency of public spending and increase accountability and transparency more generally (Sala-i Martin and Subramanian, 2012; Devarajan et al., 2011; Van Parijs, 2004). In addition, Plante (2014) presents theoretical evidence that replacing subsidies with uniform cash transfers may reduce long-run aggregate welfare losses by a factor of 15 to 25.

Although universal cash transfer schemes have frequently been used as a compensation measure, there is little evidence that they have been used as long-term redistribution programs in conjunction with a FFS reform. There are some successful real world examples, however. The Alaska Permanent Fund – a sovereign wealth fund – directly applies the concept of universal cash transfers. Since 1982, it has redistributed resource revenues by paying an average unconditional annual dividend of $1,200 to every resident of Alaska (Widerquist and Howard, 2012a,b).

Other types of funds for managing resource rents exist in a large number of developing and developed countries (Makhlouf, 2010; Gelb et al., 2014). In some cases (e.g. Norway, Malaysia), these funds are thought to be at the core of sustainable resource revenue management and successful economic development. This suggests that reforming FFS is not only about removing subsidies, but can also be an opportunity to reform the management of resource revenues to promote a country's long-term development and to improve fiscal governance more broadly.

Complementary tax reform and the double dividend

There is a prominent strand in the environmental taxation literature suggesting that there is a "double dividend" – i.e. that if environmental taxes are increased but other distortionary taxes are reduced (while maintaining revenue neutrality), then not only can environmental benefits be reaped, but also fiscal efficiency can be increased (Goulder, 1995b; Fullerton and Metcalf, 1997). Especially given the significant economic efficiency costs of labour and consumption taxes (Goulder, 1995a; Bovenberg and Goulder, 1996; Parry, 1997), there may be a rationale for using FFS reform revenues to reduce these taxes. However, there is a trade-off between efficiency and distributional effects (Parry and Williams, 2010). That is, income tax reductions are economically efficient, but regressive, while cash transfers are progressive, but less efficient.

In line with this literature, Chapter 6 has investigated both cash transfers and complementary tax reform (i.e. reduction of pre-existing labour and production taxes) as ways to redistribute FFS reform revenues, while taking into account illicit activities. The results also suggest the presence of a trade-off: On the one hand, cash transfers are strongly progressive and can reduce fuel smuggling activities, but they are not effective at reducing tax evasion. On the other hand, labour and production tax reductions do not have strong progressive effects, but are highly effective at reducing both smuggling and tax evasion activities.

Ultimately, whether it is practical to use tax cuts to redistribute FFS reform revenues depends largely on country-specific characteristics. For example, in economies with large informal sectors, tax cuts may not evenly reach the entire population. In such circumstances the reduction of pre-existing distortionary taxes may yield long-term welfare benefits as tax evasion is reduced (as demonstrated in Chapter 6); however, such tax cuts may need to be complemented with other measures (in particular direct transfers) to mitigate short-term cost shocks.

8.3.4 Complementary measures

Although there are differences in practice, FFS are essentially equivalent to a negative carbon tax. Economists have long favoured such price-based instruments for addressing environmental externalities. In fact, in the global debate on climate change mitigation policies, the implementation of carbon taxes has been one of the most frequently and prominently proposed measures (Sterner, 2007; World Bank, 2014). However, although the implementation of carbon taxes and FFS reforms are indeed crucial steps toward accounting for the external costs of carbon and thus for reducing greenhouse gas emissions, Chapter 7 has argued that complementary policies are required to ensure that these price-based measures are effective and publicly acceptable. In line with the theory of the second best, such complementary measures can counteract existing market distortions and result in a more efficient outcome than the first best approach on its own.

For instance, Avner et al. (2014) find that in an urban setting the effectiveness of carbon and fuel taxes is cut in half when they are not complemented by investments in public transport infrastructure. This is because even if fuel prices increase, people will continue to rely on fossil fuel intensive private transport if there are no public transport alternatives.

This example highlights that even if subsidies are reduced and fuel prices increased, there may be significant barriers that make households and firms unable or unwilling to adjust their behaviour or invest in more efficient technology. Chapter 7 has provided a detailed discussion of the role and prevalence of these barriers. In summary, these barriers may include information, capacity or financial constraints, or may be related to infrastructure, fiscal mismanagement, market structures, or systemic risks and uncertainty (including the long term credibility of such fiscal policy). This means that it cannot be taken for granted that the removal of subsidies per se will automatically trigger large environmental benefits. For instance, trade or information barriers may prevent firms from having access to modern, energy efficient technology, which they could install once energy prices increase. Capacity or financial constraints may cause firms to struggle to implement energy efficiency measures, or prevent households from retrofitting their dwellings to increase energy efficiency. As emphasised by the World Bank (Fay et al., 2015), environmental taxes or FFS reforms alone cannot address the complexity of existing market and government failures.

Based on insights from Fay et al. (2015) and Rentschler et al. (2016), Chapter 7 has provided an overview of the types of complementary policy measures that may be needed alongside carbon taxes and FFS reforms. These measures cover a wide range, including government support for research, development and innovation, performance standards, fiscal incentives for green investments, and social policies. Broadly speaking, the objective of such complementary measures is to (i) ensure that the necessary technologies are available and affordable, (ii) ensure that there is adequate infrastructure (e.g. for transport or electricity transmission), and (iii) account for biases and barriers that prevent behavioural change (Fay et al., 2015; Rozenberg et al., 2014).

In practice, complementary policies for FFS reforms can comprise a large variety of measures, which ultimately depend on country specific needs and circumstances. For example, in the case of Indonesia, the government was concerned that removing subsidies for kerosene (frequently used as a cooking fuel) would prompt poor households to switch to energy sources which are more harmful to health and environment (e.g. charcoal, biomass; IMF, 2013a,c). To prevent this, the government complemented its subsidy reform program (which began in 1997) by providing support to households to convert to liquefied petroleum gas (LPG), for example by offering free LPG ovens. Similar measures were undertaken in Niger in 2010 and the Philippines in 1998. Other governments have addressed financial constraints by establishing dedicated loan facilities to finance firms' investments in energy efficiency (e.g. Iran in 2010). In another example, Kenya complemented its 2005 fuel subsidy reform with large scale investments in electricity infrastructure, allowing households to switch away from fossil fuels (such as kerosene or charcoal) for domestic needs (IMF, 2013a,c).

Finally, in Ecuador, complementary measures form the foundation for the government's ongoing FFS reform program. Rather than focusing on the removal of FFS, the government has been implementing the Efficient Cooking Program, which subsidises electricity and provides low-cost electric induction stoves to households. The aim is to radically reduce demand for subsidised LPG. With residential demand in Ecuador accounting for 92% of LPG usage, by incentivising a large-scale fuel switch away from LPG, the government can maintain existing LPG subsidies until LPG demand has diminished, and remove FFS thereafter in a formal, inconsequential step (Ministerio del Ambiente, 2015).

8.3.5   Timing and price smoothing

This section argues that an effective FFS reform includes (step-wise) subsidy removal, but also depends on the careful timing of complementary measures (such as communication and compensation; see Figure 8.1).

The potential for a reform to be successful depends to a large extent on external factors (e.g. fuel prices) and political circumstances (Fattouh and El-Katiri, 2013). This underscores the vital role of getting the timing right: Falling fossil fuel prices may temporarily ease the fiscal pressures of subsidies, but they also provide an opportunity for governments to eliminate FFS. Fuel

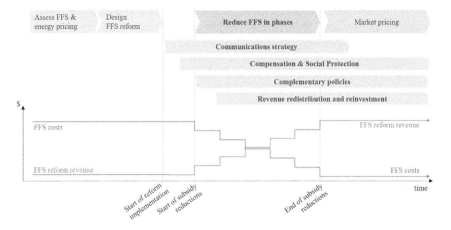

Figure 8.1 The timing and sequencing of FFS reform components (Author's illustration).

subsidy reforms in India (Nov. 2014) and Indonesia (Dec. 2014) have highlighted how political will for reform paired with low oil prices can pave the way for a smooth implementation of FFS reforms (Benes et al., 2015). However, these successful reforms were preceded by a thorough process of planning and preparation.

In addition, the study of Nigeria's smuggling market in Chapter 6 has demonstrated another role of fluctuations of international fuel market prices: The price differentials between international prices and subsidised domestic prices are the main incentive for fuel smuggling to take place. At times of low international prices (or low neighbouring country prices), fuel smuggling activities may appear low – however, these are likely to rebound once the price differential increases.

Timing is crucial not only for determining *when* but also *how* to reform. GSI (2013) underscores the importance of avoiding large sudden price shocks and thus recommends reducing subsidies gradually. The mostly unsuccessful reform attempt in Nigeria (2012) illustrates why: With little advance notice, the government removed FFS entirely, causing a one-time 117% increase in fuel prices. The benefits of removing subsidies and planned compensation programmes had not been sufficiently communicated to the population, and intense public protest ensued (Chapter 3; Bazilian and Onyeji, 2012). Chapter 3 has shown that such large one-off energy price increases can indeed have significant and immediate adverse effects on overall poverty levels, thus illustrating that instant one-off subsidy removals carry significant risks.

In contrast, the experience in Iran (2010), which phased in subsidy reductions over five years, shows that gradual adjustments and well timed reform measures can be successful. Moreover, in Iran, the benefits of reform were clearly communicated in advance and compensatory cash payments were provided to 70%-80% of the population before the first stage of the fuel price increase (Salehi-Isfahani et al., 2015).[4]

The issue of "price smoothing" is relevant not only during reform implementation, but also concerns the post-reform energy pricing regime. Indeed, instead of pure market pricing, many countries have implemented pricing mechanisms that prevent fluctuations in the international fuel price from translating uniformly into domestic retail prices. Such pricing mechanisms can be important when liberalising fossil fuel prices, as the removal of subsidies typically not only increases energy price levels, but also exposes households and firms (thus tax revenues) to the risk of price volatility. Coady et al. (2012) provide guidance for designing and implementing automatic fuel pricing mechanisms with smoothing functions that avoid adverse consequences on tax revenues. Implementing such pricing mechanisms can help governments to protect post-reform fiscal stability against volatility. Based on data for 68 resource-rich countries, Sugawara (2014) finds that stabilisation funds can indeed help governments to smooth expenditure. However, Coady et al. (2012) emphasise that to protect low-income households, direct measures are needed in addition to automatic pricing mechanisms.

8.4   Towards effective green fiscal reforms

8.4.1   *Key messages for policy makers*

Based on the main insights from previous chapters, and based on existing case studies and literature, this chapter has presented key principles for FFS reform design. It has suggested how FFS reforms can not only serve as a fiscal emergency measure, but also be more fully integrated into a country's long-term development strategy. This chapter – and indeed this book – have emphasised that FFS reform is not only about removing subsidies; it requires an integrated strategy comprising a range of carefully designed and sequenced policy measures, which help to ensure public support and social protection of vulnerable population groups. In summary, the evidence presented and discussed in this book offers the following lessons and advice for researchers and policy makers:

- **A complete assessment of the welfare costs of FFS is critical for understanding the true benefits of reform.** As Chapter 2 has shown, FFS are commonly associated with a wide range of adverse effects, such as eliminating incentives for innovation and investment, perpetuating inefficient technology and behaviour, reducing the competitiveness of the private sector, increasing fiscal imbalances, crowding out public investments, as well as aggravating inequality and local and global environmental degradation. In order to understand the true benefits of FFS reform, researchers and policy makers must take the full range of welfare costs into account, rather than focussing solely on – for instance – fiscal aspects. Moreover, Chapter 6 has shown that FFS can be associated with illicit activities such as tax evasion and fuel smuggling, which imply substantial societal welfare costs. The avoidance of such illicit activities can make a significant contribution to the benefits of FFS reform.

- **Communication and compensation are key to protecting livelihoods and managing political economy challenges.** If FFS are removed without providing compensation, both households and firms will be hurt in the short run. A transparent, timely and credible public outreach campaign is crucial for communicating the overall benefits of reform, and the government's plans for mitigating price shocks and compensating those who are adversely affected. While the rich benefit the most from subsidies, the poor may suffer the most (in relative terms) from subsidy removal as energy prices increase. Cash transfers have emerged as an effective compensation tool: Of 25 FFS reform case studies (mainly in the Middle East and North Africa), all reforms that used cash transfers and communications strategies successfully removed FFS. Without cash transfers, only 17% of reforms succeeded; and without a communication strategy, only 50% succeeded (Sdrale-vich et al., 2014).

- **FFS reform offers an opportunity to use and strengthen social protection systems.** In countries with existing social protection and cash transfer systems, this infrastructure can be used to significantly improve the cost-effectiveness and speed of delivering targeted cash compensation. For countries without such systems, FFS reforms present an opportunity to establish national social protection programmes that go beyond temporary compensation for subsidy reductions. For example, the government of Yemen established a cash transfer scheme alongside its 1996 FFS reform, which has become the country's main poverty alleviation and social assistance programme, now serving more than 1.5 million households (Bagash, Pereznieto, and Dubai, 2012). For designing effective social protection systems it is critical to recognise that income levels are an imperfect indicator of vulnerability, and that other factors (e.g. location and occupation types) need to be taken into account when identifying beneficiaries (Chapter 3).

- **Firms may require support to cope with and adapt to higher energy prices.** Rising energy costs will necessarily affect not only households, but also firms. By increasing direct energy costs, FFS removal can have significant impacts on the competitiveness of firms. Moreover, even firms relying on few direct energy inputs may incur significant adverse effects through the rising cost of capital, labour, or (energy-intensive) material inputs. While past studies have predominantly focussed on the effects on households, Chapter 5 has shown that increased energy prices can have lasting effects on the performance of firms. Rather than focussing narrowly on cost increases, it is crucial to evaluate *how* firms can adapt. As argued in Chapter 4, the ability of firms to implement response measures (i.e. absorption, efficiency, substitution, and pass-on) will eventually determine whether FFS reform results in inflation, reduced profit margins, and job losses – or promotes modernisation, innovation, and environmental benefits through increased energy efficiency and cleaner energy mixes. Complementary measures are crucial to strengthen the capacity of firms to respond (see below).

- **Establish transparent systems for reinvestment and redistribution of reform revenues.** As this chapter has discussed, FFS reforms are also an opportunity to implement transparent institutions and prudent strategies for reinvesting reform revenues in ways that are consistent with a country's long-term development goals. Especially in resource rich countries, this is closely linked to the issue of managing natural resource rents. Conventional sovereign wealth funds (following Norway's example), or investment funds for enhancing domestic infrastructure, social safety nets, or health and education systems (as in Mozambique, Tanzania, Uganda, Zambia, Kazakhstan, and Malaysia) can be effective vehicles for long-term reinvestment if operated with transparent management and oversight (Halland et al., 2014). Institutionalised 'resource dividends' can be an effective method for redistributing resource rents directly to citizens; they have a proven track record in Alaska and detailed viability studies have been undertaken in Uganda and Nigeria.
- **Manage energy price volatility through smoothing measures and smart timing.** Price smoothing is critical, both during and after the subsidy reform. Reform experiences from Namibia, Uganda, and Brazil show that gradual subsidy reductions can reduce energy price shocks and make compensation policies more manageable (IMF, 2013c). One-off complete FFS removals as 2012 in Nigeria (Chapter 3), are likely to cause significant income shocks and hence public opposition. Recent reforms in India, Indonesia, and Saudi Arabia have also shown that aligning the timing of reforms with low international energy prices can minimise price shocks (and public opposition). Moreover, the establishment of automatic pricing and smoothing mechanisms can help to stabilise domestic energy prices and associated tax revenues by moderating the pass-through of international market fluctuations (as has been done in Malaysia and Saudi Arabia).
- **Price deregulation is not enough: Complementary policies are also needed.** Similar to a carbon tax, the reduction of FFS increases energy prices, but may not be enough per se to trigger desired environmental benefits. Evidence suggests that even if fuel prices increase, households and firms may face significant barriers (e.g. information, capacity,

infrastructure, or financial constraints), which prevent them from adjusting their behaviour or investing in more efficient technology (Chapters 5 and 7). The governments of Indonesia (since 1997), the Philippines (1998), Niger (2010), Iran (2010), and Ecuador (2015) have all complemented FFS reforms with active support to households and firms to switch from fossil to clean energy sources and increase energy efficiency (Chapter 2). By complementing FFS reforms with wider energy sector reforms and investments, Kenya and Uganda have shown that subsidy reforms can not only improve financial sustainability, but also increase energy access, improve the distributional efficiency of electricity transmission and power supply, and replace unsustainable fuels such as charcoal (Chapter 2; IMF, 2013a,c,b). Without complementary measures, increased energy prices may simply result in reduced profit margins and inflation, rather than triggering environmental benefits (Chapter 5).

The need for a variety of policy measures also means that FFS reforms are not a purely fiscal task; rather, they require multi-sectoral collaboration that includes fiscal and environmental policy, the energy, transport and industrial sectors, poverty and social protection, as well as natural resource management and development financing.

Overall, past FFS reform efforts show that, despite strong incentives for reform, the record of success has been mixed. Evaluated against the reform principles highlighted above, it is evident that past reform failures have often been rooted in a violation of these principles. Considering that most environmental tax reforms tend to encounter similar political economy obstacles, the above principles for designing FFS reforms are in fact of equal relevance for carbon taxes and other green fiscal reforms.

8.4.2 Outlook

As outlined in the beginning of this book, "getting prices right" is widely regarded to be at the heart of an effective market-based solution to the climate change challenge. In its essence, this approach requires that the social and environmental costs of carbon intensive activities are reflected in their prices – i.e. by putting a price on carbon. However, the roughly $1 trillion in FFS paid every year around the world have the polar opposite effect of carbon taxes: They incentivise the overconsumption and inefficient use of carbon-intensive energy and undermine the effectiveness of any climate change mitigation effort. For this reason, reforming FFS is fundamental for achieving the climate change mitigation goals set under the 2015 Paris Agreement.

However, while subsidy reform is crucial from a climate change perspective, the wide range of economic and social externalities associated with FFS also emphasises that reform is a vital contribution to sustainable development objectives more generally. While FFS reform is formally called for by a dedicated Sustainable Development Goal (SDG 12.c), this book has shown that FFS reform has relevance and implications for a wide range of other sustainable development outcomes; such as, poverty reduction (SDG 1), sustainable agriculture (SDG 2), sustainable water usage (SDG 6), promotion of sustainable energy (SDG 7), promotion of modern and efficient industrialisation (SDG 9), reduction of inequality (SDG 10), creation of sustainable cities, in particular providing sustainable transportation and reducing local pollution (SDG 11), promotion of efficient and clean consumption and production (SDG 12), climate change mitigation (SDG 13), and reduction of illicit activities and corruption (SDG 16). FFS reform not only removes distorted incentives that undermine countries' ability to make progress towards these goals, but can also unlock significant domestic financing to facilitate and accelerate sustainable development efforts.

Nevertheless, when FFS reforms are implemented in practice, environmental objectives often play a secondary role. Instead the rationale for FFS reforms are determined within a complex – and sometimes conflicting – context of fiscal, macroeconomic, political, and social factors. In the past, governments have focussed in particular on the fiscal dimension of FFS reform, i.e. relieving public budgets by removing FFS, and avoiding public opposition by compensating the losers of reform. However, by focussing on managing the down-side risks of reforms, the full sustainable development potential associated with subsidy reform may fail to materialise. Thus, complementary measures and prudent reinvestment of reform revenues are critical to ensure that FFS reforms provide not only short-term relief in times of fiscal crisis, but also serve as a fully integrated component of a long-term sustainable development strategy.

Understanding and navigating such complexity is not only a challenge for policy makers, but an obligation for researchers. The Sustainable Development Goals have been formulated in a way to recognise the complex interlinkages and interactions between different dimensions of sustainable development, and promote an integrated approach to policy making. Similarly, assessments of FFS reforms must take into account the complex and multifaceted effects in the short- and long-run, in terms of economic, social, and environmental dimensions, for both formal and informal parts of the economy, across all income groups, and at all levels – from households to firms, and to the macro-economy. This wide range of focus areas and perspectives requires a range of different methodological approaches from the disciplines of economics and political economy.

This book has explored these perspectives by developing and applying a variety of analytical and conceptual methodologies. The aspiration is that the evidence developed and compiled here will guide future research, inform the preparation, design, and implementation of future FFS and green fiscal reforms, and thus facilitate further progress towards sustainable development.

Notes

1 *An abridged version of this chapter has been published as* Rentschler, J. E., Bazilian, M. (2017). Principles for designing effective fossil fuel subsidy reforms. *Review of Environmental Economics and Policy*. Vol. 11(1). doi:10.1093/reep/rew016.
2 For additional impact assessments of FFS reforms, see Jiang et al. (2015) and Ouyang and Lin (2014) for China, Solaymani and Kari (2014) for Malaysia, and Siddig et al. (2014) for Nigeria.
3 In-kind transfers may include any non-monetary benefits, such as food vouchers or access to free services.
4 The initial successes of Iran's subsidy reform programme were reversed to a large extent by the effects of economic sanctions.

Appendix A
Supplementary material to Chapter 5

A.1 Regional energy prices

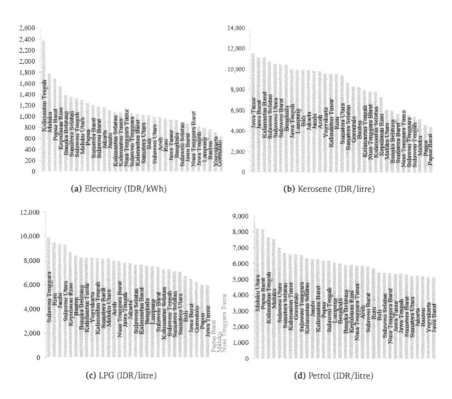

Figure A.1 Average energy price for each province, inferred from quantity and expenditure data contained in the 2013 Micro & Small Enterprise Survey for Indonesia (BPS Statistics Indonesia, 2015).

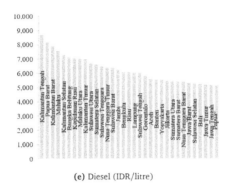

(e) Diesel (IDR/litre)

Figure A.1 (Continued)

A.2 Analytical derivation of regression equation

The regression equation can be derived analytically from a standard Constant Elasticity of Substitution (CES) production function:

$$Q_j = \gamma_j \left[\sum_h \delta_{h,j} F_{h,j}^{\eta_j} \right]^{\frac{1}{\eta_j}} \tag{A.1}$$

Q_j represents the quantity of output of firm j, $F_{h,j}$ is the quantity used of production factor h, the parameter $\delta_{h,j}$ is the input share of respective factors, and γ_j is a measure of factor productivity. Moreover, the parameter η_j is defined through the elasticity of substitution σ_j:

$$\eta_j = \frac{\sigma_j - 1}{\sigma_j} \tag{A.2}$$

The associated profit function is expressed as revenue minus the sum of factor costs:

$$\pi_j = p_j^Q Q_j - \sum_h p_h^f F_{h,j}, \tag{A.3}$$

where ρ_j denotes profits, p_j^Q the sales price, and p_h^f the price of production factor h. Standard profit optimisation yields optimal factor demand:

$$F_{h,j}^* = \left[\gamma_j^{\eta_j} \delta_{h,j} \frac{p_j^Q}{p_h^f} \right]^{\frac{1}{1-\eta_j}} Q_j \tag{A.4}$$

The profit share *PS* (i.e. percentage share of profits in total revenue, as outlined in Section 5.3.3) can be expressed as:

$$PS = \frac{\pi_j^*}{p_j^Q Q_j^*} \tag{A.5}$$

$$= \frac{p_j^Q Q_j^* - \sum_h p_h^f F_{h,j}^*}{p_j^Q Q_j^*} \tag{A.6}$$

By inserting the expression for optimal factor demand and rearranging further, the profit share can be written as

$$PS = 1 - \frac{\sum_h p_h^f \left[\gamma_j^{\eta_j} \delta_{h,j} \frac{p_j^Q}{p_h^f}\right]^{\frac{1}{1-\eta_j}} Q_j^*}{p_j^Q Q_j^*} \tag{A.7}$$

$$= 1 - \sum_h \frac{p_h^f}{p_j^Q} \left[\gamma_j^{\eta_j} \delta_{h,j} \frac{p_j^Q}{p_h^f}\right]^{\frac{1}{1-\eta_j}} \tag{A.8}$$

$$= 1 - \sum_h \left[\frac{p_h^f}{p_j^Q}\right]^{\frac{\eta_j}{1-\eta_j}} \left[\gamma_j^{\eta_j} \delta_{h,j}\right]^{\frac{1}{1-\eta_j}}. \tag{A.9}$$

By distinguishing energy and all other factors of production, the profit share can be expressed as a function of energy prices – thus yielding an estimable equation:

$$PS = 1 - (p^E)^{\frac{\eta_j}{1-\eta_j}} (p_j^Q)^{\frac{-\eta_j}{1-\eta_j}} \left[\gamma_j^{\eta_j} \delta_{E,j}\right]^{\frac{1}{1-\eta_j}} - \sum_{h\backslash E} \left[\frac{p_{h\backslash E}^f}{p_j^Q}\right]^{\frac{\eta_j}{1-\eta_j}} \left[\gamma_j^{\eta_j} \delta_{h\backslash E,j}\right]^{\frac{1}{1-\eta_j}} \tag{A.10}$$

$$= 1 - A(p^E)^{\beta_j} - B \tag{A.11}$$

The price of energy is denoted by p_E. Note, that the notation $h\backslash E$ is commonly used as "h without E". Moreover, following expressions have been defined for convenience:

$$A = (p_j^Q)^{\frac{-\eta_j}{1-\eta_j}} \left[\gamma_j^{\eta_j} \delta_{E,j}\right]^{\frac{1}{1-\eta_j}} \tag{A.12}$$

$$B = \sum_{h \backslash E} \left[\frac{p^f_{h \backslash E}}{p^Q_j} \right]^{\frac{\eta_j}{1 - \eta_j}} \left[\gamma_j^{\eta_j} \delta_{h \backslash E, j} \right]^{\frac{1}{1 - \eta_j}} \tag{A.13}$$

$$\beta_j = \frac{\eta_j}{1 - \eta_j} \tag{A.14}$$

The profit share *PS* can be rearranged to obtain the regression equation for the cost share *CS*:

$$PS = \frac{\pi^*_j}{p^Q_j Q^*_j} = 1 - A(p^E)^{\beta_j} - B \tag{A.15}$$

$$\frac{p^Q_j Q_j - \sum_h p^f_h F_{h,j}}{p^Q_j Q^*_j} = 1 - A(p^E)^{\beta_j} - B \tag{A.16}$$

$$CS = \frac{\sum_h p^f_h F_{h,j}}{p^Q_j Q^*_j} = A(p^E)^{\beta_j} + B \tag{A.17}$$

A.3   Alternative approaches to accounting for missing labour cost data

Table A.1 The first column reports baseline estimates as obtained in Section 5.1. Column (1) uses fitted values from the labour cost regression. Column (2) uses labour costs as derived from peers. Standard errors (in *italics*) are robust to heteroscedasticity, *** $p<0.001$; ** $p<0.01$; * $p< 0.05$.

	Baseline	*(1)*	*(2)*
ln (**electricity** price)	0.052***	0.034***	0.045***
	0.009	*0.008*	*0.009*
ln (**kerosene** price)	0.043	0.053	0.048
	0.043	*0.039*	*0.044*
ln (**LPG** price)	0.232***	0.180***	0.237***
	0.036	*0.031*	*0.037*
ln (**petrol** price)	0.160**	0.110*	0.209***
	0.05	*0.046*	*0.052*
ln (**diesel** price)	0.373***	0.206*	0.333**
	0.098	*0.094*	*0.102*
industry dummies	YES	YES	YES
province dummies	YES	YES	YES
N	36,759	36,742	36,742
Adjusted R^2	0.214	0.173	0.23

A.4 Parameter restrictions for the translog cost function

As discussed by Banda and Verdugo (2007), following parameter restrictions on the translog cost function are required for it to be homogeneous of degree 1 in prices; in other words, at a given level of output total cost increase proportionally in line with prices.

$$\sum_i \alpha_i = 1 \tag{A.18}$$

$$\sum_i \gamma_{Q,i} = 0 \tag{A.19}$$

$$\sum_i \sum_j \gamma_{i,j} = 0 \tag{A.20}$$

Additional parameter restrictions can be applied in order to impose assumptions on technology. For homotheticity the cost function is separable in output and input prices. This is the case for

$$\gamma_{Q,i} = 0, \ \forall i. \tag{A.21}$$

For homogeneity in output, the elasticity of costs with respect to output is constant. This is the case for

$$\gamma_{Q,i} = 0 \tag{A.22}$$

and

$$\gamma_{Q,Q} = 0. \tag{A.23}$$

A.5 Partial own and cross price elasticities (by sector)

Table A.2 Partial own and cross price elasticities by industrial sectors. Asterisks indicate the confidence level (*** 0.1%; ** 1%; * 5%) of the underlying estimate for $\gamma_{m,n}$ and $\gamma_{m,m}$ respectively.

		Electricity	Petrol	Diesel	Kerosene	LPG
	Electricity	-1.52***	0.13**	0.18***	0.25	0.10*
Mining of	Petrol	0.11**	-2.17***	0.51***	0.31***	-0.81*
coal	Diesel	0.08**	0.26***	-1.03	0.72***	0.87
lignite, peat	Kerosene	0.18	0.26***	1.21***	-5.79***	2.85***
	LPG	0.03*	-0.31*	0.66	1.28***	-2.14***
	Electricity	-1.65***	0.38	0.1	0.08	0.1
Extraction of	Petrol	0.33	-1.63***	0.27*	0.1	-0.81
crude oil,	Diesel	0.23	0.75*	-2.05***	0.24	0.87
gas, uranium	Kerosene	0.54	0.77	0.64	-5.00***	2.85***
	LPG	0.1	-0.91	0.35	0.43***	-2.52***
	Electricity	-0.59***	0.35***	0.04	0.06**	0.03
Mining of	Petrol	0.97***	-1.93***	0.12**	0.08	-0.22***
metal ores	Diesel	0.69	0.70**	-3.25***	0.18**	0.24***
& others	Kerosene	1.57**	0.72	0.29**	-1.4	0.78**
	LPG	0.29	-0.85***	0.16***	0.31**	-2.82***
Food &	Electricity	-0.84**	0.51	0.05	0.3	0.07
beverages	Petrol	0.51	-0.98	0.14**	0.38**	-0.53*
caveats due to	Diesel	0.36	1.02**	6.05***	0.88	0.56
regional	Kerosene	0.83	1.05**	0.33	1.02***	1.84
concentration	LPG	0.15	-1.24*	0.18	1.56	-2.75***
	Electricity	-1.84***	0.57**	0.33	0.05*	0.00*
Tobacco	Petrol	0.38**	0.59***	0.92	0.06*	-0.02*
products	Diesel	0.27	1.13	-0.42***	0.15	0.02*
	Kerosene	0.62*	1.16*	2.2	-1.75*	0.07**
	LPG	0.11*	-1.38*	1.20*	0.26**	10.13***
	Electricity	-0.59***	0.24	0.09	0.04	0.02
Light	Petrol	0.91	-1.88***	0.25**	0.05	-0.15
consumption	Diesel	0.64	0.49**	-2.39***	0.12	0.16
goods	Kerosene	1.47	0.5	0.6	-9.05***	0.53**
	LPG	0.27	-0.59	0.32	0.22**	-2.75***
Coke &	Electricity	-7.59***	0.03	0.11	0.01	0
refined	Petrol	0.03	-4.69**	0.31	0.02*	0
petroleum	Diesel	0.02	0.06	-1.85***	0.04	0
products	Kerosene	0.04	0.06*	0.74	-0.8	0.01
	LPG	0.01	-0.08	0.4	0.08	-19.95**
	Electricity	-0.83*	0.21**	0.2	0.01	0.02
Intermediate	Petrol	0.47**	-1.71**	0.57	0.02	-0.13
materials	Diesel	0.33	0.42	-1.28*	0.04	0.14
	Kerosene	0.76	0.43	1.37	-6.08**	0.46**
	LPG	0.14	-0.51	0.74	0.07**	-1.69*
	Electricity	-0.83***	0.41***	0.22	0.03**	0.01
Capital goods	Petrol	0.69***	-0.27***	0.63	0.04	-0.11***
& technology	Diesel	0.49	0.82	-0.53*	0.09	0.12
	Kerosene	1.12**	0.84	1.5	-2.68**	0.39
	LPG	0.21	-1.00***	0.82	0.17	-1.74*

A.6   *Partial elasticities of substitution (total sample)*

Table A.3 Allan-Uzawa partial elasticities of substitution for the five main energy
types and the total sample. Asterisks indicate the confidence level
(***0.1%; ** 1%; * 5%) of the underlying estimate for $\gamma_{m,n}$. Note
that Allen-Uzawa partial elasticities of substitution are symmetrical.

m\n	Electricity	Petrol	Diesel	Kerosene	LPG
Electricity	–	1.66***	1.18**	2.70***	0.50**
Petrol		–	3.31***	3.39*	-4.02***
Diesel			–	7.89***	4.30***
Kerosene				–	14.05***
LPG					–

Table A.4 Morishima partial elasticities of substitution for the five main energy
types and the total sample. As $\sigma_{m,n}^{MES} = \eta_{m,n} - \eta_{n,n}$, significance depends
on both $\eta_{m,n}$ and $\eta_{n,n}$ (reported in Table 5.4).

m\n	Electricity	Petrol	Diesel	Kerosene	LPG
Electricity	–	1.04	1.22	5.59	2.95
Petrol	1.79	–	1.50	5.62	2.59
Diesel	1.72	1.21	–	5.78	3.24
Kerosene	1.93	1.21	2.09	–	4.00
LPG	1.62	0.47	1.63	6.01	–

Appendix B
Supplementary material to Chapter 6

B.1 Social accounting matrix

Table B.1 The social accounting matrix (SAM), constructed for the calibration of the CGE model in Chapter 6. Variables are defined below. For detailed data sources refer to Section 6.6.1. Values in mil. Naira.

	PET	ENE	FRM	IFM	PET_SMG	CAP	LAB	TX_P	TX_CP	TX_LB
PET	604,727	234,964	1,993,673	2,017,355	99,332	0	0	0	0	0
ENE	1,216,486	476,488	1,693,525	2,411,187	0	0	0	0	0	0
FRM	191,630	1,145,244	53,129,436	38,780,013	0	0	0	0	0	0
IFM	1,433,144	1,321,968	40,453,443	38,597,984	0	0	0	0	0	0
PET_SMG	0	0	0	0		0	0	0	0	0
CAP	136,351	2,209,137	19,900,923	16,039,664	0	0	0	0	0	0
LAB	34,549	319,413	19,636,747	14,413,302	0	0	0	0	0	0
TX_P	326,540	129,178	1,792,443	224,519	0	0	0	0	0	0
TX_CP	2,177	43,698	367,013	24,059	0	0	0	0	0	0
TX_LB	8,461	89,140	5,307,798	249,350	0	0	0	0	0	0
EV_P	6,529	2,584	35,849	2,020,671	0	0	0	0	0	0
EV_CP	44	874	7,340	216,535	0	0	0	0	0	0

(Continued)

Table B.1 (Continued)

	PET	ENE	FRM	IFM	PET_SMG	CAP	LAB	TX_P	TX_CP	TX_LB
EV_LB	338	3,566	212,312	2,368,826	0	0	0	0	0	0
PL_SM	0	0	0	0	13,608	0	0	0	0	0
EC_P	0	0	0	0	0	0	0	0	0	0
EC_CP	4	87	734	21,654	0	0	0	0	0	0
EC_LB	34	356	21,231	236,883	0	0	0	0	0	0
EC_SMG	0	0	0	0	7,947	0	0	0	0	0
SB_EN	-1,348,000	-92,914	0	0	0	0	0	0	0	0
HH1	0	0	0	0	0	2,652,432	2,399,985	0	0	0
HH2	0	0	0	0	0	4,201,767	3,801,861	0	0	0
HH3	0	0	0	0	0	5,943,298	5,377,641	0	0	0
HH4	0	0	0	0	0	8,368,461	7,571,988	0	0	0
HH5	0	0	0	0	0	17,142,596	15,511,040	0	0	0
SMG	0	0	0	0	0	0	0	0	0	0
GOV	0	0	0	0	0	0	0	2,472,680	436,947	5,654,749
INV	0	0	0	0	0	0	0	0	0	0
EXT	3,599,425	786,670	11,438,614	11,267,194	0	0	0	0	0	0
Total	6,212,439	6,670,453	155,991,081	128,889,196	120,887	38,308,554	34,662,515	2,472,680	436,947	5,654,749

(Continued)

Table B.1 (Continued)

	EV_P	EV_CP	EV_LB	PI_SM	EC_P	EC_CP	EC_LB	EC_SMG	SB_EN
PET	0	0	0	0	0	0	0	7,947	0
ENE	0	0	0	0	0	0	0	0	0
FRM	0	0	0	0	0	0	0	0	0
IFM	0	0	0	0	0	0	0	0	0
PET_SMG									
CAP	0	0	0	0	0	22,479	0	0	0
LAB	0	0	0	0	0	0	258,504	0	0
TX_P	0	0	0	0	0	0	0	0	0
TX_CP	0	0	0	0	0	0	0	0	0
TX_LB	0	0	0	0	0	0	0	0	0
EV_P	0	0	0	0	0	0	0	0	0
EV_CP	0	0	0	0	0	0	0	0	0
EV_LB	0	0	0	0	0	0	0	0	0
PI_SM	0	0	0	0	0	0	0	0	0
EC_P	0	0	0	0	0	0	0	0	0
EC_CP	0	0	0	0	0	0	0	0	0

(Continued)

Table B.1 (Continued)

	EV_P	EV_CP	EV_LB	PI_SM	EC_P	EC_CP	EC_LB	EC_SMG	SB_EN
EC_LB	0	0	0	0	0	0	0	0	0
EC_SMG	0	0	0	0	0	0	0	0	0
SB_EN	0	0	0	0	0	0	0	0	0
HH1	143,022	15,564	178,985	0	0	0	0	0	0
HH2	226,563	24,656	283,533	0	0	0	0	0	0
HH3	320,468	34,875	401,051	0	0	0	0	0	0
HH4	451,235	49,106	564,699	0	0	0	0	0	0
HH5	924,345	100,592	1,156,774	0	0	0	0	0	0
SMG	0	0	0	13,608	0	0	0	0	0
GOV	0	0	0	0	0	0	0	0	0
INV	0	0	0	0	0	0	0	0	0
EXT	0	0	0	0	0	0	0	0	0
Total	2,065,633	224,793	2,585,042	13,608	0	22,479	258,504	7,947	0

(Continued)

Table B.1 (Continued)

	HH1	HH2	HH3	HH4	HH5	SMG	GOV	INV	EXT	Total
PET	12,544	37,623	75,246	188,114	940,571	33	7	7	296	6,212,439
ENE	59,689	94,553	133,743	188,316	385,761	82	6	13	10,604	6,670,453
FRM	2,770,072	4,388,127	6,206,900	8,739,626	17,902,918	3,804	7,123,443	5,730,573	9,879,295	155,991,081
IFM	2,023,719	3,218,456	4,568,112	6,490,632	13,691,226	9,689	1	1	17,080,821	128,889,196
PET_SMG	0	0	0	0	0	0	0	0	120,887	120,887
CAP	0	0	0	0	0	0	0	0	0	38,308,554
LAB	0	0	0	0	0	0	0	0	0	34,662,515
TX_P	0	0	0	0	0	0	0	0	0	2,472,680
TX_CP	0	0	0	0	0	0	0	0	0	436,947
TX_LB	0	0	0	0	0	0	0	0	0	5,654,749
EV_P	0	0	0	0	0	0	0	0	0	2,065,633
EV_CP	0	0	0	0	0	0	0	0	0	224,793
EV_LB	0	0	0	0	0	0	0	0	0	2,585,042
PLSM	0	0	0	0	0	0	0	0	0	13,608
EC_P	0	0	0	0	0	0	0	0	0	0
EC_CP	0	0	0	0	0	0	0	0	0	22,479
EC_LB	0	0	0	0	0	0	0	0	0	258,504

(Continued)

Table B.1 (Continued)

	HH1	HH2	HH3	HH4	HH5	SMG	GOV	INV	EXT	Total
EC_SMG	0	0	0	0	0	0	0	0	0	7,947
SB_EN	0	0	0	0	0	0	1,440,914	0	0	0
HH1	0	0	0	0	0	0	1	0	0	5,389,989
HH2	0	0	0	0	0	0	1	0	0	8,538,381
HH3	0	0	0	0	0	0	1	0	0	12,077,334
HH4	0	0	0	0	0	0	1	0	0	17,005,490
HH5	0	0	0	0	0	0	1	0	0	34,835,348
SMG	0	0	0	0	0	0	0	0	0	13,608
GOV	0	0	0	0	0	0	0	0	0	8,564,376
INV	523,965	799,622	1,093,333	1,398,802	1,914,872	0	0	0	0	5,730,594
EXT	0	0	0	0	0	0	0	0	0	27,091,903
Total	5,389,989	8,538,381	12,077,334	17,005,490	34,835,348	13,608	8,564,376	5,730,594	27,091,903	

Description of variables used in the SAM:

PET :	The petrol sector
ENE :	The energy sector (all energy types excluding petrol)
FRM :	The formal sector (an aggregate of all formal, non-energy sectors)
IFM :	The informal sector
PET_SMG :	Virtual account for petrol smuggling
CAP :	Factor of production: Capital
LAB :	Factor of production: Labour
TX_P :	Production tax, paid by all sectors
TX_CP :	Capital tax, paid by all sectors
TX_LB :	Labour tax, paid by all sectors
EV_P :	The total amount of production tax that is evaded by a given sector
EV_CP :	The total amount of capital tax that is evaded by a given sector
EV_LB :	The total amount of labour tax that is evaded by a given sector
PI_SM :	Net benefit of smuggling activities, accruing to the smuggler
EC_P :	Economic cost of activities related to production tax evasion
EC_CP :	Economic cost of activities related to capital tax evasion
EC_LB :	Economic cost of activities related to labour tax evasion
EC_SMG :	Economic cost of smuggling activities
SB_EN :	Fossil fuel subsidies, paid to the petrol sector
HH1 :	Household representing the poorest quintile of the income distribution
HH2 :	Household representing the second quintile of the income distribution
HH3 :	Household representing the third quintile of the income distribution
HH4 :	Household representing the fourth quintile of the income distribution
HH5 :	Household representing the richest quintile of the income distribution
SMG :	Smuggling agent
GOV :	Government
INV :	Investment account
EXT :	External account

As described in Section 6.6, the SAM obtained from GTAP has been refined by disaggregating income quintiles, and by including tax evasion and smuggling activities. Note that the external account in this (aggregated) SAM does not distinguish types of goods. For further details see Section 6.5.7 (Exports, imports, and the balance of payments) on the Armington assumption. Sectors are modelled to pay taxes (TX_*i*), while the evaded share of taxes is transferred to households via the evasion account EV_*x*. The cost of factor tax evasion takes the form of unproductive usage of production factors, paid through the evasion cost accounts EV_CB and EV_LB. The cost of production tax evasion come in the form of production losses, which are directly factored into output levels rather than the cost account EC_P. PET_SMG acts as a sector for petrol smuggling activities. It purchases petrol for illicit resale (PET) and for transportation purposes (i.e. the cost of smuggling, via EC_SMG). Moreover, it pays the smuggling profit to a small group of households (SMG) via the profit account PI_SM.

Bibliography

Acemoglu, D., Aghion, P., Bursztyn, L., Hemous, D., 2012. The environment and directed technical change. *American Economic Review* 102(1), 131–166.

Acemoglu, D., Robinson, J., 2010. The role of institutions in growth and development. In: Brady, D., Spence, M. (Eds.), *Leadership and Growth*. The World Bank, Washington, DC, Ch. 5, pp. 135–164.

Adam, L., Lestari, E., 2008. Ten years of reforms: The impact of an increase in the price of oil on welfare. *Journal of Indonesian Social Sciences and Humanities* 1, 121–139.

ADB, 2013. *Same Energy, More Power: Accelerating Energy Efficiency in Asia*. Asian Development Bank, Manila.

ADB, 2015. *Fuel-marking Programs: Helping Governments Raise Revenue, Combat Smuggling, and Improve the Environment*. Asian Development Bank, Manila.

Aghion, P., Bloom, N., Blundell, R., Griffith, R., Howitt, P., 2005. Competition and innovation: An inverted-U relationship. *The Quarterly Journal of Economics* 120 (2), 701–728.

Albrizio, S., Botta, E., Koźluk, T., Zipperer, V., 2014. *Do Environmental Policies Matter for Productivity Growth?* OECD Economics Department Working Papers 1176.

Aldy, J. E., Krupnick, A. J., Newell, R. G., Parry, I. W. H., Pizer, W. A., 2010. Designing climate mitigation policy. *Journal of Economic Literature* 48(4), 903–934.

Allwood, J. M., Ashby, M. F., Gutowski, T. G., Worrell, E., January 2011. Material efficiency: A white paper. *Resources, Conservation and Recycling* 55(3), 362–381.

Ambec, S., Cohen, M. A., Elgie, S., Lanoie, P., January 2013. The porter hypothesis at 20: Can environmental regulation enhance innovation and competitiveness? *Review of Environmental Economics and Policy* 7(1), 2–22.

Anand, R., Coady, D., Mohommad, A., Thakoor, V. V., Walsh, J. P., 2013. The fiscal and welfare impacts of reforming fuel subsidies in India. *IMF Working Papers* 13(128), 1.

Anderson, S. T., Newell, R. G., 2004. Information programs for technology adoption: The case of energy-efficiency audits. *Resource and Energy Economics* 26(1), 27–50.

Andrikopoulos, A. A., Brox, J. A., Paraskevopoulos, C. C., December 1989. Inter-fuel and inter-factor substitution in Ontario manufacturing, 1962–82. *Applied Economics* 21(12), 1667–1681.

APEC, 2013. *2013 Leaders' Declaration*. Bali Declaration – Resilient Asia-Pacific, Engine of Global Growth, 8 October 2013.

Araar, A., Choueiri, N., Verme, P., 2015. *The Quest for Subsidy Reforms in Libya*. World Bank Policy Research Working Papers 7225.

Araar, A., Verme, P., 2012. *Reforming Subsidies a Tool-kit for Policy Simulations*. World Bank Policy Research Working Papers 6148.

Arlinghaus, J., 2015. Impacts of carbon prices on indicators of competitiveness: A review of empirical findings. *OECD Working Papers* 87, 36.

Armington, S. P., 1969. A theory of demand for products distinguished by place of production. *IMF Staff Papers* 16(1), 159–178.

Arnold, J. M., Mattoo, A., Narciso, G., 2008. Services inputs and firm productivity in Sub-Saharan Africa: Evidence from firm-level data. *Journal of African Economies* 17(4), 578–599.

Arzaghi, M., Squalli, J., July 2015. How price inelastic is demand for gasoline in fuel-subsidizing economies? *Energy Economics* 50, 117–124.

Arze del Granado, F. J., Coady, D., Gillingham, R., November 2012. The unequal benefits of fuel subsidies: A review of evidence for developing countries. *World Development* 40(11), 2234–2248.

Avner, P., Rentschler, J., Hallegatte, S., 2014. *Carbon Price Efficiency Lock-in and Path Dependence in Urban Forms and Transport Infrastructure*. World Bank Policy Research Working Papers 6941.

Azlina, A., Anang, Z., Alipiah, R. M., 2013. Interfactor and interfuel substitution in the industrial sector of three major energy producer in developing countries. *International Review of Business Research Papers* 9(September), 139–153.

Baffes, J., Kose, M. A., Ohnsorge, F., Stocker, M., 2015. *The Great Plunge in Oil Prices: Causes, Consequences, and Policy Responses*. The World Bank, Washington, DC.

Bagash, T., Pereznieto, P., Dubai, K., 2012. *Transforming Cash Transfers: Beneficiary and Community Perspectives on the Social Welfare Fund in Yemen*. Overseas Development Institute, London.

Banda, H., Verdugo, L., 2007. *Translog Cost Functions: An Application for Mexican Manufacturing*. Banco de Mexico Working Papers 8.

Banerjee, A., Duflo, E., 2005. Growth theory through the lens of development economics. In: Philippe, A., Durlauf, S. (Eds.), *Handbook of Economic Growth*. North Holland, Amsterdam, pp. 473–552.

Baron, D. P., 1985. Regulation of prices and pollution under incomplete information. *Journal of Public Economics* 28(2), 211–231.

Bassi, A. M., Yudken, J. S., Ruth, M., August 2009. Climate policy impacts on the competitiveness of energy-intensive manufacturing sectors. *Energy Policy* 37(8), 3052–3060.

Bast, E., Doukas, A., Pickard, S., Van Der Burg, L., Whitley, S., 2015. *Empty Promises: G20 Subsidies to Oil, Gas and Coal Production*. Oil Change International, Washington, DC.

Bast, E., Makhijani, S., Pickard, S., Whitley, S., 2014. *The Fossil Fuel Bailout: G20 Subsidies for Oil, Gas, and Coal Exploration*. ODI and OCI, London and Washington, DC.

Bastein, T., Koers, W., Dittrich, K., Becker, J., Lopez, F., 2014. *Business Barriers to the Uptake of Resource Efficiency Measures*. POLFREE Deliverable 1.5. Policy Options for a Resource Efficient Economy (POLFREE).

Bazilian, M., Onyeji, I., 2012. Fossil fuel subsidy removal and inadequate public power supply: Implications for businesses. *Energy Policy* 45, 1–5.

Benes, K., Cheon, A., Urpelainen, J., Yang, J., 2015. *Low Oil Prices: An Opportunity for Fuel Subsidy Reform*. Policy Paper, Columbia Center on Global Energy Policy.

Bento, A. M., Jacobsen, M., January 2007. Ricardian rents, environmental policy and the 'double-dividend' hypothesis. *Journal of Environmental Economics and Management* 53(1), 17–31.

Bento, A. M., Jacobsen, M., Liu, A. A., 2017. Environmental policy in the presence of an informal sector. *Toulouse School of Economics*. Discussion paper. URL https://www.tse-fr.eu/sites/default/files/TSE/documents/sem2017/environment/jacobsen.pdf

Blackorby, C., Russell, R. R., 1989. Will the real elasticity of substitution please stand up? (A comparison of the Allen/Uzawa and Morishima Elasticities). *The American Economic Review* 79(4), 882–888.

Blaug, M., 2007. The fundamental theorems of modern welfare economics, historically contemplated. *History of Political Economy* 39(2), 185.

Bleischwitz, R., 2010. International economics of resource productivity – Relevance, measurement, empirical trends, innovation, resource policies. *International Economics and Economic Policy* 7, 227–244.

Bleischwitz, R., 2012. Towards a resource policy—Unleashing productivity dynamics and balancing international distortions. *Mineral Economics* 24(2–3), 135–144.

Bleischwitz, R., Giljum, S., Kuhndt, M., Schmidt-Bleek, F., 2009. Eco-innovation: Putting the EU on the path to a resource and energy efficient economy. *Wuppertal Spezial* 38.

Bleischwitz, R., Hennicke, P., 2004. *Eco-efficiency, Regulation, and Sustainable Business: Towards a Governance Structure for Sustainable Development.* Edward Elgar Publishing, Cheltenham.

Bleischwitz, R., Hoff, H., Spataru, C., van der Voet, E., VanDeveer, S., 2017. *Routledge Handbook of the Resource Nexus.* Routledge, London.

Bleischwitz, R., Johnson, C. M., Dozler, M. G., 2013. Re-assessing resource dependency and criticality. Linking future food and water stress with global resource supply vulnerabilities for foresight analysis. *European Journal of Futures Research* 2(1), 34.

Bloom, N., Van Reenen, J., 2007. Measuring and explaining management practices across firms and countries. *The Quarterly Journal of Economics* 122(4), 1351–1408.

Bontems, P., Bourgeon, J.-M., 2005. Optimal environmental taxation and enforcement policy. *European Economic Review* 49(2), 409–435.

Bovenberg, A. L., 1999. Green tax reforms and the double dividend: An updated reader's guide. *International Tax and Public Finance* 6(3), 421–443.

Bovenberg, A. L., Goulder, L. H., 1996. Optimal environmental taxation in the presence of other taxes: General-equilibrium analyses. *The American Economic Review* 86(4), 985–1000.

Bowen, A., Fankhauser, S., 2011. Low-carbon development for the least developed countries. *World Economics* 12(1).

BP, 2016. *Approximate Conversion Factors – BP Statistical Review of World Energy 2016.* BP, London.

BPS, 2016. *Provincial Minimum Wage Per Year and Average National Wages (Rupiah), 1997–2016.* URL www.bps.go.id/linkTableDinamis/view/id/917

BPS Statistics Indonesia, 2015. *Indonesia Micro and Small Industries Survey 2013.* Badan Pusat Statistik, Jakarta.

Bringezu, S., Schütz, H., 2010. *Material Use Indicators for Measuring Resource Productivity and Environmental Impacts: Material Efficiency & Resource Conservation Background Paper.* Wuppertal Institute Resource Efficiency Papers 6.1.

Brunner, S., Flachsland, C., Marschinski, R., 2012. Credible commitment in carbon policy. *Climate Policy* 12(2), 255–271.

Burniaux, J.M., Chateau, J., 2014. Greenhouse gases mitigation potential and economic efficiency of phasing-out fossil fuel subsidies. *International Economics*, 140, 71–88.

Cagno, E., Worrell, E., Trianni, A., Pugliese, G., 2013. A novel approach for barriers to industrial energy efficiency. *Renewable and Sustainable Energy Reviews* 19, 290–308.

Calvo-Gonzales, O., Cunha, B., Trezzi, R., 2015. *When Winners Feel Like Losers – Evidence From an Energy Subsidy Reform*. World Bank Policy Research Working Papers 7227.

Carpenter, C., Khan, S., 2015. *U.A.E. Removes Fuel Subsidy as Oil Drop Hurts Arab Economies*. URL www.bloomberg.com/news/articles/2015-07-22/u-a-e-to-link-gasoline-price-to-global-markets-effect-aug-1

Carson, R. T., Jacobsen, M. R., Liu, A. A., 2014. *Comparing the Cost of a Carbon Tax in China and the United States*. American Economic Association Conference 2015 Working Paper. URL www.aeaweb.org/conference/2015/retrieve.php?pdfid=634{&}usg=AFQjCNGhW1bl9fFYsDXU3ujw-Wfyv7BW3A{&}sig2=DeUCH

Castagneto-Gissey, G., 2014. How competitive are EU electricity markets? An assessment of ETS Phase II. *Energy Policy* 73, 278–297.

CFR, 2015. *Fuel Subsidy Reform Insights From a CFR Workshop*. Council on Foreign Relations, Maurice R. Greenberg Center for Geoeconomic Studies, New York.

Chambers, R. G., 1988. *Applied Production Analysis: A Dual Approach*. Cambridge University Press, Cambridge, UK.

Chattopadhyay, D., Jha, S., May 2014. The impact of energy subsidies on the power sector in Southeast Asia. *The Electricity Journal* 27(4), 70–83.

Cheon, A., Lackner, M., Urpelainen, J., 2015. Instruments of political control: National oil companies, oil prices, and petroleum subsidies. *Comparative Political Studies* 48(3), 370–402.

Cheon, A., Urpelainen, J., Lackner, M., 2013. Why do governments subsidize gasoline consumption? An empirical analysis of global gasoline prices, 2002–2009. *Energy Policy* 56, 382–390.

Cho, W. G., Nam, K., Pagán, J. A., January 2004. Economic growth and interfactor/interfuel substitution in Korea. *Energy Economics* 26(1), 31–50.

Christensen, L. R., Jorgenson, D. W., Lau, L. J., 1973. Transcendental logarithmic production frontiers. *The Review of Economics and Statistics*, 28–45.

Clements, B., Jung, H.-S., Gupta, S., 2007. Real and distributive effects of petroleum price liberalization: The case of Indonesia. *The Developing Economies* 45(2), 220–237.

Coady, D., 2006. Indirect tax and public pricing reforms. In: Coudouel, A., Paternostro, S. (Eds.), *Analyzing the Distributional Impact of Reforms: A Practitioner's Guide to Pension, Health, Labor Markets, Public Sector Downsizing, Taxation, Decentralization and Macroeconomic Modeling*. The World Bank, Washington, DC, pp. 255–312.

Coady, D., Arze, J., Eyraud, L., Jin, H., Thakoor, V., Tuladhar, A., Nemeth, L., 2012. *Automatic Fuel Pricing Mechanisms With Price Smoothing: Design, Implementation, and Fiscal Implications*. International Monetary Fund, Washington, DC.

Coady, D., Flamini, V., Sears, L., 2015a. *The Unequal Benefits of Fuel Subsidies Revisited: Evidence for Developing Countries*. IMF Working Papers WP/15/250.

Coady, D., Gillingham, R., Ossowski, R., Piotrowski, J., Tareq, S., Tyson, J., 2010. *Petroleum Product Subsidies: Costly, Inequitable, and Rising*. IMF Staff Position Note SPN/10/05.

Coady, D., Parry, I., Sears, L., Shang, B., 2015b. *How Large Are Global Energy Subsidies?* IMF Working Papers WP/15/105.

Coady, D., Parry, I., Sears, L., Shang, B., March 2017. How large are global fossil fuel subsidies? *World Development* 91, 11–27.

Commander, S., 2012. *A Guide to the Political Economy of Reforming Energy Subsidies*. IZA Policy Paper No. 52.

Commander, S., Nikoloski, Z., Vagliasindi, M., 2015. *Estimating the Size of External Effects of Energy Subsidies in Transport and Agriculture*. World Bank Policy Research Working Papers 7227.

Dahl, C., 1994. A survey of energy demand elasticities for the developing world. *Journal of Energy and Development* 28(1).

D'Amato, A., Dijkstra, B. R., 2015. Technology choice and environmental regulation under asymmetric information. *Resource and Energy Economics* 41, 224–247.

Dansie, G., Lanteigne, M., Overland, I., 2010. Reducing energy subsidies in China, India and Russia: Dilemmas for decision makers. *Sustainability* 2(2), 475–493.

Davis, L. W., December 2013. The economic cost of global fuel subsidies. *American Economic Review, Papers and Proceedings 2014* 104(5), 581–585.

Deaton, A., 2003. Household surveys, consumption, and the measurement of poverty. *Economic Systems Research* 15(2), 135–159.

DeCanio, S. J., 1993. Barriers within firms to energy-efficient investments. *Energy Policy* 21(9), 906–914.

DeCanio, S. J., Dibble, C., Amir-Atefi, K., 2000. The importance of organizational structure for the adoption of innovations. *Management Science* 46(10), 1285–1299.

DeCanio, S. J., Watkins, W. E., 1998. Investment in energy efficiency: Do the characteristics of firms matter? *Review of Economics and Statistics* 80(1), 95–107.

Dechezlepretre, A., Sato, M., 2014. *The Impacts of Environmental Regulations on Competitiveness*. Grantham Research Institute on Climate Change and the Environment, London.

del Granado, F. J., Coady, D., Gillingham, R., 2012. The unequal benefits of fuel subsidies: A review of evidence for developing countries. *World Development* 40(11), 2234–2248.

De Oliveira, A., Laan, T., 2010. *Lessons Learned From Brazil's Experience With Fossil Fuel Subsidies and Their Reform*. International Institute for Sustainable Development, Geneva.

Dethier, J.-J., Hirn, M., Straub, S., 2011. Explaining enterprise performance in developing countries with business climate survey data. *The World Bank Research Observer* 26(2), 258–309.

Devarajan, S., Ehrhart, H., Le, T. M., Raballand, G., 2011. *Direct Redistribution, Taxation, and Accountability in Oil-Rich Economies: A Proposal*. CGDEV Working Paper Series 281.

Devarajan, S., Mottaghi, L., Iqbal, F., Mundaca, G., Laursen, M., Vagliasindi, M., Commander, S., Chaal-Dabi, I., 2014. *MENA Economic Monitor: Corrosive Subsidies*. The World Bank, Washington, DC.

Dickinson, T., 2015. Universal price subsidies in Cameroon: Cost, impact, and avenues for reform. In: Angwafo, M. S., Chuhan-Pole, P. (Eds.), *From Evidence to Policy: Innovations in Shaping Reforms in Africa*. The World Bank, Washington, DC, pp. 5–9.

Dijk, M., Kemp, R., 2016. *Understanding the Web of Constraints on Resource Efficiency in Europe*. Policy Brief March 2016. Policy Options for a Resource Efficient Economy (POLFREE).

Domenech, T., Bleischwitz, R., Ekins, P., O'Keeffe, M., Drummond, P., 2014. *Lessons From the EU Policy Experiences*. POLFREE Deliverable 1.2. Policy Options for a Resource Efficient Economy (POLFREE).

Dube, I., 2003. Impact of energy subsidies on energy consumption and supply in Zimbabwe. Do the urban poor really benefit? *Energy Policy* 31(15), 1635–1645.

Durand-Lasserve, O., Campagnolo, L., Chateau, J., Dellink, R., 2015. *Modelling of Distributional Impacts of Energy Subsidy Reforms: An Illustration With Indonesia*. OECD Environment Working Papers 86.

Durbin, S., September 2004. *Workplace Skills, Technology Adoption and Firm Productivity: A Review*. New Zealand Treasury Working Paper 04/16.

Ebrahim, Z., Inderwildi, O. R., King, D. A., January 2014. Macroeconomic impacts of oil price volatility: Mitigation and resilience. *Frontiers in Energy* 8(1), 9–24.

EBRD, 2010. *Management, Organisation, and Innovation (MOI) Survey*. URL www.ebrd.com/pages/research/economics/data/moi.shtml

Economist, 2015. Finance and economics: Energy prices – Pump aligning. *The Economist*, January 17th 2015, 45.

EIA, 2016. *Energy Conversion Calculator*. URL https://www.eia.gov/energyexplained/index.cfm?page=about_energy_conversion_calculator

Ekins, P., Speck, S. 2008. Environmental Tax Reform in Europe: Energy Tax Rates and Competitiveness. In: Chalifour, N., Milnet, J.E., Ashiabor, H., Deketalaere, K., Kreiser, L. (Eds.), *2008 Critical Issues in Environmental Taxation Volume V*, Oxford University Press, pp. 77–105.

Ekins, P., Speck, S., March 2010. *Competitiveness and Environmental Tax Reform*. Technical Report. Green Fiscal Commission. URL http://www.greenfiscalcommission.org.uk/images/uploads/gfcBriefing7_PDF_isbn_v8.pdf

Ellis, J., 2010. *The Effects of Fossil-fuel Subsidy Reform: A Review of Modelling and Empirical Studies*. Global Subsidies Initiative, Geneva.

Enevoldsen, M., Ryelund, A., Andersen, M., 2009. The impact of energy taxes on competitiveness: A panel regression study of 56 European Industry sectors. In: Andersen, M., Ekins, P. (Eds.), *Carbon-Energy Taxation: Lessons From Europe*. Oxford University Press, Oxford, Ch. 5.

European Commission, 1999. *Council Directive 1999/31/EC of 26 April 1999 on the Landfill of Waste*. European Commission, Brussels.

European Commission, 2008. *Directive 2008/98/EC of the European Parliament and the Council of 19 November 2008 on Waste*. European Commission, Brussels.

European Commission, 2011. *Roadmap to a Resource Efficient Europe*. Communication from the Commission to the European Parliament, the Council, the European Economic and Social Committee and the Committee of the Regions.

European Commission, 2012. *Directive 2012/27/EU of the European Parliament and the Council of 25 October 2012 on Energy Efficiency*. European Commission, Brussels.

European Commission, 2013. *Eurobarometer: SMEs, Resource Efficiency and Green Markets*. European Commission, Brussels.

Fankhauser, S., Bowen, A., Calel, R., Dechezleprêtre, A., Grover, D., Rydge, J., Sato, M., 2013. Who will win the green race? In search of environmental competitiveness and innovation. *Global Environmental Change* 23(5), 902–913.

Fankhauser, S., Hepburn, C., Park, J., 2010. Combining multiple climate policy instruments: How not to do it. *Climate Change Economics* 1(3), 209–225.

Farzin, Y. H., Kort, P. M., 2000. Pollution abatement investment when environmental regulation is uncertain. *Journal of Public Economic Theory* 2(2), 183–212.

Fattouh, B., El-Katiri, L., June 2013. Energy subsidies in the Middle East and North Africa. *Energy Strategy Reviews* 2(1), 108–115.

Fattouh, B., El-Katiri, L., 2015. *A Brief Political Economy of Energy Subsidies in the Middle East and North Africa*. The Oxford Institute for Energy Studies, Oxford.

Fattouh, B., Sen, A., Moerenhout, T., May 2016. *Striking the Right Balance?* GCC Energy Pricing Reforms in a Low Price Environment. Oxford Energy Comment.

Fay, M., Hallegatte, S., Vogt-Schilb, A., Rozenberg, J., Narloch, U., Kerr, T., 2015. *Decarbonizing Development: Three Steps to a Zero-Carbon Future.* The World Bank, Washington, DC.

FFFSR, 2015. *Friends of Fossil Fuel Subsidy Reform – Communiqué.* URL http://fffsr.org/communique/

Fischer, C., 2008. Emissions pricing, spillovers, and public investment in environmentally friendly technologies. *Energy Economics* 30(2), 487–502.

Fischer, C., Greaker, M., Rosendahl, K., 2015. *Strategic Subsidies for Renewable Energy.* Conference Paper. Green Growth Knowledge Platform (GGKP) Third Annual Conference, 29–30 January, 2015.

Flachenecker, F., 2017. The causal impact of material productivity on macroeconomic competitiveness in the European Union. *Environmental Economics and Policy Studies* 20(1), 17–46.

Flachenecker, F., Bleischwitz, R., Rentschler, J. E., 2016. Investments in material efficiency: The introduction and application of a comprehensive cost–benefit framework. *Journal of Environmental Economics and Policy,* 1–14.

Flachenecker, F., Rentschler, J., 2015. *Investments in Resource Efficiency – Costs and Benefits, Investment Barriers, and Intervention Measures.* University College London, European Bank for Reconstruction and Development, London.

Flues, F., Lutz, B. J., 2015. *Competitiveness Impacts of the German Electricity Tax.* OECD Environment Working Papers 88.

Frishammar, J., Åke Hörte, S., 2005. Managing external information in manufacturing firms: The impact on innovation performance. *Journal of Product Innovation Management* 22(3), 251–266.

Frondel, M., 2010. *Substitution Elasticities: A Theoretical and Empirical Comparison.* German Collaborative Research Center Discussion Paper SFB 823.

Fullerton, D., Metcalf, G. E., 1997. *Environmental Taxes and the Double-Dividend Hypothesis: Did You Really Expect Something for Nothing?* National Bureau of Economic Research Working Paper Series No. 6199.

G20, 2009. *G20 Leaders' Statement.* Pittsburgh Summit, September 2009.

G20, 2014. *G20 Leaders' Communique.* Brisbane Summit, November 2014.

Gangopadhyay, S., Ramaswami, B., Wadhwa, W., 2005. Reducing subsidies on household fuels in India: How will it affect the poor? *Energy Policy* 31(2), 125–137.

Gelb, A., 1988. *Oil Windfalls: Blessing or Curse?* The World Bank, Washington, DC.

Gelb, A., Majerowicz, S., 2011. *Oil for Uganda – Or Ugandans? Can Cash Transfers Prevent the Resource Curse?* CGDEV Working Paper Series 261.

Gelb, A., Tordo, S., Halland, H., Arfaa, N., Smith, G., 2014. *Sovereign Wealth Funds and Long-Term Development Finance Risks and Opportunities.* World Bank Policy Research Working Papers 6776.

Ghisetti, C., Mancinelli, S., Mazzanti, M., Zoli, M., December 2016. Financial barriers and environmental innovations: Evidence from EU manufacturing firms. *Climate Policy,* 1–17.

Gill, I. S., Izvorski, I., van Eeghen, W., de Rosa, D., 2014. *Diversified Development – Making the Most of Natural Resources in Eurasia.* The World Bank, Washington, DC.

Gillingham, K., Newell, R. G., Palmer, K., 2009. Energy efficiency economics and policy. *Annual Review of Resource Economics* 1(1), 597–620.

GIZ, 2014. *Energypedia: International Fuel Prices.* URL https://energypedia.info/wiki/

Gollier, C., 2002. Discounting an uncertain future. *Journal of Public Economics* 85 (2), 149–166.

Gonseth, C., Cadot, O., Mathys, N. A., Thalmann, P., March 2015. Energy-tax changes and competitiveness: The role of adaptive capacity. *Energy Economics* 48, 127–135.

Goulder, L. H., 1995a. Effects of carbon taxes in an economy with prior tax distortions – An intertemporal general equilibrium analysis.pdf. *Journal of Environmental Economics and Management* 29, 271–297.

Goulder, L. H., 1995b. Environmental taxation and the double dividend: A reader's guide. *International Tax and Public Finance* 2(2), 157–183.

Goulder, L. H., 2013. Climate change policy's interactions with the tax system. *Energy Economics* 40, S3–S11.

Grave, K., Hazrat, M., Boeve, S., von Blücher, F., Bourgault, C., Breitschopf, B., Friedrichsen, N., Arens, M., Aydemir, A., Pudlik, M., Duscha, V., Ordonez, J., Lutz, C., Großmann, A., Flaute, M., 2015. *Electricity Costs of Energy Intensive Industries an International Comparison.* Fraunhofer ISI & ECOFYS, Berlin.

Grubb, M., Ulph, D., 2002. Energy, the environment, and innovation. *Oxford Review of Economic Policy* 18(1), 92–106.

GSI, 2010a. *A How-to Guide: Measuring Subsidies to Fossil Fuel Producers.* Global Subsidies Initiative, Geneva.

GSI, 2010b. *Defining Fossil-fuel Subsidies for the G-20: Which Approach Is Best?* Global Subsidies Initiative, Geneva.

GSI, 2011. *A Citizens' Guide to Energy Subsidies in Indonesia.* Global Subsidies Initiative, Geneva.

GSI, 2012a. *A Citizens' Guide to Energy Subsidies in Nigeria.* International Institute for Sustainable Development: Global Subsidies Initiative, Geneva.

GSI, 2012b. *Fossil Fuels – At What Cost? Government Support for Upstream Oil and Gas Activities in Russia.* Global Subsidies Initiative, Geneva.

GSI, 2013. *A Guidebook to Fossil-fuel Subsidy Reform for Policy-makers in Southeast Asia.* GSI, Geneva.

Halland, H., Beardsworth, J., Land, B., Schmidt, J., 2014. *Resource Financed Infrastructure – A Discussion on a New Form on Infrastructure Financing.* The World Bank, Washington, DC.

Hallegatte, S., Bangalore, M., Bonzanigo, L., Fay, M., Narloch, U., Vogt-Schilb, A., Rozenberg, J., 2014. *Climate Change and Poverty: An Analytical Framework.* World Bank Policy Research Working Papers 7126.

Hallegatte, S., Fay, M., Vogt-Schilb, A., October 2013. *Green Industrial Policies – When and How.* World Bank Policy Research Working Papers 66776.

Hammar, H., Lofgren, A., Sterner, T., 2004. Political economy obstacles to fuel taxation. *The Energy Journal* 25(3), 1–18.

Hassan, M., Schneider, F., 2016. *Size and Development of the Shadow Economies of 157 Countries Worldwide: Updated and New Measures From 1999 to 2013.* IZA Discussion Paper Series IZA DP No.

HM Revenue and Customs, 2014. *VAT Rates on Different Goods and Services.* URL www.gov.uk/rates-of-vat-on-different-goods-and-services

Hosoe, N., Gasawa, K., Hashimoto, H., 2010. *Textbook of Computable General Equilibrium Modelling.* Palgrave Macmillan, New York.

Howarth, R. B., Andersson, B., 1993. Market barriers to energy efficiency. *Energy Economics* 15(4), 262–272.

Hyytinen, A., Toivanen, O., 2005. Do financial constraints hold back innovation and growth?: Evidence on the role of public policy. *Research Policy* 34(9), 1385–1403.

IEA, 2010. *World Energy Outlook 2010.* International Energy Agency, Paris.

IEA, 2011. *World Energy Outlook 2011.* International Energy Agency, Paris.

IEA, 2013. *World Energy Outlook 2013.* International Energy Agency, Paris.

IEA, 2014a. *Database: Fossil Fuel Subsidy Rates as a Proportion of the Full Cost of Supply, 2012*. URL www.iea.org/subsidy/index.html

IEA, 2014b. *Energy Supply Security – Indonesia*. International Energy Agency, Paris.

IEA, 2014c. *World Energy Outlook 2014*. International Energy Agency, Paris.

IEA, 2015a. *Indonesia 2015 – Energy Policy Beyond IEA Countries*. International Energy Agency, Paris.

IEA, 2015b. *World Energy Outlook 2015*. International Energy Agency, Paris.

IEA, 2016. *International Energy Agency: Energy Statistics*. URL www.iea.org/statistics/

IEA, 2017. *Fossil Fuel Subsidies – Methodology and Assumptions*. URL www.worldenergyoutlook.org/resources/energysubsidies/methodology/

IEA, OECD, World Bank, 2010a. *The Scope of Fossil Fuel Subsidies in 2009 and a Roadmap for Phasing Out Fossil Fuel Subsidies*. Joint Report Prepared for the G20 Summit in Seoul (Republic of Korea), 11–12 November, 2010.

IEA, OPEC, OECD, World Bank, 2010b. *Analysis of the Scope of Energy Subsidies and Suggestions for the G-20 Initiative*. Prepared for Submission to the G-20 Summit Meeting Toronto (Canada), 26–27 June, 2010.

IFC, 2011. *Resource Efficiency in the Ferrous Foundry Industry in Russia*. International Finance Corporation, Washington, DC.

IMF, 2008a. *Fuel and Food Price Subsidies: Issues and Reform Options*. The World Bank, Washington, DC.

IMF, 2008b. *Poverty and Social Impact Analysis by the IMF Review of Methodology and Selected Evidence*. International Monetary Fund, Washington, DC.

IMF, 2013a. *Case Studies on Energy Subsidy Reform Lessons and Implications*. International Monetary Fund, Washington, DC.

IMF, 2013b. *Energy Subsidy Reform in Sub-Saharan Africa: Experiences and Lessons*. The World Bank, Washington, DC.

IMF, 2013c. *Energy Subsidy Reform Lessons and Implications*. International Monetary Fund, Washington, DC.

IMF, 2015. *Luxembourg – Selected Issues*. International Monetary Fund, Washington, DC.

IMF, 2016a. *IMF and Reforming Energy Subsidies: Distributional Analysis of Fuel Subsidy Reform*. URL www.imf.org/external/np/fad/subsidies/

IMF, 2016b. *Who Benefits From Energy Subsidies: An Update*. URL www.imf.org/external/np/fad/subsidies/

Inchauste, G., Victor, D., 2017. *The Political Economy of Energy Subsidy Reform*. The World Bank, Washington, DC.

IPCC, 2006. *Guidelines for National Greenhouse Gas Inventories – National Greenhouse Gas Inventories Programme*. Intergovernmental Panel on Climate Change, Geneva.

IPCC, 2014. Summary for policymakers. In: Edenhofer, O., Pichs-Madruga, R., Sokona, Y., Farahani, E., Kadner, S., Seyboth, K., Adler, A., Baum, I., Brunner, S., Eicke-Meier, P., Kriemann, B., Savolainen, J., Schlömer, S., von Stechow, C., Zwickel, T., Minx, J. (Eds.), *Climate Change 2014: Mitigation of Climate Change. Contribution of Working Group III to the Fifth Assessment Report of the Intergovernmental Panel on Climate Change*. Cambridge University Press, Cambridge, UK.

Iwayemi, A., Adenikinju, A., Babatunde, M. A., January 2010. Estimating petroleum products demand elasticities in Nigeria: A multivariate cointegration approach. *Energy Economics* 32(1), 73–85.

Jamal, M., Ayarkwa, A., 2014. Fuel price adjustments and growth of SMEs in the New Juaben Municipality, Ghana. *International Journal of Small Business and Entrepreneurship Research* 2(3), 13–22.

Jiang, Z., Ouyang, X., Huang, G., April 2015. The distributional impacts of removing energy subsidies in China. *China Economic Review* 33, 111–122.

Johnston, A., Heffron, R. J., McCauley, D., September 2014. Rethinking the scope and necessity of energy subsidies in the United Kingdom. *Energy Research & Social Science* 3, 1–4.

Jordan, N. D., Lemken, T., Liedtke, C., September 2014. Barriers to resource efficiency innovations and opportunities for smart regulations: The case of Germany. *Environmental Policy and Governance* 24(5), 307–323.

Kammerlander, M., 2014. *Individual Behavioural Barriers to Resource Efficiency*. Deliverable 1.6 of POLFREE Project, SERI, MU-ICIS and UCL.

KfW, 2013. *BMU-Umweltinnovationsprogramm Neuer Förderschwerpunkt "Material-effizienz in der Produktion"*. Kreditanstalt für Wiederaufbau.

Khattab, A., 2007. *Assessing the Impacts of Removing Energy Subsidies on Energy Intensive Industries in Egypt*. The Egyptian Center for Economic Study, Cairo, Working Paper ECESWP124-.

Kilian, L., 2008. The economic effects of energy price shocks. *Journal of Economic Literature* 46(4), 871–909.

Kim, S. E., Urpelainen, J., 2015. Democracy, autocracy and the Urban Bias: Evidence from petroleum subsidies. *Political Studies* 64(3), 552–572.

Kim, W., Chattopadhyay, D., Park, J.-B., August 2010. Impact of carbon cost on wholesale electricity price: A note on price pass-through issues. *Energy* 35(8), 3441–3448.

Kojima, M., 2009. *Government Response to Oil Price Volatility: Experience of 49 Developing Countries*. Extractive Industries for Development Series. The World Bank, Washington, DC.

Kojima, M., 2016. *Fossil Fuel Subsidy and Pricing Policies: Recent Developing Country Experience*. World Bank Policy Research Working Papers WPS 7531.

Kojima, M., Bacon, R., Trimble, C., 2014. *Political Economy of Power Sector Subsidies: A Review With Reference to Sub-Saharan Africa*. The World Bank, Washington, DC.

Kojima, M., Koplow, D., 2015. *Fossil Fuel Subsidies: Approaches and Valuation*. World Bank Policy Research Working Papers 7220.

Koplow, D., 2014. Global energy subsidies: Scale, opportunity costs, and barriers to reform. In: Halff, A., Sovacool, B., Rozhon, J. (Eds.), *Energy Poverty: Global Challenges and Local Solutions*. Oxford University Press, Oxford.

Koskela, E., Sinn, H.-W., Schöb, R., 2001. Green tax reform and competitiveness. *German Economic Review* 2(1), 19–30.

Kostka, G., Moslener, U., Andreas, J., 2013. Barriers to increasing energy efficiency: Evidence from small-and medium-sized enterprises in China. *Journal of Cleaner Production* 57, 59–68.

Krishna, P., Mitra, D., 1998. Trade liberalization, market discipline and productivity growth: New evidence from India. *Journal of Development Economics* 56(2), 447–462.

Krysiak, F. C., 2008. Prices vs. quantities: The effects on technology choice. *Journal of Public Economics* 92(5), 1275–1287.

Kuralbayeva, K., 2013. *Effects of Carbon Taxes in an Economy With Large Informal Sector and Rural-Urban Migration*. Grantham Research Institute on Climate Change and the Environment Working Paper 156.

Laffont, J. J., 1994. Regulation of Pollution with Asymmetric Information. In: Dosi, C., Tomasi, T. (Eds.), *Nonpoint Source Pollution Regulation: Issues and Analysis*. Economics, Energy and Environment, Vol. 3. Springer, Dordrecht.

Lang, K., 2011. *The First Year of the G-20 Commitment on Fossil-fuel Subsidies: A Commentary on Lessons Learned and the Path Forward*. Global Subsidies Initiative, Geneva.

Lecuyer, O., Quirion, P., 2013. Can uncertainty justify overlapping policy instruments to mitigate emissions? *Ecological Economics* 93, 177–191.

Legeida, N., 2002. *The Economic Implications of Government Support for the Steel Industry: The Case of Ukraine*. Association for Studies in Public Economics – The Fifth International Conference on "Public Sector Transition".

Lipsey, R. G., Lancaster, K., 1956. The general theory of second best. *The Review of Economic Studies* 24(1), 11–32.

Liu, A. A., 2013. Tax evasion and optimal environmental taxes. *Journal of Environmental Economics and Management* 66(3), 656–670.

Lockwood, M., 2015. Fossil fuel subsidy reform, rent management and political fragmentation in developing countries. *New Political Economy* 20(4), 475–494.

Makhlouf, H. H., 2010. Sovereign wealth funds. *International Journal of Government Financial Management* 10(1), 35.

Marcu, A., Genoese, F., Renda, A., Wieczorkiewicz, J., Roth, S., Infelise, F., Luchetta, G., Colantoni, L., Stoefs, W., Timini, J., Simonelli, F., 2014. *Composition and Drivers of Energy Prices and Costs in Energy Intensive Industries*. CEPS Special Report 85.

Mas-Colell, A., Whinston, M. D., Green, J. R., 1995. *Microeconomic Theory*. Vol. 1. Oxford University Press, New York.

MEES, 2016. *Riyadh Cuts Fuel Subsidies, Petchem Producers Count the Cost*. URL http://archives.mees.com/issues/1618/articles/53472

Merrill, L., Bassi, A., Bridle, R., Toft Christensen, L., 2015. *Tackling Fossil Fuel Subsidies and Climate Change: Levelling the Energy Playing Field*. Nordic Council of Ministers, Copenhagen.

Michael, B., 2014. *Moody's Says India's Diesel Deregulation Timed Aptly*. Credit Positive. URL www.ibtimes.co.uk/moodys-indias-deregulation-diesel-prices-will-ease-inflationary-pressure-1471043

Ministerio del Ambiente, 2015. *Folleto: Reduction of Greenhouse Gas Emissions in Ecuador*. Ministry of Environment of Ecuador, Quito.

Mlachila, M., Ruggiero, E., Corvino, D., 2016. *Unintended Consequences: Spillovers From Nigeria's Fuel Pricing Policies to Its Neighbors*. IMF Working Papers WP/15/17.

Montero, J.-P., 2002. Permits, standards, and technology innovation. *Journal of Environmental Economics and Management* 44(1), 23–44.

Morris, J. R., Phillips, P. S., Read, A. D., 1998. The UK landfill tax: An analysis of its contribution to sustainable waste management. *Resources, Conservation and Recycling* 23(4), 259–270.

Morris, M. G., Venkatesh, V., 2000. Age differences in technology adoption decisions: Implications for a changing work force. *Personnel Psychology* 53(2), 375–403.

Moss, T., Young, L., 2009. *Saving Ghana From Its Oil: The Case for Direct Cash Distribution*. CGDEV Working Paper Series 186.

Mourougane, A., 2010. *Phasing Out Energy Subsidies in Indonesia*. OECD Economics Department Working Papers 808.

National Bureau of Statistics, 2010. *Nigeria Poverty Profile 2010*. National Bureau of Statistics, FCT Abuja.

National Bureau of Statistics, 2013. *National Bureau of Statistics: Central Data Catalogue*. URL www.nigerianstat.gov.ng/nada/index.php/catalog

NCE, 2016. *The Sustainable Infrastructure Imperative: Financing for Better Growth and Development*. The New Climate Economy, Washington, DC.

Neary, J. P., 2006. Measuring competitiveness. *Economic and Social Review* 37(2), 197.

OECD, 2004. *Principles of Corporate Governance*. Organisation for Economic Cooperation and Development, Paris.

OECD, 2011. *Fossil Fuel Support: OECD Secretariat Background Report for G20 Meeting of Finance Ministers*. Organisation for Economic Cooperation and Development, Paris.

OECD, 2013. *Inventory of Estimated Budgetary Support and Tax Expenditures for Fossil Fuels 2013*. URL http://oecdinsights.org/2013/02/11/fossil-fuel/subsidies-billions-up-in-smoke/

OECD, 2015a. *OECD Companion to the Inventory of Support Measures for Fossil Fuels 2015*. OECD, Paris.

OECD, 2015b. *OECD Inventory of Support Measures for Fossil Fuels 2015*. Organisation for Economic Cooperation and Development, Paris.

O'Leary, F., Howley, M., Ó'Gallachóir, B., 2007. *Energy in Industry*. Sustainable Energy Ireland – Energy Policy Statistical Support Unit, Dublin.

Omisakin, O., Oyinlola, A., Oluwatosin, A., 2012. Structural breaks, parameter stability and energy demand modeling in Nigeria. *International Journal of Economic Sciences and Applied Research* 2, 129–144.

Onischka, M., Liedtke, C., Jordan, N. D., 2012. How to sensitize the financial industry to resource efficiency considerations and climate change related risks. *Journal of Environmental Assessment Policy and Management* 14(3), 1250017.

Ouyang, X., Lin, B., September 2014. Impacts of increasing renewable energy subsidies and phasing out fossil fuel subsidies in China. *Renewable and Sustainable Energy Reviews* 37, 933–942.

Pamukcu, T., 2003. Trade liberalization and innovation decisions of firms: Lessons from post-1980 Turkey. *World Development* 31(8), 1443–1458.

Pande, R., Udry, C. R., 2005. *Institutions and Development: A View From Below*. Yale University Economic Growth Center Discussion Paper 928.

Parry, I. W. H., 1997. Environmental taxes and quotas in the presence of distorting taxes in factor markets. *Resource and Energy Economics* 19, 202–203.

Parry, I. W. H., Evans, D., Oates, W. E., 2014. Are energy efficiency standards justified? *Journal of Environmental Economics and Management* 67(2), 104–125.

Parry, I. W. H., Williams, R. C., 2010. What are the costs of meeting distributional objectives for climate policy? *The B.E. Journal of Economic Analysis & Policy* 10(2).

Parry, I. W. H., Williams III, R. C., Goulder, L. H., 1999. When can carbon abatement policies increase welfare? The fundamental role of distorted factor markets. *Journal of Environmental Economics and Management* 37(1), 52–84.

Pigou, A. C., 1920. *The Economics of Welfare*. Macmillan and Co., London.

Pindyck, R. S., 1979. Interfuel substitution and the industrial demand for energy: An international comparison. *The Review of Economics and Statistics* 61(2), 169–179.

Pindyck, R. S., 1990. *Irreversibility, Uncertainty, and Investment*. NBER Working Paper 3307.

Pindyck, R. S., 2007. Uncertainty in environmental economics. *Review of Environmental Economics and Policy* 1(1), 45–65.

Plante, M., 2014. The long-run macroeconomic impacts of fuel subsidies. *Journal of Development Economics* 107, 129–143.

Ploeg, R. V. D., Stefanski, R., Wills, S., 2011. *Harnessing Oil Revenues in Ghana*. Working Paper.

Pogge, T. W., 2001. Eradicating systemic poverty: Brief for a global resources dividend. *Journal of Human Development* 2(1), 59–77.

Popp, D., 2006. R&D subsidies and climate policy: Is there a "free lunch"? *Climatic Change* 77(3), 311–341.

Porter, M. E., March–April 1990. The competitive advantage of nations. *Harvard Business Review* 1990(2), 73–95.

Pritchett, L., 2005. *A Lecture on the Political Economy of Targeted Safety Nets.* World Bank Social Protection Discussion Paper 0501.

Rao, N. D., 2012. Kerosene subsidies in India: When energy policy fails as social policy. *Energy for Sustainable Development* 16(1), 35–43.

Reddy, B. S., 2013. Barriers and drivers to energy efficiency–a new taxonomical approach. *Energy Conversion and Management* 74, 403–416.

Rentschler, J. E., 2015. *Incidence and Impact: A Disaggregated Poverty Analysis of Fossil Fuel Subsidy Reform.* Oxford Institute for Energy Studies, Oxford.

Rentschler, J. E., 2016. Incidence and impact: The regional variation of poverty effects due to fossil fuel subsidy reform. *Energy Policy* 96, 491–503.

Rentschler, J. E., Bazilian, M., 2016. Reforming fossil fuel subsidies: Drivers, barriers and the state of progress. *Climate Policy* 17(7), 891–914.

Rentschler, J. E., Bazilian, M., 2017. Principles for the effective design of fossil fuel subsidy reforms. *Review of Environmental Economics and Policy* 11(1).

Rentschler, J. E., Bleischwitz, R., Flachenecker, F., 2016. On imperfect competition and market distortions: The causes of corporate under-investment in energy and material efficiency. *International Economics and Economic Policy*, 1–25.

Rentschler, J. E., Flachenecker, F., Kornejew, M., 2017. *Assessing Carbon Emission Savings From Corporate Resource Efficiency Investments: Theory and Practice.* Working Paper.

Rentschler, J. E., Hosoe, N., 2017. *Illicit Dealings: Fossil Fuel Subsidy Reform and the Role of Tax Evasion and Smuggling.* Tokyo: National Graduate Institute for Policy Studies. GRIPS Discussion Paper DP17-05.

Rentschler, J. E., Kornejew, M., 2016. *Energy Subsidy Reforms and the Impacts on Firms: Transmission Channels and Coping Mechanisms.* Oxford Energy Comment – Oxford Institute for Energy Studies, Oxford.

Requate, T., 1998. Incentives to innovate under emission taxes and tradeable permits. *European Journal of Political Economy* 14(1), 139–165.

Requate, T., 2005. Timing and commitment of environmental policy, adoption of new technology, and repercussions on R&D. *Environmental and Resource Economics* 31(2), 175–199.

Requate, T., 2006. Environmental policy under imperfect competition. In: Tietenberg, T., Folmer, H., (Eds.), *The International Yearbook of Environmental and Resource Economics 2007*, pp. 120–207. Edward Elgar Publishing, Cheltenham.

Requate, T., Unold, W., 2003. Environmental policy incentives to adopt advanced abatement technology: Will the true ranking please stand up? *European Economic Review* 47(1), 125–146.

Rodrik, D., 1988. *Closing the Technology Gap: Does Trade Liberalization Really Help?* NBER Working Paper No. 2654.

Rohdin, P., Thollander, P., Solding, P., 2007. Barriers to and drivers for energy efficiency in the Swedish foundry industry. *Energy Policy* 35(1), 672–677.

Rozenberg, J., Vogt-Schilb, A., Hallegatte, S., May 2014. *Transition to Clean Capital, Irreversible Investment and Stranded Assets.* World Bank Policy Research Working Papers 6859.

Ruggeri Laderchi, C., Olivier, A., Trimble, C., 2013. *Balancing Act: Cutting Energy Subsidies While Protecting Affordability.* No. 76820. The World Bank, Washington, DC.

Sala-i-Martin, X., Subramanian, A., 2012. Addressing the natural resource curse: An illustration from Nigeria. *Journal of African Economies* 22(4), 570–615.

Salehi-Isfahani, D., Wilson Stucki, B., Deutschmann, J., 2015. The reform of energy subsidies in Iran: The role of cash transfers. *Emerging Markets Finance and Trade* 51(6), 1144–1162.

Schwanitz, V. J., Piontek, F., Bertram, C., Luderer, G., April 2014. Long-term climate policy implications of phasing out fossil fuel subsidies. *Energy Policy* 67, 882–894.

Sdralevich, C., Sab, R., Zouhar, Y., Albertin, G., 2014. *Subsidy Reform in the Middle East and North Africa: Recent Progress and Challenges Ahead*. International Monetary Fund, Washington, DC.

Segal, P., 2011. Resource rents, redistribution, and halving global poverty: The resource dividend. *World Development* 39(4), 475–489.

Segal, P., 2012. How to spend it: Resource wealth and the distribution of resource rents. *Energy Policy* 51(May), 340–348.

Shleifer, A., 1998. *State Versus Private Ownership*. NBER Working Paper 6665.

Siddig, K., Aguiar, A., Grethe, H., Minor, P., Walmsley, T., 2014. Impacts of removing fuel import subsidies in Nigeria on poverty. *Energy Policy* 69, 165–178.

Siggel, E., 2006. International competitiveness and comparative advantage: A survey and a proposal for measurement. *Journal of Industry, Competition and Trade* 6(2), 137–159.

Sijm, J., Neuhoff, K., Chen, Y., 2006. CO2 cost pass-through and windfall profits in the power sector. *Climate Policy* 6(1), 49–72.

Slemrod, J., 2007. Cheating ourselves: The economics of tax evasion. *Journal of Economic Perspectives* 21(1), 25–48.

Soile, I., Mu, X., 2015. Who benefit most from fuel subsidies? Evidence from Nigeria. *Energy Policy* 87, 314–324.

Solaymani, S., Kari, F., 2014. Impacts of energy subsidy reform on the Malaysian economy and transportation sector. *Energy Policy* 70, 115–125.

Sorrell, S., Sijm, J., 2003. Carbon trading in the policy mix. *Oxford Review of Economic Policy* 19(3), 420–437.

Standing, A., 2014. Ghana's extractive industries and community benefit sharing: The case for cash transfers. *Resources Policy* 40, 74–82.

Stefanski, R., 2014. Dirty little secrets: Inferring fossil-fuel subsidies from patterns in emission intensities. *OxCarre Research Paper 134* 44, 1–52.

Sterner, T., 2007. Fuel taxes: An important instrument for climate policy. *Energy Policy* 35, 3194–3202.

Strand, J., 2013. *Political Economy Aspects of Fuel Subsidies: A Conceptual Framework*. World Bank Policy Research Working Papers 6392.

Sugawara, N., 2014. *From Volatility to Stability in Expenditure: Stabilization Funds in Resource-Rich Countries*. IMF Working Paper 14.

Sutherland, R. J., 1991. Market barriers to energy-efficiency investments. *The Energy Journal*, 15–34.

Swedish National Tax Agency, 2008. *Tax Gap Map for Sweden*. Report 2008:1B.

Tambunan, T., 2015. *Impacts of Energy Subsidy Reform on Micro, Small and Medium-Sized Enterprises (MSMEs) and Their Adjustment Strategies*. Global Subsidies Initiative, Geneva.

Terton, A., Gass, P., Merrill, L., Wagner, A., Meyer, E., 2015. *Fiscal Instruments in INDCs: How Countries Are Looking to Fiscal Policies to Support INDC Implementation*. IISD Discussion Paper.

Trade Arabia, 2015. *Energy Price Hike to Cost Saudi Cement $18m*. URL www.tradearabia.com/news/CONS{_}297717.html

Trianni, A., Cagno, E., Thollander, P., Backlund, S., 2013. Barriers to industrial energy efficiency in foundries: A European comparison. *Journal of Cleaner Production* 40, 161–176.

Udo, B., 2015. *Nigerian Govt Re-launches Failed Scheme to Enforce N50 Kerosene Price.* URL www.premiumtimesng.com/business/175215-nigerian-govt-re-launches-failed-scheme-enforce-n50-kerosene-price.html

UN, 2015a. *Addis Ababa Action Agenda.* Outcome Document of the Third International Conference on Financing for Development Addis Ababa, 13–16 July 2015, United Nations, Addis Ababa.

UN, 2015b. *Open Working Group Proposal for Sustainable Development Goals.* United Nations, New York.

UN, 2016. *Transforming Our World: The 2030 Agenda for Sustainable Development.* United Nations, New York.

UNEP, 2003. *Energy Subsidies: Lessons Learnt in Assessing Their Impact and Designing Policy Reforms.* United Nations, Geneva.

US Dept. of Commerce, 2001. *Report to the President.* Global Steel Trade: Structural Problems. International Trade Administration.

Uzawa, H., 1962. Production functions with constant elasticities of substitution. *The Review of Economic Studies* 29(4), 291–299.

Vagliasindi, M., July 2012a. *Implementing Energy Subsidy Reforms: An Overview of the Key Issues.* World Bank Policy Research Working Papers 6122.

Vagliasindi, M., 2012b. *Implementing Energy Subsidy Reforms: Evidence From Developing Countries.* The World Bank, Washington, DC.

Van Parijs, P., March 2004. Basic income: A simple and powerful idea for the twenty-first century. *Politics & Society* 32(1), 7–39.

Vasilev, A., 2016. *VAT Evasion in Bulgaria: A General-Equilibrium Approach.* Bulgarian Economic Papers BEP 09-201.

Verme, P., El-Massnaoui, K., 2015. *An Evaluation of the 2014 Subsidy Reforms in Morocco and a Simulation of Further Reforms.* World Bank Policy Research Working Papers 7224.

Victor, D., 2009. *The Politics of Fossil-fuel Subsidies.* Global Subsidies Initiative, Geneva.

Vogt-Schilb, A., Hallegatte, S., 2014. Marginal abatement cost curves and the optimal timing of mitigation measures. *Energy Policy* 66, 645–653.

WEF, 2013. *The Global Competitiveness Report 2013-2014.* World Economic Forum, Cologny.

WEF, 2016. *The Global Competitiveness Report 2015-2016.* World Economic Forum, Cologny.

Whitley, S., 2013. *Time to Change the Game: Fossil Fuel Subsidies and Climate.* Overseas Development Institute, London.

Whitley, S., van der Burg, L., 2015. *Fossil Fuel Subsidy Reform From Rhetoric to Reality.* New Climate Economy, London.

Widerquist, K., Howard, M. W., 2012a. *Alaska's Permanent Fund Dividend Examining Its Suitability as a Model.* Palgrave Macmillan, Basingstoke.

Widerquist, K., Howard, M. W., 2012b. *Exporting the Alaska Model Adapting the Permanent Fund Dividend for Reform Around the World.* Palgrave Macmillan, Basingstoke.

Willenbockel, D., Hoa, H., 2011. *Fossil Fuel Prices and Taxes: Effects on Economic Development and Income Distribution in Viet Nam (Package 2 Report for UNDP Viet Nam).* Hanoi Central Institute for Economic Management (CIEM), Hanoi.

Williams, R. C., 2002. Environmental tax interactions when pollution affects health or productivity. *Journal of Environmental Economics and Management* 44(2), 261–270.

World Bank, 2004a. *Corporate Governance Country Assessment: Moldova.* The World Bank, Washington, DC.

World Bank, 2004b. *Corporate Governance Country Assessment: Romania*. The World Bank, Washington, DC.

World Bank, 2006. *Corporate Governance Country Assessment: Ukraine*. The World Bank, Washington, DC.

World Bank, July 2010. *Subsidies in the Energy Sector: An Overview. Background Paper for the World Bank Group Energy Sector Strategy*. The World Bank, Washington, DC.

World Bank, 2013. *World Development Report 2014 – Risk and Opportunity: Managing Risk for Development*. The World Bank, Washington, DC.

World Bank, 2014. *State and Trends of Carbon Pricing 2014*. The World Bank, Washington, DC.

World Bank, 2015a. *Global Economic Prospects – January 2015*. The World Bank, Washington, DC.

World Bank, 2015b. *World Development Indicators*. URL http://data.worldbank.org/indicator

World Bank, 2016. *Doing Business 2016: Measuring Regulatory Quality and Efficiency*. The World Bank, Washington, DC.

WTO, 2006. *World Trade Report 2006*. World Trade Organisation, Geneva.

Yeo, M., 2010. *Natural Resource Subsidies*. World Trade Organization, Geneva.

Yilmaz, I., Akcaoz, H., Ozkan, B., 2005. An analysis of energy use and input costs for cotton production in Turkey. *Renewable Energy* 30(2), 145–155.

Zairi, M., 1994. Benchmarking: The best tool for measuring competitiveness. *Benchmarking for Quality Management & Technology* 1(1), 11–24.

Zhang, F., 2011. *Distributional Impact Analysis of the Energy Price Reform in Turkey*. World Bank Policy Research Working Papers 5831.

Zhang, Z., Baranzini, A., 2004. What do we know about carbon taxes? An inquiry into their impacts on competitiveness and distribution of income. *Energy Policy* 32(4), 507–518.

Zhao, J., 2003. Irreversible abatement investment under cost uncertainties: Tradable emission permits and emissions charges. *Journal of Public Economics* 87(12), 2765–2789.

Index

For Product Safety Concerns and Information please contact our EU
representative GPSR@taylorandfrancis.com
Taylor & Francis Verlag GmbH, Kaufingerstraße 24, 80331 München, Germany